The Invisible People

©2014-2020 Mariana Stjerna and SoulLink Publisher
All Rights Reserved

ISBN 978-91-985785-3-9   (paperback)
ISBN 978-91-985785-4-6   (haedcover)
ISBN 978-91-985785-5-3   (e-book)
First printed in Swedish

Other books in English by Mariana Stjerna:
Agartha — The Earth's Inner World
On Angels' Wings
Mission Space
Time Journey to the Origin and the Future
The Bible Bluff

SoulLink Publisher
www.SoulLink.se
info@SoulLink.se

Mariana Stjerna

The Invisible People

In the Magical World of Nature

SoulLink Publisher

Jan Fridegard (1897-1968) grew up as a farm laborer and tried several professions before the debut of his writings: *One Night in July* (1933). His autobiographical novel trilogy about Lars Hard is perhaps his finest work. The death of his father aroused a latent interest in the supernatural, which came to be reflected in *The Tower Rooster* (1941).

Contents

Introduction

Outer Space is infinite. How then is it possible for humans to be so arrogant as to assume they are the only living beings in the entire universe?

How can human beings be so presumptuous that they only believe in that which can be seen with their physical eyes? How can they encourage their limitations to such a degree that these define their only acceptable truth?

Why not simply admit that we limit our field of vision, and accept the fact that there are those able to see behind the veils we generally have in front of our eyes? For there are indeed veils, but it has not always been so.

When the notion of writing this book about Mother Earth, magic, and Nature spirits came about, a magical memory appeared in my consciousness. I shall never forget it, even though it happened a very long time ago. I call it "my memory from the Plant Kingdom."

I ran across the lawn and out onto the narrow, gravel pathway, leading to our neighbor's house. I then jumped over the shallow ditch and clambered up the wooded hillside, where I usually picked the first flowers of spring. In the ditch the coltsfoot would raise their golden, ruffled heads. Further up the hillside, underneath an old birch tree, the very first hepaticas popped their bluish-green buds up towards the sun, continuing to unfold until they became a blue veil covering the ground. There were not only blue hepaticas, but red ones, too. Just a small patch, but oh, so pretty! Those I was forbidden to pick, for they were called "rare."

Above the hill swept the Ulriksdal forest. There were some tracks in there that I knew like the back of my hand, but one day I went along an unfamiliar, winding animal track leading to some big trees encircling a spring. I had never come across it before and I cheered, danced, and sang for joy over this magnificent, prodigious discovery. This became my very own secret spring, barely a few yards wide and rather deep. The water was clear; I could see right down to the bottom, where the pine needles and moss tumbled about as in a rhythmic dance. A few small leaves sailed around on the surface and I saw with delight how the roots of the trees formed walls around the spring. In the very same root meanderings, the fairies dwelt. Of this I was completely certain, for I had read the book *Peter Pan,* and I was convinced that every word in it was true. I was six years of age and much alone, described as "an imaginative child" by my unimaginative mother.

The spring in the forest became my own clandestine place of consolation. There I could sit and daydream at great length, without anyone missing me. My mother liked to take a nap in the afternoon, while the housemaid and the cook had better things to do than chasing the "little miss" out in the forest. In my childish fashion I would sit and meditate by the spring, my head filled with fairy-tales, breathing in the lovely scent of the mixture of deciduous and evergreen trees.

During the summer I would, without permission, splash my feet in the spring water; other seasons I simply enjoyed watching and feeling the atmosphere. I clearly saw fairies and goblins all the time, although I can't swear if it was with my physical eyes or my mind's eye. Anyhow, they became my friends, and even if they were invisible, I spoke to them. They were the kindest of friends, precisely the sort a lonely child needs.

That was how it began. I lived within two worlds, the mundane one, ruled by my dominating mother and dearly beloved, kindly father, and the daydream one by the spring in the forest - acting as a source of inspiration. Throughout my adult life I have longed to revisit it, but now new settlements have devastated the beautiful piece of forest where natural life and inspiration penetrated the listening ear of a small child.

Another vivid memory comes from the Animal Kingdom. It's a memory of a less pleasant nature; nevertheless it has also persecuted me. I was even smaller then, perhaps three years of age. I was walking through the forest with my nanny when we suddenly came upon a tiny baby squirrel, which had apparently fallen out of its nest. We brought it home with us, to my mother's great dismay. She was not particularly fond of animals - which is perhaps why I have become all the more so. However, this occurrence has haunted my mind many times during my adulthood and I've never really understood it. I was allowed to keep the baby squirrel in my doll's bed and I clearly remember that we fed it cream and sponge cake crumbs. But still, it died in an unpleasant way.

I can see this scene clearly: I was standing in the serving room, adjacent to the dining room, together with the housemaid. The baby squirrel sat on a bench, just underneath the china cabinet. It had just stuffed itself with sponge cake and I'd held it in both hands, wishing to say how much I liked it to its face. I squeezed it too hard. To this day I can still feel its soft body between my hands as the housemaid shouted so loudly that the cook rushed away from her pots and pans to see what the commotion was.

Both of the women scolded me and took care of the little animal, but it was already dead. My mother, rudely aroused from her beauty sleep, also scolded me. I don't recollect whether my father scolded me as well, but I don't believe so. Neither do I remember if I got beaten, however I remember how terribly unhappy I was and can still recall the despair I felt at having killed a small animal. No one tried to understand me, comfort me, or at least talk to me. Instead, everyone merely blamed me. I felt a terrible guilt.

As mentioned earlier, my strong love for animals might be rooted in this event. I have had many animals: horses, sheep, goats, chickens, and of course cats and dogs. Somehow I have, during my entire life, tried to atone for that incident. Yet it is crystal clearly imprinted in my memory in the form of guilt, even though I have forgiven myself a long time ago. I do know how important it is to truly forgive oneself.

I have a memory from the Mineral Kingdom as well. This is one in adulthood, when I was cycling together with my two daughters along a gravel road in the countryside on a beautiful summer's day. I was the one farthest back. All of a sudden I spotted a stone, about the size of the palm of my hand, and felt compelled to stop my bike. It was as though someone inside of me commanded me to take up the stone and hold it to my ear. I did so - and it sang! I could swear, it truly did sing to me. Shells can sing, but I've never heard of stones on a gravel road in the countryside that can sing. The girls impatiently called to me, reminding me that the bun-dough rising back at home might be ruined. I put the stone in my pocket and biked after them.

The stone never ceased singing. I don't know where it is now. Unfortunately it disappeared, but it inspired me to start artistically painting stones, and I later had an exhibition in Stockholm displaying my art stones. Somehow it also became a sort of inner song, a stone's secret message to me, and it still remains inside of me. It told me that everything in Nature is alive. If a small stone can sing, then a big rock can rumble and a mountain can transmit an icy melody. I still have a special love for stones, both precious ones and those naturally polished by time, creating remarkable shapes and colors. To most people, stones are just stones. Not to me. Every grain of sand, every stone, every cliff, every rock, and every mountain has life. Life takes care of life: Nature's living (and to us) *Invisible People* take care of Mother Earth's physical creations. You doubt this? Well, that's why I'm writing this book.

My adventurous angel friend Jan has not abandoned me. He would like to tell about his latest adventures *in the Magical World of Nature*. He is assigned to the most remarkable missions in the dimension in which he dwells. After having completed his mission as a truth seeker in the world of the New Testament (see *The Bible Bluff*), he has now proceeded to the magical book of Nature, with all its millions of written and unwritten pages.

Magic of any kind is exciting. It's like a prism of crystal, full of multicolored alternations, full of superstition, but also full of a deep wisdom. The latter is the most interesting. Our dreams, daydreams, visions, hidden hopes, and undisclosed experiences - the things we hold secret, call supernatural, and don't understand - are all concealed in the magic. Yet the most magical and mysterious of all is the Nature in which we live and which we compete to destroy. We see only what we want to see in a world that contains vastly more than what our eyes

1

perceive. We wander around blind in our everyday lives, dismissing the unseen around us as mere delusion and superstition. In an attempt to alter this attitude, Jan has delved deeply into the greatest, most magical, and mysterious of all worlds: Nature.

Mariana Stjerna

1. A Yawning Jan Has the Floor

I enjoyed being able to hand over new information concerning the historical events of the New Testament. It was fun making peep-holes into such an interesting era, and delving into the lives of the "celebrities" of that time, who in many ways proved to resemble their modern counterparts. Throughout all time there have always existed "modern" people, because feelings and thoughts stem from the same original source. I am now sitting at home in the Angelic Realm, contemplating what will happen next. So far nothing has happened, and that's why I'm yawning. Even angels can yawn. Angels need to be fully occupied, just like humans do. We don't get hungry for food, but we get hungry for knowledge. We also get hungry for energies. What you call energies is an infinite amount of rays in all colors and more, both light and dark ones.

Who invented the word "energies," by the way? In our time it has become a trendy word. The world of energies is for us deafening and tumultuous, full of surprises, but also of wisdom. You never tire of the discoveries in this world, but in fact, they have to do with feelings, perceptions, and to some degree radiation.

I have been told that I should rest, but this is something I find really hard. Perhaps I'm just a restless spirit, but I dearly wish to feel that I am accomplishing something worthwhile. Many also find it difficult to understand how I can reason in such a human-like manner. It's not hard at all. In my thinking, much of the human remains - my medium on Earth is well aware of that. Otherwise I wouldn't have been assigned to my previous missions, and I hope for more of these to come. I also hope that someone noticed I yawned. It's not easy to have any secrets here. That's probably why there was a knocking at my door right now!

In came my good friend and former religious historian, the lovely spirit Lydia. Her long brown hair gleamed like old copper and her radiant brown-green eyes shone. All her lovely appearance looked as if she had something important to communicate, and I was certainly not mistaken!

"Look at you, sitting here yawning!" she exclaimed, laughing. "It could be heard all the way to the school, where I was. But now I will tell you something most exciting: You and I are to embark on a new adventure once again. We are going to make peep-holes in the Nature World."

"Nature?" I repeated, startled. "What on Earth for?"

"Dear Jan," she replied, winking at me. "We are going to teach humans about the magic of Nature. We'll visit different time periods and various aspects of Nature, different kinds of magicians in Nature, and some occult, transcendental phenomena. We'll also try to get humans to understand that Nature's infinite variety of beings truly exists. So what do you think of that?"

I jumped up out of my comfortable chair. Gone were my former tiredness and boredom, gone was the source of my yawning. Life - that is, my angelic life - had once again become exciting.

"May we become humans sometimes?" I asked.

"It may not always be that popular in this context," she said, smiling. "Perhaps, if necessary. However, we'll also have a great deal of magical help from our escorts. We'll be four persons this time. Please enter, Balthori and Thesa!"

The gently smiling man who came towards me was quite tall and was wearing a dark violet cloak. He had a very peculiar face. It was thin, with high cheekbones, and his eyes were slanted and honey-colored. His eyebrows were almost grown together over the root of his nose and they were as fair as his shoulder-length hair. His nose was large, but not bent, and his mouth, albeit narrow, was well shaped. His hollow cheeks were as though sculpted with deep lines. His gaze was sharp, and it instilled a feeling of deep wisdom. The body underneath the shimmering silk cloak seemed thin, but at the same time lithe.

A female being appeared at his side; she was called Thesa. She, too, was wearing a violet cloak. When she pushed back her hood, she showed a beautiful, although unusual, face. She appeared as her companion: thin, almost transparent. Her face was pale and her large eyes were a dark honey color. Her cheekbones were high and gave an almost Asian impression. She seemed more vivacious than the man, and she smiled gently the whole time. Her pointed ears were adorned with exquisite pearl earrings, and I glimpsed a pearl necklace around her neck. Who were these: humans, angels, or ... well, what?

"We are elves," announced the woman in a soft, melodic voice. "We are half Nature spirits, and without us you will not get far on your planned trip. We belong to a soon extinct branch of elves who once inhabited the Earth."

"We will accompany you, Jan and Lydia, on a remarkable journey," the man continued. In contrast to his slender, thin figure, his voice was surprisingly dark and deep. There was something compelling, something unknown, strong, and strange in his entire appearance. I noticed that his hands were well shaped and that his unusually lengthy fingers had long, pointed nails. On his right hand he wore a gold ring, which was wide and very ornate. In its patterns, stones were glittering that I supposed were amethysts, turquoise, and rubies.

"You're welcome," I replied. "Who are you?"

"Balthori is one of the most skilled sorcerers, wizards, mystics, and magicians you could meet," interjected Lydia in his place. "His wife, Thesa, carries the four elements - earth, water, air, and fire - within her body, and she masters them completely. She is a necessary complement to her husband."

"Unfortunately, I wasn't quick enough to prevent this hardly-modest introduction of us," said the man, gently smiling. "But since we are going to examine what the magic of Nature contains, both of us will be needed."

"I've never heard of either you or your wife before," I objected. "Are you from the Angelic Realm and, if so, are Balthori and Thesa your real names? Do elves exist here, too?"

"Don't you know that a sorcerer never reveals his real name?" was his counter-question. "If you find Balthori too long, then among friends,

Balt will do! Among the elves you will find a magic that certainly can be likened to what humans perceive of the word, but it also has its own meaning and effect."

"One might say that it is more powerful, but perhaps also more dangerous," his wife filled in. "In answer to your second question: We don't exist among the angels. We come from our own planet, and Melchizedek has summoned us here."

"Jan, Balt, Thesa, and Lydia," giggled Lydia. "What a team! Magic and occultism are all part of a religious historian's competence, which is why I asked to join in when I was notified of these plans. By the way, maybe I'll just go with you in order to keep a watchful eye on Jan, so he isn't mesmerized off by some alluring fairy."

"I wasn't informed of any plans," I grumbled. "Melchizedek hasn't summoned me."

"But he has now!" Melchizedek was standing in the room, tall and radiant, as the high Master he was.

2. The First Meeting with Mother Earth in Her Green Cave

I forgave him instantly. Probably he had his reasons for holding back the information. Maybe I wasn't always obedient or easy to find, and perhaps he wanted to see my reaction when it came to the elves. Well, to be honest, I never thought that elves were for real - only that they existed in fairy-tales and legends. It was certainly true that we needed company to penetrate the secrets of Nature - a magic-skilled and fascinating company who could lead us on the right track in all dangerous nooks and crannies.

The Earth was our original home - Lydia's and mine - which we knew well and which we loved. To discover new, hidden parts of it seemed like a hair-raising adventure. Maybe we would get to experience the wood nymphs and the trolls for real! I reveled in the thought. But the thought was read by Melchizedek, who gave a hearty laugh.

"Easy now, Janne!" he said. "I can see that Lydia is needed by your side. You are not going to take part in old tales. You are going to enter and discover the reality that is invisible to ordinary human eyes, but which exists as tangibly as humans themselves. You do not own the Earth you walk on. The Earth, including everything that grows on it, has both a physical and an invisible life - invisible to your eyes. We'll show you these things, because humans need to take better care of their Earth. It is not fashionable to believe in the existence of the elemental spirits. It is not fashionable to believe in Nature's enchanting beings. But the fashion in that respect has not fundamentally changed. Nature has permanent properties which are derived from the dawn of time, and you will soon experience that."

The way to move from the Angelic Realm to the object of our

investigation had not changed significantly. Now we stood together hand in hand, Thesa on my side and Balthori at Lydia's side. We closed our eyes, a buzzing sound was heard, and all of a sudden we were on our way. Hey presto, and we had also reached our destination. I wasn't thinking in terms of time on those trips. It was long ago since I had stopped thinking of time, this troublesome human invention. Suddenly you were here, and just as suddenly there. Movement was no problem and was free of charge, as far as fuel cost was concerned. But this time Balthori and Thesa led us. Melchizedek was gone.

We found ourselves in an intense green light. At first I saw only greenish, but after a short while I could make out more details. We stood in a cave. At least, it resembled the caves I've visited - although still not. The walls were rocky and uneven, but not mossy. They shifted in gold and silver, and everywhere streaks of different colored gemstones seemed to be interspersed. It was very beautiful. We stood on a deep green carpet of moss, which first caught our eyes. Here and there were stalactites and stalagmites, stalactite structures just as in ordinary caves, but more beautiful, brighter and more brilliant. From a bench at the far end of the cave a woman dressed in glittering green stood up. She proceeded, rather than walked, up to us and embraced each one of us. As usual, the embrace was not felt, but that's how it is when you are an ethereal spirit, I thought. But it was nice anyway. I enjoy being hugged!

"Welcome to the Earth's innermost cave!" The woman's voice was loud and clear. It's hard to explain, but it sounded more like a song than words. I observed her. She was tall and sheer, but neither young nor old. Her hair was white and fluffy, in large, shimmering waves and curls. Her face was thin and beautiful, but was marked by time. Her eyes were both sharp and deep, melancholic and joyful, and their color shifted between green, brown, and dark blue. As a sea wave during a storm, I thought.

"I am Mother Earth, or perhaps you'd prefer to call me an aspect of Mother Earth - for she has many aspects," continued the woman. "From here begins your journey into the secrets of Nature, since it was here that everything began. The substance of this cave existed in the first grain of gravel that grew and developed into our Earth. A seed becomes a flower, so why can't a grain of gravel become an Earth? Nature's potencies are infinite."

"Where are we?" I asked eagerly. "Are we in the midst of the Earth's
•o?
core?"

The woman nodded. I looked at my companions. Lydia stood smiling at my side and watched the green-clad woman. Thesa and Balthori walked around and touched the cave walls and looked curiously into the huge obelisks of the stalagmites.

"You know the Nature on Earth, you who have lived there so recently," continued the woman who called herself Mother Earth. "But you don't know the invisible beings that live around you, who you face each day without you knowing it, and who you kill with your toxins, your violence, and your ignorance. You will see how they live. You will get to visit the time when humans were aware of their brothers and sisters in Nature. You shall be together with them, like Peter Pan, and maybe you will meet the God Pan, the uncrowned ruler of Nature. You will return here to the innermost cave now and then, because your journey starts from the cradle of Nature, from me. I have many peep-holes that you are going to visit. When I'm finished with you, your message to the humans on the surface of the Earth will be that there is a world inside the world, a world with an equally magical past as the one you call your world. Are you ready?" Our "Yes" was unanimous.

"Will we experience magic?" I asked breathlessly, "both black and white?"

"There is only white magic," said the Earth's Mother, smiling. "The black magic is created by humans, the evil humans, the power-hungry humans. There are actually no evil humans, either. Evil is in close proximity to humans, waiting for them to grab the lust for power and violence to usurp power. Then evil sees its chance, and jealousy, envy, and other negative emotions and energies prevail. The energies are all around humans, but it is up to them what they choose. The good is always near. Additionally, dear Jan, all that you experience from now on as a human is magic - you just have to take care of it properly."

I sighed, but chose not to respond. She was right. I had asked a stupid question.

"Not stupid, but perhaps unnecessary," whispered Lydia. "You could have asked me. I knew that!"

"We will begin to unravel from the proper end," continued the green-clad woman. "More than twenty-two million years ago, at a time when Earth's humans certainly were primitive - and according to your current scientists didn't even exist - extraterrestrial, human-like beings visited our globe and intermingled with the inhabitants here. You have probably heard about that before. They brought with them a highly developed culture, and some of them were what you nowadays call elves. I want you to be involved from the beginning, when elementals roamed completely visible, although with a slightly different structure than yours.

"At that time, many millions of years ago, there were three kinds of human beings here: aboriginal inhabitants, elves, and extraterrestrial humans. These three kinds of people got on well together and shared valuable knowledge, enabling Nature to thrive in a favorable way for humans. I'm talking about a time that is not in your scientific studies and discoveries on the surface of my Earth."

"Were there animals then?" I wondered.

"Oh yes, lots of animal species and lots of plant species," was the reply. "The plants came first. That happened after the oceans had contracted and left open, dry areas of soil. All life began in the ocean; surely you must have learned that? But the extraterrestrials brought with them seeds, some birds, and knowledge to manage the burgeoning soil. Furthermore, you are probably aware of the fact that repeated periods of disasters have happened in the form of earthquakes, floods, and volcanic eruptions thereafter. The time you consider to be man's first advent on Earth is incorrect.

"The time of the humans that you are about to visit now is more than twenty million years ago. The Earth was developing and was completely habitable. It was just waiting to share both its beauty and its contents. You talk about monkeys. Certainly they are related to humans, but in a completely different way than you think, and during a later development era. Humans were fully developed in their bodies and had a fairly developed brain when the elves settled here. However, the difference was quite large, both in appearance and intelligence.

"The elves were superior in everything and then became a type of lords, or at least leaders. They were magicians of a new variety, which was both new and foreign to the humans. It took thousands of years and many mixed marriages for envy, competitive desire, and lust for power to emerge. The Earth has perished many times because of this, but never completely. The globe has remained, and I've been here all along. Come with me, Jan and Lydia, Thesa and Balthori. You will understand all tongues you meet, otherwise these trips would be meaningless."

Mother Earth asked us with a graceful gesture to follow her. We discovered a golden door in the farthest part of the cave. When we got closer we saw that it consisted of a bright, sparkling mineral in which gold veins were interspersed. It shimmered so much it hurt my eyes. Our green-clad leader took out a gold key and opened the door. Outside the door only a slightly yellow mist was seen. She handed the key to Balthori.

"Turn this in the air when you want to come back here." She smiled. "I'm waiting for you."

It was not the first time my companions and I stepped out into a mysterious cloud of smoke of an unknown misty vapor.

3. A Meadow Full of Tiny Elementals

A meadow is a meadow. Back home in Swede,n a meadow during summer is a flowering, idyllic place with succulent green grass that sometimes is shaggy and sometimes grows in tussocks with cornflowers, poppies, clover, timothy-grass, yarrow, many kinds of hawkbits, oxeye daisies, bluebells, and buttercups. That wasn't the case with this meadow. It was no ordinary meadow, and yet it was a real, flowering meadow. It contained the enumerated flowers and hundreds of others, new, I had never seen.

There were also groves. Groves usually consist of groups of trees and bushes here and there in big meadows. We saw several such. The oaks we recognized, hazel, ash, and linden I could make out, but there were other nameless trees and bushes as well. Only because of their shape could I call them trees and bushes and other things. Everything grew neat and defined, as if each plant had been put into the soil with uttermost accuracy. It was beautiful, sun-drenched and without limits. Yet it smelled like a Swedish summer meadow. This is a very special smell that only exists in Sweden. I know because I grew up with it.

"The meadow has an end," said Thesa, smiling. "We'll track down the road to some settlements, but look carefully around all the time. You will see more than the meadow."

Indeed, she was absolutely right! I had been so fascinated by the vegetation that the life around it had escaped me. Lydia pinched my arm in her usual mischievous way and then I woke up. There were not only flowers, bushes, and trees in the meadow, there were people too! I call them "people," but that is not the correct word. Everywhere beings of different kinds were moving. They had heads and bodies with arms and legs like us, but they were not as physically stout. I understood that they were fairies and gnomes of various kinds.

"Here the beings of Nature live completely visible to humans," explained Balthori. "They simply take care of Nature. As simple as that."

"Do they still exist on Earth today?" I asked, even if my question seemed a little unnecessary.

"In a way they do and in another way they don't," was his cryptic reply.

"Those who are still on Earth now have proceeded to form units for each plant species," Thesa hastened to explain, when she saw my puzzled face.

"Units?"

"Yes, a kind of group souls if you wish," replied Thesa.

We wandered slowly along the meadow, and now I saw high boulders that obscured the view and prevented me from seeing the end of the meadow. The beings of Nature were working with their plants, apparently totally unaware of us. They floated, laid down and dug, knelt, sat next to their plants, and seemed to enjoy themselves. Bumblebees, bees, butterflies, and other insects glistened, glittered, and flew as multicolored rays across the splendor of the plants. It was like learning anew, learning about plants and insects and the multifaceted Nature spirits who let their thin bodies blend into the diversity of colors.

"If you look a really long time," said Lydia thoughtfully, "you can distinguish the beings of the four elements from each other." I must have looked bewildered, since Balthori laughed.

"You must know the four elements, Jan," he explained, "earth, water, air, and fire. They have their representatives everywhere here: gnomes, undines, sylphs, and salamanders. I preferred to choose this meadow as the starting point for our visit in this time, which takes place eons of years ago. We will end the excursions in a similar way when you have had your experiences. You must get familiar with the different beings of Nature if you are to accomplish your mission. I suppose your mission is composed of passing on the lessons you learn here?"

I nodded. Lydia laughed and put her arm under mine.

"Puzzled writer?" she whispered. "We are actually on the Earth, the Earth you thought you knew from beginning to end."

"But this is beyond all scientific research. It doesn't reach this far back in time," I added, and sighed. "I've actually skimmed a little of what Rudolf Steiner has written, but I dismissed it as mythology."

"You don't skim anymore; you experience a reality, even if it's ancient," she replied. "As a historian, I find this extremely fascinating. And just wait, you'll see things that will make your eyes stand on stem!"

Thesa and Balthori had stopped a bit ahead of us. The elf held a budding sunflower gently between his hands. Several sunflowers grew close to a large boulder, and small beings floated around them.

"I will let you see down into the earth, Jan," said Balthori. "Look, what do you see?"

The root spirit (gnome) was about a hand's breadth high.

It felt as if my eyes burst out in some strange way. I could see straight down into the earth, all the way to the roots of the sunflower, which branched out in a jumble of soil and a dense pattern of other roots. The funniest thing was the gnomes, who were everywhere. I call them gnomes because it was the closest description I came up with. They were the root spirits. They were about a hand's breadth high and had very different, quite human, appearances. Their skin color was gray-green, although it also varied with yellow and brown features. Their tight clothes were of the same color as their bodies. Their eyes

25

were yellow or green. Their long thin fingers with claw-like nails worked diligently, but the pace was not very fast.

First I thought they moved around in slow motion, but then I understood that their pace was adapted to the root system. I felt like Gulliver, not yet imprisoned in the nets of the Lilliputians.

I rubbed my eyes, which felt normal again. Balthori observed me with a loving, yet at the same time a bit quirky, smile.

"Now you'll get to meet the undines, the water spirits, a very strange species," he promised. "You can see them using your regular angelic eyes."

Undine, or water spirit.
Undines float around in dancing waves near the ground.

I moved my gaze to the Earth's surface, i.e., to the undulating ocean of plants in the meadow. Near the ground, beings were floating around in dancing waves. I had no idea what their task was, so I asked Balthori.

"When the root spirits send up the plants from their roots and they reach the Earth's surface, the plants would dry out in the rapid air exchange unless the undines existed," he replied.

"Actually, water is the proper element of the undines, but when they are working with the plants they emit rays that surround the plant in a humidifying way. Other undines live in the water, but maybe you already know that."

I nodded and didn't pretend that I knew much about the secret part of growing in Nature. Instead I observed the sheer beings that resembled multi-colored, bluish light rays. They behaved differently than ordinary light rays, which shine outward or upward and are always straight. These beings could wriggle around the plants; they formed spirals and rings around a newly awakened, and by daylight a little shocked, plant. These elemental spirits united, in some mysterious way, water and air, which apparently are what plants need, I thought.

"The sylphs are the elemental spirits of the air," the handsome elf continued. He made a sweeping gesture with his hand. "They develop the leaves and the flowers of the plant, causing it to wake up properly, and giving it a desire to unite with the light. Look carefully at the sunflower!"

I did. Then I discovered tiny, almost translucent figures flying around the plant, seemingly working on different parts of it. They unfolded the leaves and provided stability to the flower. The undines had no visible figures to me, but the sylphs did. I got a perception of their wings and I was almost blinded by their shimmering movement. They were extremely fast.

"The sylphs are dwelling in the air currents." Now it was Thesa who spoke. "You see them around the sunflower here, but they are almost everywhere. For example, the draft that a bird makes in its flight in the air is the home of the sylphs. The draft creates a tone which the sylphs pick up. Look closely at them and you will see how beautiful they are."

Sylph, or air spirit. These are almost translucent beings flying around,
seemingly working on different parts of the plant.

I leaned forward and studied the tiny beings. They were as big as my thumb, brightly pastel-colored, and despite their tininess, very human-like. I saw them making different faces; they laughed, smiled, frowned their little foreheads, sang, and held up their thin arms towards the light.

"Yes, of course they sing," said Thesa, laughing. "Their tones are in accordance with the sound of the air and the air currents. They celebrate the light and they ensure that the plants can receive exactly the right amount of light. Other than that, the birds are their best friends and they follow in the wake of the birds' flight."

"Finally we come to the fire spirits, who are also called salamanders." Balthori pointed out and upwards. I hadn't seen them before, but up there hovered small figures in shades from yellow to deepest red. At first I thought they seemed to swim aimlessly around in the air, but Thesa explained how they worked.

"They collect heat," she said. "For example, they collect solar heat and carry it into the plants, so that they are permeated by it. Even if it rains or is overcast, the plant maintains the heat for a certain period of time, thanks to the salamanders. But salamanders also work inside fire. They love fire, and it develops their powers and multiplies them."

Fire spirit, or salamander. These beings collect solar heat
and carry it into the plants. They also work inside fire.

"As in a fire disaster," I added dryly and scrutinized the little creeps. They didn't look quite human, more like flames without bodies. Now and then something resembling figures with high conical heads could be glimpsed inside the flame. Their dance up in the air was almost like a crackling fire, but without heat and sparks.

"You have gotten to see how the Nature spirits of the Plant Kingdom are working," said Balthori. "Now we have to move on; there is much to learn here."

Large stones were around us, and Balthori leaned against a big gray boulder that looked like a healing stone. It had a pit with a hole at the top. I climbed up onto it to look a little closer, while the other three stood and laughed below. I might have looked a little "clumsy Swedish," but my long legs didn't deny themselves. Up I got with a bang. I was not used to sudden noises any longer and reacted strongly when my physical butt hit the stone in a very earthly way. I even wiped the sweat from my forehead. Then I realized that I was in a highly physical state. I looked at my legs and saw that I wore a pair of white pants - well, they were not that white after the climb. I apparently had a red striped shirt, too, so I felt like a big lollipop. The giggle that followed my thought came from down below. Lydia read my thoughts, as usual.

There was a depression in the stone. I crawled forward to watch the moss-edged hole. It was deep, a little bigger than my spread hand. It was dark, and seemed a lot deeper than I had imagined. I wished I had a flashlight, and I actually had one when I felt in my pocket.

Thoughtful angels, I thought contentedly, and let the light flash right into the hole. A pair of large, angry, reddish eyes met mine. A broad, warty nose was glimpsed and then a huge mouth roared some words I didn't understand, but which sounded very angry.

"Come down, Janne!" Balthori cried. "You must not awaken the wrath of the mountain spirit."

I had already done so, and horrified, I scuffled back towards the edge of the stone. Up from the hole appeared a greenish thatch, which more resembled moss than hair, and below it was the hideous face I had glimpsed down there. I shuffled quickly towards the edge, and after that I don't remember anything.

"Jan, oh Jan, you scared me so!" I woke up with my head in Lydia's lap. Thesa and Balthori stood next to us, chanting something. I thought I had been dreaming, because trolls don't exist for real and I had seen a troll. A nasty troll who came creeping closer and closer and then I fell ...

"There are no trolls," I said angrily and stood up. I stretched my arms and legs and felt my back. It was as usual; I had apparently taken no harm. "That was not a troll," I continued challenging.

"We call them mountain spirits or stone spirits," Balthori replied. "They are not always pleasant. You fell down, but we have healed you. You received no serious injuries. Can we continue on to the village?"

"How many thousands of years ago have we arrived at?" I asked.

"Not thousands, we count millions," said Thesa, smiling. She and Lydia supported me on either side and it was so nice that I limped a little extra now and then. But then we stopped. We found ourselves on the edge of a high hill and Balthori pointed at the landscape before us.

4. Visiting Humans and Elves in an Ancient Village

A gathering of houses met my astonished eyes. They were not just any houses, but there were actually two types. Some resembled huts made of clay and the others were braided from a material which I didn't recognize. Thus they were braided houses, where the braids stood upright and formed four sides. The roofs were made of moss that probably rested on a framework of unknown material. All the houses had chimneys, while the huts had holes in their round roofs.

"The village!" cried Balthori delightedly, and he started running down the hill. We followed after him, of course.

It was pretty nice to see humans, after all the little monstrous Nature creeps, I thought, a little mean. Lydia cast an angry glance in my direction, but she remained silent, because now we found ourselves in a real crowd. It teemed with brown-skinned, stout humans. We hurried, led by our elves, across a square that was surprisingly large. There was apparently some kind of ongoing market, since humans sat on the ground with goods lined up in front of them. I would have liked to have had a closer look at the goods, but Balt seemed to be in a hurry.

One braided house was larger than the others and it was apparently the goal of our visit. Balt turned around and beckoned us to follow him into the house. There was no door, only a rather large, square opening.

"This is the meeting house in the village," said Thesa. "Absolutely everything takes place here."

We entered a large, oblong room. It was also full of people, gathered in smaller groups. There was no furniture other than long, wooden logs and folded, colorful blankets to sit on. Balthori brought us to a smaller group that consisted of both elves and humans. In its center sat a man who appeared significant. He was old, and his brown face was furrowed. His closely adjacent eyes were pale and slightly walleyed, but occasionally they were lit up by an inner fire. His body was haggard. He was dressed in a yellow cape, much like an Indian guru. Some humans were dressed in cloths, more or less artistically wrapped around their bodies, while others only wore a loincloth.

It was quite warm, both outdoors and indoors. In the middle of the room, a low fire was burning. Inside the fire, fully visible salamanders were moving around in a frisky dance. Balthori bowed deeply to the old man. The old man stood up, unfolded his hands, and smiled kindly at us. When he spoke I understood what he said.

"Welcome, descendants of the recent human race, and most welcome, sister and brother of the elf race!" He bowed his head in a graceful manner. "The flattened time is imprinted in the mystery of the ether. We remain as an echo of our own time and our own power. We live in our own reality that we now share with you. Here are representatives of earth, water, air, and fire, who are keen to share their wisdom of the elements. What do you wish to know?"

"Um, doesn't it get a bit crowded with all the elementals together with the humans?" I dared to ask. Lydia rolled her eyes and put her hand to her mouth, presumably to stop giggling. But the old man looked serious. There was something about him that made me react strongly. At that moment I couldn't explain why. I understood it much later. He gestured for us to sit down on the floor.

"My name is Haak," he replied, "and I speak for the entire village when I say that your question is superfluous. Humans and elves live in the same village in perfect harmony. The extraterrestrials live in their area, the five golden towers on the outskirts of the village, and they travel back and forth in their own vehicles to their different worlds. The Earth is not the only inhabited planet in the Universe. The extraterrestrials are in contact with us in order to give us the information we need. They teach us how to cultivate our soil, which of the animals we can tame as pets, and much more. We haven't noticed any crowding; each one handles their own occupation. The market can be very busy, since it's open only certain days. If you mean the elementals, they don't require much space, and no space at all for dwellings. They are only active in their atmospheres in their own areas."

"It's hard to conceive as far back as to this time," I muttered apologetically. "Everything seems so different; everything except the ground, the soil, and Nature. It is similar to our present time, even though you have many species which must be extinct in our time."

"Then I ask you a question." Haak smiled gently and looked with his warped look straight into my eyes. Somehow it felt creepy. "What kind of magic do you have in your time?"

"Magic is not very popular," answered Lydia in my place. "It is considered quixotic and is often called flights of fancy. There are sorcerers, but they are only skilled with their hands; nothing comes from within. There are a few genuine magicians, but they are obliged to work in secret."

Haak shook his head and frowned. A low murmuring noise arose from the people sitting around, a murmuring noise that sounded threatening.

"So the power to practice the magic of Nature has thus degenerated," the old man stated. "We don't care about inventing things; we are living close to Nature and are utilizing what is offered there in all its diversified forms. Nature's magic is the most important thing we have. The body is satisfied, but the spirit must also be satisfied. That is more important than anything else."

"Maybe we define magic differently," I suggested. "I think of magic as a more advanced kind of sorcery, such as changing appearance or stemming blood ..."

"Changing appearance is not magic," interrupted Balthori, hitherto quiet and observing, just like Thesa. "We elves make use of that whenever it's necessary. Also for the purpose of demonstration."

Thesa stood up. Gradually she faded to light. I couldn't distinguish her features as she, to my amazement, appeared again - as a white hind. The whole group laughed. Gone was the threatening atmosphere that existed a while ago. The hind ran around for a while, after which it returned to its position beside Balthori and was gradually transformed back to Thesa. Both Lydia and I stared. We probably looked silly, since the laughter continued. Apparently, the humans who lived millions of years ago were used to what we call magic.

"What you saw was Thesa perverting the vision of everyone in this room. It's an ancient knowledge of the simpler kind. The genuine magic has its origin in the interaction between Nature and human," resumed Haak. "The interaction must be conducted consciously and purposefully for a reason, a desire, or a task that is in alignment with the light or the dark. Both exist. Do you understand?"

Lydia and I nodded. Actually I didn't really understand what he meant, but I was going to ask Balthori at a later point. Anyway, "in alignment with the dark" boded no good. A brown-skinned, young woman bent down and put something in front of us. It was a meal, laid out on a flat piece of wood and decorated with green leaves. The meal consisted of bread, fruit, and dried meat. The drink served was fresh and delicious spring water. Probably they had not learned to cook here yet. Haak signed to the four of us to eat, and so we ate. We dared nothing else, although we shouldn't eat meat in our temporary bodies. The dried meat tasted good, even though some spices would have been needed. We didn't want to expose ourselves to the group's unwillingness once more. They watched us very intrusively, following every move we made, especially Lydia's and mine.

"This village is representative of its age," explained Balthori, just as if he could read my thoughts. "They're certainly not very fond of strangers; we are accepted at the moment, but not more. When you have finished your meal, we will leave for the five towers."

As we walked from there, Haak sat in some sort of meditation posture. He didn't say goodbye to us; instead he had his eyes closed and seemed completely gone. The group now ignored our existence. Yet, it was as if something invisible forced me to turn around. A large, brown-skinned man with a dark brown beard and bushy eyebrows, squinting so that you almost saw only one of his eyes, followed us with his gaze. I would not call his looks friendly glances. Were they full of hatred? So

34

I would have interpreted it if I hadn't heard so much about how good this village was. But I memorized his nasty glances.

We followed Balthori. Thesa went on my left side. A sunny smile played on her lips.

"Well, how does it feel to be millions of years back in time?" she asked.

"Exciting," said Lydia, laughing. "We should have known about this when we lived on Earth. But of course, no scientist would have believed us."

"I agree," I said, clearing my throat. "Is it far to the five towers?" I'd better lie low, I thought. I completely trusted Balt and Thesa. Melchizedek had confidence in them. But old Haak seemed to be a rascal, not to mention his company. I recognize rascals when I see them. I have met too many of them during my different lives. Hypocrisy is also something I sense. I glanced at Lydia's clean, beautiful profile. She was seemingly unaffected by my thoughts, or perhaps she was disconnected from them. I was hoping for the latter.

5. The Five Towers and
the Monster in the Cave

I could not imagine anything so unlike and different from the rest of the village than the five towers. I actually felt reverent as we stood in front of them, after a walk through the village and the small woodland. The five towers stood in a ring, with forest on one side and meadow on the other. They looked as if they were made of gold - and yet not. It must be a golden material, I thought, but it wasn't as dense as gold, and it shimmered and glittered in a different way than our precious metal. I understood that it was an extraterrestrial metal, which later turned out to be a correct assumption.

"The towers are built in a circle, and in its center is a plateau that is a landing site for extraterrestrial crafts," explained Balthori. "Let's knock on the door to see if someone is home."

A rather narrow door was opened. At first I hadn't taken any notice of it, and I thought it was pretty smart to hide a door so you didn't suspect its existence. A blond woman stood in the doorway. She was human-like and very beautiful. Yet, she didn't resemble any human. Now I contradict myself. It's perhaps because of the feeling I got that she belonged to an alien race. Her hair was so bright it was almost white. Her facial color was very pale, and somehow transparent, much like the elves.

She smiled gently in recognition towards the elves, and then she pointed at us. Balthori replied with a smile and said something in a language I didn't understand. The woman replied with a friendly smile and we were allowed to enter.

"Heth is the guardian of this tower," said Balt. "We've met a couple of times before. Soon you will witness the landing of a ship that is on its way here."

After I had entered the tower I stopped. All the towers were round and quite high, but as shiny golden was the outside, as crystal clear was the inside. The interior of each tower was probably made of window glass. I didn't see any glass, but when I tried to step farther forward I walked into something. Heth laughed heartily. Balt had to explain again.

"The walls in the innermost half of the towers are made of a transparent material unknown to us. These towers are here right now, during this period of time we have chosen to visit, but they will disappear when the extraterrestrials' mission on Earth comes to an end. Keep track of Jan, Lydia, so he's not getting himself into trouble. Now, let's move on."

I had nothing against Lydia putting her arm under mine. Heth conversed vividly with our elves and I looked curiously around. It glistened in my eyes, making it difficult to discern the details. However, I got the impression that this part of the tower was sparsely furnished with tables and high stools, and there were seats here and there. We walked up a spiral staircase. Finally we reached a room that was a little different from the rest of the tower.

The walls were painted in variegated colors, and although the figures were only implied, I understood that they represented different stages in human life. For example, there was a woman in labor, and you could see how the baby developed from birth into something uncertain, which was impossible to decipher. It seemed as if the child became a warrior. The last picture was showing a battle. Consequently, they had already at that time understood to portray the warlike part of human nature. But there was also a large window, and Heth signed to Lydia and me to look out.

The circular field below glistened as much as the towers. But the remarkable thing was the craft that calmly and quietly descended towards the shiny, golden landing site. Not a round flying saucer, I thought, no ordinary UFO. Rather, I wanted to call it an unusual UFO. There was no doubt it was a UFO. That's how these must have looked like in the beginning, I thought further.

The craft was shaped much like a dolphin. From its tail a long beam of multicolored light was sent out, looking almost like a rainbow, although the violet light was dark purple and overrode the other colors. After it had landed, its "head" swayed softly above the ground, and also the tail was bent upward. A ladder was folded down and humans climbed onto the ground. At least they looked like humans. From one of the towers came several beings running. They were all dressed in tight, gold-colored jump suits.

"It looks like a modern disembarkation from an ultra-modern craft," I whispered in Lydia's rosy ear. Balthori probably heard us, because he gave me a cheery smile.

"These are visitors from Sirius," he exclaimed. "They have an excellent line to Earth, one that will actually work many times in the future as well."

"The Dogon people?" I asked, and he nodded. I was thinking of the African people in Mali, who, according to their thousands of years old preserved petroglyphs and stories, have been visited by Sirians.

"They will intermingle with the Earth humans," he continued, "but first they must undergo a kind of treatment for preparatory purposes."

"When their work is finished," continued Thesa, "they will not return, and the five towers will disappear. They have a particular task in teaching the Earth humans how to cultivate their soil and how to take charge of the gifts of the Earth."

"Which will be forgotten in the coming disasters," sighed Lydia, who knew her history.

"Some of it will remain, and is yet there," said Balthori, smiling. Whether Heth understood our language or not was impossible to say, but she smiled too. We bowed our heads to say goodbye, and sadly, we never saw the delightful lady again.

"You are not allowed to see more of this area," explained Thesa.

"Now we'll return to the village, and then we're heading back home. We have many ages to visit, both good and evil. We take the shortest route back!" She put her arm around Lydia, and Balt put his arm around me. The transport was as fast as when you switch TV channels with your remote control. Instantly we were back in the village, in the middle of the crowd in the square.

"I think we are getting to the meadow where we first arrived," said Balt. Before he had time to continue, we suddenly were surrounded by large, densely hairy men, resembling gorillas with human faces, long hair, and beards. I recognized some of them from our previous meeting with Haak. Even then they looked threatening. One of them was the squinting one who looked like a caveman.

"What do you want?" asked Balthori. He looked stern. I felt scared. Those types were not to be trifled with.

"We've been ordered to take you to the cave," said one of them. "Haak has some questions for you."

To my surprise, Balt let the large men carry us off. I looked with astonishment at Lydia, but her face was completely flattened. She showed no fear, and neither did Thesa. I pretended to take it easy, but inside of me there was chaos. What did Balt and Thesa mean? For a moment I had the horrible thought that they had some funny business together with Haak, but I let it pass quickly.

The walk wasn't long. Just outside the village we went into woods that looked like an ordinary Swedish forest with lots of mountains. We were immediately taken to a high mountain, in which there was a cave. I knew we could have cleared ourselves from this trouble by just disappearing, but obviously Balthori had other plans. We just had to hang on.

This was not a pleasant, glittering cave like Mother Earth's. It was dark and damp, water ran down the walls, and a pungent smell stung my nose. Haak sat on a piece of cloth on the ground and leaned against a rough, damp wall. What scared me even more was a rock that naturally rose in the middle of the cave. Probably this rock had made the cave become a meeting place and, from what I understood, a place for some kind of sacrifice. I felt terrible disgust when I saw that the rock was stained with blood. Was it human blood or animal blood?

Lydia turned to me and frowned. She sent tranquility to me and I tried to liberate myself from my unpleasant thoughts. We were angels already and couldn't die once again, so in fact I was being very stupid. I even laughed at my own stupidity, but then I got an angry shove. I almost fell, since the man who pushed me was a pair of heads taller than me, with bulging muscles and a brutal countenance. I kept silent, but I gave him an angry look. At least I thought so, but on his lips played an unpleasant grin.

"Listen to me!" It was Haak who raised his voice. "We think you are some kind of sniffer dogs, dispatched from another planet. Here the penalty for poking your nose into our affairs is only one: death."

"I've understood that you use the wrong kind of magic," said Balthori seriously. He fixed his eyes on Haak and held up both his hands towards the old man. Soon our jailers ceased to hold us and Haak flinched. He looked as if he wanted to sink into the cliff. His face was all gray.

"Call on your master of magic!" roared Balt. His eyes were flashing. "I propose a duel between him and me."

A tall dark figure detached himself from an outcrop of rock behind Haak. Once upon a time he had probably looked like the other villagers, but now he was completely covered with brownish-black hair. He resembled a bear with human features. Only his eyes appeared, and they were horrific. They sent out flashes of lightning in yellow and red. Whoever he was, he was certainly a monster.

"Home-made monster," Lydia's thought whispered to my brain. "This is a form of fear tactics."

Haak knelt before the apparition and the other villagers followed his example. The creature apparently was their god, since they worshiped him. The hairy one stood silent for a moment, and then he stretched out his arms and waved a little bit with his hands in the air, while he growled low as a Pekingese. There was a thunderclap in the cave, and after a short while a flash of lightning. Small hissing fire worms whizzed around and the villagers lay motionless with their foreheads to the floor.

The four of us stood straight and Balt raised his hand towards the monster. The monster opened his red mouth and lots of smoke came out of it. The smoke put out the fire worms and flowed into the whole cave, making everything except the monster's own body invisible. He looked triumphantly at us. I only knew where I was standing and that the others were somewhere nearby. The thick, gray smoke settled like dirty cotton around us and it smelled unpleasant. Apparently, this was the monster's way of showing us what an extraordinary sorcerer he was.

"Hocus-pocus," I heard Balthori mutter. I could vaguely make out that Balt, who was standing right in front of me, stretched out his right arm and pointed his finger at the evil "god." The monster let out a roar and started to shrink. When he was barely a yard in height, Balt stopped. The smoke dissipated in an instant. Haak and all the others were paralyzed. They didn't dare move. Their old leader got up painstakingly and fell down on the piece of cloth at the rock wall. The little monster ran around whimpering, but nobody cared about him. He slipped away and disappeared like a rat into a narrow crack in the rock wall.

Balthori nodded to the three of us and proceeded slowly out of the cave. None of the men were moving; they seemed completely petrified.

"They will move as usual when we have disappeared," he said. "Black magic is certainly evil and dangerous, but when the evil master isn't there anymore, we hope that they'll find a better master. I actually spoke a few words with Heth before we left the five towers. The extraterrestrials are aware that there is black magic going on here, and I promised them I would destroy the so-called master."

"But what about Haak?" I exclaimed. "He surely has bad influence on the villagers here."

"Not anymore." Balt's gentle smile was introverted. "I think he will be both scared and uncomfortably affected when he wakes up from the trance that I put him into. He can do a lot of good things as well, and he can actually be a good leader when he's not captured in the black magic."

"The monster you saw has kept the village in fear for quite some time," continued Thesa. "He will never return; he will soon surely be eaten by some larger animal. I knew Balthori had a task to perform here, and he has done it with verve. Now we can go home and tell them that the first mission is completed!" She put her hands on Lydia's and my shoulders, and Balt did the same. I only had time to cast a brief glance at the black cave entrance and the tall pine trees surrounding it, and then everything disappeared.

We were back in Mother Earth's cave.

6. Visiting the Same Place
Several Million Years Later

"Twenty million years back; that was awesome!" I groaned and wiped the sweat from my forehead. It was an unnecessary gesture; I had become an angel again, and consequently I didn't sweat. "I wouldn't have imagined that the Earth had developed such a high culture back then."

"Beings from other planets assisted," said Mother Earth, smiling. "From the perspective of the planets, it was a kind of teamwork to populate the beautiful Earth with humans who would make it become even lovelier. The intermingling of the original humans with highly developed planetary beings was a step that should have been successful. And it was - as long as the negative qualities within humans didn't become predominant."

We sat on benches around a stone table in Mother Earth's cave. There was a pleasant heat; no damp walls or bad smell. We enjoyed the smell of moss, mixed with the scent of a kind of tallow candle our hostess used - at least it looked like tallow candles. Mother Earth smiled when she saw my wondering eyes.

"It is possible to extract tallow from plants without hurting them," she said. "Among other things, Dipterocarpaceae, the oil-rich fruit tree, and Sapium, the tallow tree, have seeds that are useful for that purpose. It's very old knowledge, Jan. There is so much practical knowledge and wisdom that is forgotten in your time. The same applies to the beings of Nature. The cooperation with them is totally forgotten. If this cooperation instead had continued through the ages, so much misery could have been avoided, especially all the environmental destruction and poisoning that occur in the time you two angels come from. The beings of Nature had healing powers, but they also had recipes for miraculous medicines, ointments, and tinctures, which they shared during the ages when they were visible to humans."

"Where does the next peep-hole lead?" I asked, and Lydia nodded in agreement.

"Now you will only go one million years back in time," replied Mother Earth, with a roguish expression on her beautiful face. "The elves have their missions, and you just follow them. There is much you can learn on such trips. One million years ago, there were humans in certain places on Earth for a period."

"But if we think of Lydia's and my present time, approximately where did we find ourselves in our recent peep-hole twenty million years ago?" I asked. "Geographically speaking, I mean."

"In France, my dear, in southern France!" It was the historian Lydia who responded this time. "Didn't you get that?" I made an ugly face to her and everybody laughed. She continued, "A great many prehistoric discoveries have been made in France, and the Frenchmen are skilled geologists. Is that where we're going now?" Mother Earth nodded.

"To begin with. Much happens in so many millions of years. If you arrive at about the same location, you will notice the developments that have taken place. Do you have the strength to continue?" We nodded, smiling. Mother Earth stood up and walked over to the door that led to all the past years of the Earth.

We held each other's hands tightly and walked right out into the mist, with the two elves in the lead. I thought we would end up in the same flourishing meadow as previously, but we didn't at all. Instead we ended up on a high mountain. It could have been any mountain anywhere.

"A grain of sand has formed a mountain," commented Lydia on my thought. "First it became the hill we were standing on the last time we were here, but in many thousands of years the hill became this mountain. Are you with me?"

"The wings of change are flying continuously," I said, nodding. I peered cautiously into the valley below. The vegetation was quite low along the mountainside and I saw a valley where a river foamed and fizzed over stocks and stones, but I didn't see any village. Balthori stood close behind me.

"Villages move after millions of years," he stated. "We'll probably have to look for houses somewhere else."

"Aren't the extraterrestrials still here?" I asked, fully alarmed.

"Oh no!" It was Thesa who responded. "Their mission was done and they returned to their home planet. They were to sow certain grains of knowledge within the Earth humans and mix their seed with them. Presumably, new extraterrestrials will eventually come here again. Now we shall look for a village, if there is any." She turned sharply around and went across the top of the mountain to the other side. Up on the mountain there were signs indicating that humans were located there occasionally. Large stones were carved like human faces, coarse and ugly, but made with a certain artistry. They stood in a semicircle, and in front of them was a flat stone with faded flowers on top of it.

"These represent gods," said Balthori, pointing to the strange stone sculptures. "Victims are carried to the altar stone. The humans get up here on the road you see over there."

We saw a long and steep road that wriggled up the mountain. Balt and Thesa started to walk down the road and motioned for us to follow. Far below, we could distinguish round rooftops. A white, sheer mist lay like a blanket over the village. It will be exciting to see how far these humans have evolved, I thought. And exciting it became.

The roofs of the round houses were not roofs in the usual sense. On a framework of flexible tree branches, animal hides had been placed and were tied together with wicker at the top in order to create a hole, a chimney, in the middle. It looked very primitive, but apparently it worked, since a thin smoke oozed out of the holes from several of the huts.

We ventured closer when a big man came out of the hut by pulling aside one of the skins on the wooden framework. He stretched himself and yawned, but then he caught sight of us. Balthori stood in front of us with his hands stretched out toward the man. The man was rather hairy, just like the villagers from the previous trip. He wore a loincloth of skin and an animal hide over his shoulders. His head was quite round, with coarse facial features and small, grayish-brown eyes. His lips were wide and he smacked them. A woman looked out of the hut, and soon several small children came gently crawling. The woman had only a loincloth of skin, which was a bit longer than the man's. She had straight, dark hair that hung in wisps far down her back. Her nose was wide and her mouth was plump. The kids resembled her. I wondered if they were Stone Age people.

"Oh, don't be silly, the Stone Age was much later. This age we don't know much about," whispered Lydia, a bit superior because of her continuous historical knowledge. "That's why we're here."

The man bent down and picked up something from the ground. It proved to be a cudgel. He swung the weapon above his head and looked menacingly at us. Then Balthori raised his voice. The wild man - I thought he looked like a savage - gave a jump and lowered his cudgel. First he listened with a frown, and then a grin that exposed his big strong teeth broke out. I'm using the term "broke out" because the grin came fiercely, until it lay there like a rumbling cave full of white bone chips.

He approached Balthori, grabbed the elf's thin shoulders, and led him past the gathering of huts. They chatted in a friendly way and the Stone Age man (I still thought he looked like one) often showed his teeth. We, of course, followed in their tracks. We walked along a river, which apparently flowed through the village. It was certainly the same river we had seen from the other side of the mountain. In my eyes it resembled the Swedish river Dalalven, but I'm, of course, thinking in a far too modern manner.

Suddenly the village man and the elf stopped. I was walking between Lydia and Thesa and we stopped as well. In front of our eyes a light mist swept and it was filled with beings that continuously danced and moved gracefully. Fairies! Could it be fairies?

Dancing fairies.

Balt, who was speaking the villagers' language, had asked if there were any elementals and if the villagers had contact with them, explained Thesa. This was the answer: A being freed itself from the misty dance and floated up to Balt and the man from the village. The three of them had a conversation. The being, who resembled a fairy, seemed to have no gender. Its body was so slender and jointless, you could not tell if it was a man or a woman. Its hair was long and yellow-green. Its facial features were finely chiseled and its eyes, beneath the half-closed eyelids, appeared green. This strange being smiled at us and thereby bared its small, pointed teeth. It nodded and brought both of its small, neat hands to its heart and smiled even wider. The being's mouth didn't seem large when it was closed, but it stretched almost from ear to ear when it laughed.

"Surely the fairy people communicate with the villagers," explained

Balthori. "Fairies and elves are closely related, but the elves have evolved a little differently, more human-like. We can speak the fairy language, but they don't speak the language of the currently living humans. Dogob here wants us to come into his hut and dine with them. Do you mind that?"

A being with many names: dwarf, gnome, hobgoblin, goblin.

7. Meeting with Little People
and a Tree Spirit

The fairy smiled broadly the whole time while we were talking, but then it drifted up in the mist, which had thickened and settled like happy beads on all the leaves. "The Stone Age man" called Dogob beckoned us to follow him, and after a little while we were standing in front of a hut. He pulled apart the hides and we entered. There were hides on the inside as well. Balt explained that it was a protection against the various weather conditions that occurred here. But there was something else in the hut, too.

In the middle glowed a fire on the floor, which consisted of trampled down clay. Dogob's wife skillfully balanced several sticks - in modern language called skewers - with pieces of meat neatly strung. It actually smelled pretty good. However, the strangest thing in front of Lydia's and my eyes was several very small figures running around in there. They were not children. They had to be gnomes or dwarves. They received small, fried pieces of meat from Dogob's wife, who nodded and smiled at them all the time. In addition, she poured up a couple of small goblets with a mead-like drink for them. They zestfully slurped the drink that perhaps was a little intoxicating, as they both giggled and staggered around after they had consumed it.

"Now, let's eat," commanded Balt. "We have dense bodies, so we can probably endure this diet. Show your appreciation by smiling, nodding, and stomping easily with your feet. If you don't eat, our hosts will become offended, and then you don't know what they can do. Don't forget to smile!"

I unwillingly went for a skewer. Lydia sat close to me so we could push each other's sides. We chewed and smiled and smiled and chewed.

The meat was served together with large pieces of yeasted bread, which tasted really good. On the contrary, the meat tasted not particularly good; it was fat and without spices. The meat was pork-like; a wild boar had most certainly lost its life. But I thought that grimacing could be mistaken for smiling in this early civilization, so I managed to eat the whole skewer.

I saw that the elves had it even harder than us to consume the meat. Their small, even teeth were not designed for meat consumption, so I assume they swallowed their food unchewed. But they smiled all the time, and we all stomped the floor lightly. Our hosts seemed delighted. But when the next skewers arrived at our table we shook our heads and I understood that Balt explained that our stomachs were full, because he eagerly rubbed his flat, invisible belly. We were served beverage from a giant jar and my assumption regarding mead was absolutely correct. If the meat was tasteless, the mead was quite the opposite. Luckily, all drank from the same jar, so you could take just a small sip without anyone noticing. It was stronger than schnapps!

The little dwarves had partaken of enough meat and drink, and now they examined us thoroughly. We looked back at them and didn't forget to smile. They actually resembled some pictures I've seen of little people. They were human-like, but their features were coarser, their eyes were smaller, and their foreheads sloped very much backward. They were dressed in green or brown frocks that seemed woven. Maybe they would teach this primitive people to weave? Perhaps, I thought, the little people and the elves have been teachers for the primitive humans since quite far back in time, after the extraterrestrials had disappeared.

I had seen shaggy sheep on our little walk in the fairy mist, but they had seemed bigger than the present day's sheep, much like the size of deer. (When I talk about the present day, I mean the twentieth century.)

"The kinds of dwarves and gnomes you see in here also exist together with the other villagers," explained Thesa. "There was a very strong cooperation between elementals and humans at this time on Earth. Then came the major natural disasters that wiped out a large part of both the animals and the humans."

The dwarves were human-like,
dressed in green or brown frocks and peaked stocking caps.

"And then?" I asked. I didn't remember much of my knowledge about Earth's history.

"Then came the ages described in the history books on Earth," said Lydia. "We historians didn't really know that much, so we had to adapt to the geological findings that were made and figure out, in our own way, how the humans came into existence and which epochs the Earth has undergone."

"Darwin and all that?" I suggested, with a short laugh.

"There were different opinions, Darwin's was, and still is, one of them," she sighed. "The original cosmic Truth was not accepted in the time we both come from. The most common opinion was the ape theory; that humans began walking upright about five million years ago. There was even an ape that lived in Africa fourteen million years ago, who is considered to be the ancestor of the human race. And about two million years ago there was an ape-like human called the 1470 Man, who had a more developed brain than the human apes. She even manufactured tools. Homo Erectus, the upright man, was found in areas of Asia, Africa, and actually even in Europe about 500,000 years ago ... "

"Stop!" I cried. "I didn't need a thesis of human evolution; I just wanted to know where we are right now."

Lydia was like a running water tap when she began with historical information. At times it was informative and interesting, but perhaps a bit disturbing when we found ourselves in a place about one million years ago.

I noticed that Thesa looked at us with an amused smile. Balthori was engaged in a conversation with Dogob, so she must feel lonely. Lydia probably thought the same, because she took Thesa under her arm and whispered something to her - probably about me - which made the elf woman laugh excitedly and accompany her out of the smoky hut. I took the opportunity to follow the two women's example, but I walked in the opposite direction. At a distance I saw water glisten. Lakes and streams have never ceased to enchant me. When I got to the river, I faced the next surprise.

Dusk had just started to cover the Earth with its amazing shadow theater. The river was running clear and calm, with silvery fringes on the ripples, and the birds' music had slowly subsided. It was quiet and wonderfully beautiful and the landscape looked so classically Swedish that it might as well have been one million years later. But one thing was different from the 1900s. Lots of fairies danced on the silvery fringes.

To my amazement, I got to see a figure slowly detach itself right out of the trunk of a huge chestnut tree near the river. The figure was almost man-high and came straight towards me, so I could examine it more closely. If it had a gender, it must be a man. He was thin, wiry, and gnarled. His skin was brownish and full of wrinkles and crinkles. His brown-green eyes scrutinized me curiously. Actually, he looked ancient, and I understood he was the tree's spirit. He smiled kindly at me and welcomingly stretched out his lean, uneven hands that more resembled twigs shooting out from his branched body. He started talking and I understood what he said.

"Human, you are welcome here with us. I do not recognize you, but I hope our cooperation will be good."

"I'm an angel," I replied and returned his smile. "I'm sent here to see how the cooperation between humans and elementals works among you."

"That's good, that's good," replied the tree spirit. "As long as the humans in the village don't cut us - the trees - down for their own self-interest, we can have nice chats together." He motioned for me to sit down with my back against the trunk of the chestnut tree and then he put himself next to me. "I have seen many human ages disappear, but never before have I seen an angel. The relations between Nature spirits and humans have not always been good, but in the last fifty thousand years they have developed well. As a reward for that, I have given this village many chestnut trees."

"So the villagers can see the Nature spirits?" I wondered. I heard a tinkling laugh behind me and I turned around, terrified. An undine, that is, a water spirit, stood behind me and laughed. It must have been a female being; she was dizzyingly beauteous, but at the same time unreal. There are no such women, I thought, looking at her long, thin, but well-shaped body with tiny, barely visible breasts and slender hips.

Her face was indescribable. I've never seen anything so beautiful, and her wet green-golden hair closed tightly around her forehead and then billowed down to the ground. But she was real to the fullest. She wrapped her soft, balmy arms around me and kissed me on my forehead ... I jumped high when the voice of the gnarled tree spirit reached me through the shimmer of the undine's aura.

"Beware, angel! Undines are good and happy spirits, but they like to trap humans in their nets. If you want to return to the heavenly kingdom, you'd better keep her at a distance! She wants to drag you down into the river and amuse herself with you underwater, way down to the bottom ..."

"Jaaan!" Lydia's voice was heard, and I saw her and Thesa come running. Behind them I caught a glimpse of Dogob's wife. "What are you doing?"

The Undine rippled as when you throw a stone into the water and quickly disappeared out into the river. I breathed a sigh of relief and the gnarled man by my side let out a half-suppressed laugh. When the two women came up to us they stopped, terrified, but the tree spirit stood up and bowed politely to both of them.

"Welcome to our village," he pattered between his yellow, uneven teeth. "All humans are welcome to rest for a while at my trunk. May I offer you a chestnut?" He scooped up three chestnuts from an invisible pocket and then he settled down with his arms crossed.

"How come the other village doesn't exist anymore, the one on the other side of the mountain?" I asked. "We visited it many million years ago from now. But you and your tree were not living then, right?"

"No, we are youngsters, only 500 years old," beamed the tree spirit. Lydia and Thesa sat down in the grass in front of him. Of course we couldn't eat raw chestnuts, but we put them in our pockets.

"There was an earthquake here about one million years ago," the tree spirit continued. "The ground isn't the same as the one you visited the last time you were here. But the seed of my tree was here, and it grew well because of the proximity to the river. The landscape changed, but a certain basic structure remained, such as the river, for example. As you can see, it is lush and nice here. I believe that humans, to a degree, were to blame for the earthquake. There was a lot of evil that developed after the extraterrestrials left the place. They were no babysitters; they had to leave the people in order for them to develop at their own pace and in their own way. The villagers over there are not descendants of them. They are wanderers who came here and decided to settle down here. They are a good people. We get on well together."

"We must continue our walk through the centuries," remarked Lydia. "Maybe we will return someday to see if you are still here."

The tree spirit's bony fingers closed around my hands. "Welcome back," he said. "We Nature spirits greet the good humans welcome here - and of course, angels and elves as well!" He grinned broadly and his eyes shone like beacons. Balt came back and his friendly face was the last thing I saw when the usual haze betokened the permanent proximity of the borderland.

8. In the Underground Headquarters
of the Dwarves

The feeling of warmth and snug coziness struck us again in Mother Earth's emerald green cave. Her loving embrace and gentle smile gave us strength and balance.

"The epochs of time don't resemble each other, do they?" she asked. "Yet, the Nature spirits have had an important position longer than you bother to count. Among them the changes are not significant. They have neither changed their different appearances or their way of living and moving on many levels. On the contrary, the collaboration and contact between Nature spirits and humans has undergone major changes over the years, and eventually it has disappeared completely. That is what we are investigating and what we hope to improve eventually. This time you will experience the Earth's industrious workers, the earth spirits, or dwarves, and examine their attitudes towards humans. Are you ready for another peep-hole?"

We hurried out through the misty port to a new adventure, accompanied by both of our lovely elves. We got out in a storm that was about to take our breath away and a downpour that lashed our bodies violently. Balthori, in the lead of our little troop as usual, cried out with a thunderous voice:

"Form a protection around you with your thoughts. Create a dry void around you NOW!"

We did as we were told, and even though we already had gotten wet, it felt good to walk in a dry and warm bubble that eventually also dried our clothes. We followed closely in our leader's tracks. The only thing I could register was that we were in a dense forest and that tree trunks were cracking like matchsticks around us. Tree branches swished around our heads and in front of our feet, but our dry bubbles also protected us against them. The bubble slid forward; it felt kind of like ice skating. I have learned how to protect myself on my trips in the Universe, but that was long ago, and this particular knowledge was new to me. The thunder rumbled and frequent lightning lit up the pieces of the sky we saw between the canopies. Suddenly we were standing at the edge of a rather steep depression.

"Here we're going down!" cried Balthori. "Keep together!" He took Thesa's hand, she grabbed Lydia's, and Lydia took mine. We flew, rather than walked, downwards and I don't even believe my feet touched the ground. The wind whistled as if possessed, and had we not held so tightly together, we probably would have flown away in different directions.

Soon I felt sand under my feet. There was a significant difference between the sand and the previous needled-covered moss, so I understood that we were standing in the bottom of the depression. Balthori held a luminous wand in his free hand. Where he got it from, I have no idea. He planted the wand in the ground with a hard thrust, and there we stood, all four of us, anchored at the bottom of an unknown sandy depression. Our "dry bubbles" still remained, which was comfortable, because the rain showed itself from its most bounteous side. When we started walking again it wasn't a walk over damp sand, but instead we were splashing our thin sandals in sandy water. We headed in the direction of a dark hole, which could be glimpsed through our bubbles.

When we had arrived in the dark hole we halted, and shook our bodies like wet dogs. Our dry bubbles disappeared and then we could distinguish each other in the semi-darkness. Our clothes were dry and it felt good, even though we heard the roar of Nature outside the hole. I can't come up with any better expression than "hole," because there was no gate, no door, not even a hatch. The floor inclined slightly downwards and the brown walls smelled of damp soil. It was reminiscent of a cave, but if so, more of a sand cave.

"We are heading into the headquarters of the dwarves," explained

Balthori, "the way it looked about one million years ago. Just follow me, and don't take any side steps, my friends."

There was nothing to see and no side roads either, so at first I didn't understand what he meant. The passage was illuminated by small, crawling lights: glow worms. I then understood that Balt had referred to them. They stuck to the uneven walls, but occasionally they happened to end up on the ground. We made sure to avoid stepping on these little creatures.

It felt like an eternity before the dim passage led to a large hall. Hammer blows and throbbing were heard a long while before we reached the hall. The closer we got, the more the sound turned into a loud cacophony, but as soon as we entered the hall it ended abruptly in an almost shocking way. Hundreds of eyes were turned towards us and we saw no end to the huge room that was packed to the brim with dwarves. We must have appeared like giants to these small beings.

They looked very different. The tallest ones were up to around a yard in height, but their sizes varied tremendously. Their faces were furrowed and gnarled, but it certainly had nothing to do with their age. Some were hunchbacked, some were really fat, while others were thin and almost transparent. Their hair color ranged from white, gray, and greenish. Their eyes were small and narrow or very round and shined brightly in green and yellow. Their clothes were green or brown, and most of them wore a hip-length frock and tight pants. I thought they just looked like I had always imagined dwarves.

The hall was dead silent. The fall of a needle would have sounded like thunder. One of the larger dwarves detached himself from the front row and came up to us. He wore a green frock and a peaked stocking cap that went down over his ears. His green, somewhat shaggy clothes gave the impression of a wandering pyramid-shaped bush. White tufts of hair hung over both his fringe and neck, but his eyes were sharp and wise. His greeting was not particularly inviting.

"What are you doing here? What do you want? Get lost, preferably the same way you came!" Oddly enough, we understood him. Lydia and I looked at each other. But Balthori remained standing, tall and stately.

"The Master Melchizedek greets you through Pan, the God of Nature," he said seriously. "We are friends of Pan. None of us are human. Thesa and I are elves, while Lydia and Jan are angels. Mother Earth has sent us here. We would like to know when your friendship with the humans ceased."

The dwarf observed us in silence. With his hands he then showed us a gangway between the worktables and went before us. The hall was still breathlessly silent. We followed in the wake of the bushy dwarf and we dared not say a word. The looks I met from the other dwarves were not friendly and some of them sent red flashes. These flashes stung, but didn't cause any major harm. Pan was certainly their god, and you don't protest against your own god, I thought.

After a while we ended up in some kind of kitchen. Fires were lit everywhere and dwarves were working at the boiling pots and the baking boards. One end of the room was furnished with low tables and benches, and there we were brought. The wandering bushy pyramid motioned for us to sit down, as best we could. We folded ourselves and ended up in a very uncomfortable position near the floor. Lydia's giggle was on its way and I gave her a warning glance. After all, this dwarf didn't exactly look like he encouraged outbursts of joy. It was once again a quiet moment while he watched us without changing his facial expression the slightest. Finally, he thundered:

"The humans have tried to exterminate us. They are forever our enemies. We have introduced invisibility and silence in connection with humans. They consider us as prey and chase us indiscriminately as if we were animals. Now we live in dark chambers underground, where we work with roots, seeds, and forging work. Is that enough information or do you want to know more? Since you can see us, we understand that you are telling the truth and that you are not humans."

"Are there more dwarves than the ones who live here?" asked Thesa with her sunshine smile.

"We are found in many places throughout the Earth's crust," replied the green one, straightening himself up proudly. His short, sparse beard waggled and he almost smiled. "We are as numerous as the grains of sand in our subterranean abode. We actually could eradicate humanity if we wanted to."

"But you surely don't want that, do you?" I exclaimed, terrified.

The dwarf's eyes became cold as steel.

"We probably would like to," he replied, "but our ruler, Pan, doesn't allow us. He loves the Earth and he wants to preserve it and he believes that humans are needed to cultivate it and to nurture it. He says that there are good humans, too."

"There certainly are," assured Balt. "Soon there will come a time on Earth when humans and elementals again come together in harmony."

Hallelujah, I thought, and smiled sourly. I had trouble imagining that there would come such a time, considering the way that humans lived when I last spent time on Earth. Instead, I asked:

"Would you tell us your name, dear dwarf?" I'd better be polite, I thought, and remembered how my mother had taught me to take off my hat for big shots. So I kindly bent my head.

"Vrang," the green one replied. "And it's probably best that I bring you farther in the underground. We work with many different things. Humans would envy us if they had any idea what we do. I'll bring you to our forge. It is not for making hoes, that I promise!"

He went to a heavy wooden door in one corner of the room and took out a large key. Slowly the door swung up and we went inside. A smell of iron, fire, and beer swept towards us in an almost suffocating cloud. It was indeed a cool forge!

The small smiths worked tirelessly with their heavy materials. They forged swords, arrows, shields, coats of mail, saddle accessories, mysterious locks, and much more. We stood fascinated and just watched. Each smith had his own beer mug from which he sipped. They often sip, I thought excitedly. At least they had that in common with humans. I heard Lydia's stifled giggles at my thought. Yet, none of the dwarves seemed to be drunk, so they probably could withstand the drink. Vrang saw that I watched the mugs with disbelief. He almost smiled.

"The smiths need something to strengthen them. The beer has an exhilarating effect and it brings them power. It's not the same kind of brew that destroys humans. We have completely different herbs and completely different purposes."

"But this is war material," objected Balt. "Why do you manufacture that?"

"Eventually it could probably be needed," replied the dwarf angrily. "Don't you understand - with the great amount of dwarf species that exist, they won't always get along in the long run? Have you never read about dwarf wars? And just think about humans! They are much worse; they are fighting constantly. Maybe they will utilize dwarf weapons in a distant future."

"Yes, certainly," answered Lydia. "That which existed in humans' imagination when I lived on Earth are things that have an ancient heritage. In the same way that you dwarves were called gnomes during the millennium in which I lived, the many millennia gave you different faces. Somewhere the Truth is always hidden, even if its form changes. That's what Jan and I have learned during our journeys."

"Furthermore, I have read that dwarf smithery was considered extremely valuable during the first centuries BC," I exclaimed. "And at that time there were human warriors who got on well with you that got their armor from your forges."

"It may well be so," snapped Vrang, "I can't predict the future you're talking about. I can only show you what we're doing now and hope that you will tell Pan about our skills."

I smiled gently on the sly. Vrang wanted to keep in good with the gods. But the shining armors were just the beginning of what we were allowed to see. There were several wooden doors and many heavy locks. Vrang had softened a bit; he was constantly engaged in lively conversations with Balthori. When we got into the next hall I was astounded.

It was certainly a cave. The damp, rough walls dripped with water, and right through the middle of the hall ran a stream which was several yards wide. This was the boat builders' hall, where hammering, nailing, and singing were heard. At least ten boat hulls turned their dark, rough backs toward the ceiling, where rows of spectators in the form of the night aviators, the bats, hung in long, close rows. On some boats the dwarves worked with the ribs, while others made exquisitely carved oars. It smelled pleasantly of wood, varnish, and lacquers. I've always liked boats, so here I could have stayed for a long while. But Vrang brought us forth.

Again we came to a forge, but of a different kind than the first one. Here jewelry was manufactured, dwarf jewelry. Lydia gave a cry of delight. Both of the ladies were enthused, and in fact, I was too. It was shining and glittering everywhere, and in some strange way the finished jewelry emitted some kind of very pleasant radiation. Balt pointed out that this was magical jewelry.

There was an elevation in the center of the hall. Upon this podium sat a little, crooked dwarf, wearing some kind of red variegated cowl. The variegation turned out to be magical signs and insignia. The dwarf held his thin hands with long, claw-like fingers curved around a piece of jewelry.

"He gives the piece of jewelry a certain power," explained Vrang. "All gemstones have different powers, and our magical Master here amplifies them. On the right bearer, such a piece of jewelry becomes a blessing, which gives its owner positive abilities of various kinds. On the wrong carrier, the spell can be turned into completely different negative properties, such as power and wealth through deception and false promises."

"Who receives the jewelry?" wondered Thesa. "Of course, you don't socialize with humans."

"It is sold by certain intermediation, partly to various elementals, partly it happens that it ends up in human hands," answered the dwarf. "There are many explanations. Sometimes we need money, and then we sell jewelry on the markets; sometimes we just want to test the humans, and then we follow up on the items we have sold."

"In any case, it must be quite fun," said the mischievous Lydia, smiling. Indeed, I recognized how desirous she was to follow up a piece of jewelry on its migration. Vrang must have noticed that, too. He walked up to the old dwarf magician on the podium and whispered something in his ear. Then he stretched out his hand and I saw one or more items changing hands. Vrang thereafter returned and gave Lydia and Thesa each a pendant, and I got a ring. Balthori got a gemstone without a bezel, which glowed in various shimmering colors in the elf's hand.

Thesa's pendant was white and clear, like a diamond, but it could adopt different colors when necessary. My ring was green, and in its center was sort of a glimmer of fire. In Lydia's chain hung an opal of incomparable beauty. It shifted color according to mood, but also as a warning against dangers, we were told later. My ring had similar properties. We understood that our jewelry was not physical because we ourselves weren't, but we could enjoy them now on our journey. When we got home they would probably disappear, since angels don't wear jewelry.

"Each of the stones given to you is a talisman," proclaimed the dwarf. "I will not tell you which abilities they have; that you have to find out for yourselves. There are more halls here to explore, but the locks to them are sealed. You will not get farther than this. I now bid you farewell!"

Only a light green smoke was seen on the spot where the green dwarf had been standing. Balt hastened to take my hand and I grabbed Lydia's, who in turn took Thesa's. As by a gust, we were blown right up through the ceiling, which gave way to our spirit bodies. I closed my eyes and I had no time to think before we were back in Mother Earth's cave.

9. Mother Earth Tells a True Story about Our "Free Will"

"Now you have gotten to know the grim dwarves," Mother Earth said, smiling. She wore a bright yellow dress that shone like a sunbeam and she had put up a table with delicious refreshments in the middle of her cave.

"Surely Vrang was grumpy," I acknowledged, "but he gave us lovely stones."

"Eventually you will see more of Vrang," Mother Earth told us. "He's an eternal wanderer in the worlds of the dwarves. But his grumpiness is just an attitude. I must say, you have received valuable gifts. I felt their magical power as soon as you landed in here. They are the proof that he liked you."

"What do you mean by saying we'll see more of Vrang?" asked Lydia. "Isn't he stuck in the world he showed us?"

"Absolutely not," replied our lovely hostess. "Vrang is a vitrigo."

"What is a vitrigo?" I exclaimed, startled.

"A smith, and a smith of words," she replied. "A highly developed spiritual teacher and wanderer on the roads of wisdom. There were smiths who were magicians, and he belongs to them. They are a remarkable and extraordinarily skillful species, and even if they surround themselves with grimness, they have warm hearts and are good teachers. They have power - more than you can imagine - but it's a good power. They are immortal. I can only congratulate you that you got Vrang as your guide."

"It felt like the dwarves thought they owned the Earth!" I exclaimed. "They were so furious with the humans." Mother Earth shook her head, making her long, lustrous curls whisk around her forehead.

"The Earth owns us," she replied, "as it actually owns all of Nature. The forest owns the ground on which it stands, as well as the grass and the plants. The water owns the skies that are mirrored in it, and the skies own the stars that hide behind them. The light owns the darkness, like the sun owns the moon. But who owns the humans, those who think they own everything?"

"It is Prime Creator, the great God Consciousness, who owns them and leads its puppet theater, where the threads sometimes form patterns and sometimes get tangled up," answered Lydia, smiling. "It owns us all, visible and invisible, but it lets us be just the way we are. That is the great wonder." Mother Earth chuckled.

"Sorry," she said, "Sorry, you are not quite right. The wonder of free will has gone too far. Free will is used in the wrong way and in the wrong context. That's why it's so beneficial for you to find out more about the worlds of the Nature spirits. Nothing is quite as you think, since your faith so far is humanly pervaded - Balthori and Thesa excluded. Because of the divine generosity and the lack of visible Nature spirits, things have turned out the way they have on Earth."

"In that case," I interrupted, "I ask, what God do we have? Shouldn't he have had the power to see which way things were heading already thousands of years ago? Why didn't he prevent the alienation between humans and Nature spirits at an early stage?"

"Because of free will and a good portion of envy between humans and spirits," replied Mother Earth, with eyes of steel.

"If we didn't have our free will, we would be God's slaves," I protested. "Is slavery better than liberty?"

"You've got it all wrong, Jan," interjected Balthori, and Thesa nodded eagerly.

"Slaves, that is exactly what humans are in the present time on Earth. What makes a human a slave? Envy and jealousy, power and abuse of power, negative thinking followed by negative actions, the worship of the golden calf, and so on. When humans became slaves of hatred and evil in a too substantial way, then we elves moved from the Earth. We thought it had become a kind of prison. There humans still live, unaware of the shackles that bind them and the power that controls them. To be a slave to the Love of the Great Spirit is something completely different."

"What do you mean by saying that humans are unaware of the power that controls them?" I interrupted. "Then there must exist a lot of powers that control everywhere?"

"I think you need a little lecture before you go ahead," decided Mother Earth. "I will tell you a true story. It's thousands and thousands of years old, but I took part at that time too, and I shiver when I think of what humanity has gone through. Poor wretches, there was no reasonable person who could tell you the Truth then. I was locked up here during certain phases, so I wouldn't come up with the idea of trying to save my brothers and sisters who wander up there.

"Everything isn't what you believe it is. Well, there was certainly nothing new under the sun there, I think. But truly, everything isn't what the humans on my Earth believe it is; far from it. Will they never wake up and understand who they really are? After so many thousands of generations, they are still living in the same pattern of silence, separation, and finally, as in the present Earth time, self-destruction. Their materialism is incredibly well riveted in their brains and leaves no room for other things than fanatically religious thinking, vindictiveness, and destruction. That is completely incomprehensible to me."

"What shall we do about it?" I sighed. "To be sure, there are decent people there, too. You only see it from a Nature spirit's point of view." Mother Earth laughed.

"You talk about God," she continued. "We talk about First Source. First Source is All of us who exist on Earth (and inside of it), our collective Beingness. God doesn't live in human form somewhere in an unknown heaven or an equally unknown universe.

"First Source isn't burdened with human individual souls. We are all part of it. In the beginning we lived in non-material dimensions that eventually got denser during the phases of Creation. But our interdimensional bodies were tempted to enter human bodies. How do you think that happened? Listen:

"In the time of Atlantis, about 11,000 years ago in a kingdom called Annunaki, there was a king named Anu who needed slaves to harvest the gold that was found in abundance on Earth. Therefore, a small evolved people of the Atlanteans was persuaded by King Anu to take physical form. At the same time, the cunning king understood that he must provide them with a sort of soul system that would prevent them from developing their true gifts. Anu had a staff of skilled scientists who helped him in this terrible mission.

"The God-Spirit-Soul system became the basis for separation. That means Anu created a myth that was converted to religion. And that was exactly what he wanted. This resulted in a situation where the human's true identity had to be preserved and developed anew in order for the Earth's residents to be able to perceive all of Nature's wonderful intrinsic essence.

"But how would Anu get his 'slaves' to keep toiling for him? Well, by providing them with a brain system that reduced their possibilities to express their original abilities and instead use programs that Anu and his scientists had invented and which suited them. Why did the God-Spirit-Soul system become the anchor of separation? There were two ways: religion and spirituality. Clever as he was, Anu knew that humans eventually would evolve, and he feared that they finally would figure out who they truly were.

"The chosen Atlanteans were highly evolved beings before they were turned into Anu's slaves. Now the king hurried up to create a sort of prison, formed by illusions and disappointments in their brains. He couldn't destroy the soul, so he embedded it as much as possible and called it the life force, that which gave life to the body. Another aspect was drawn forth in the visual field: fear of death, separation anxiety, the fear of not truly existing for real.

"This strong fear inside humans gave rise to the creation of a particular (false) God, who sent out a particular Spirit that filled the whole universe with its light and began creating humans, one at a time. The fact was that Anu, king of the Anunnaki, positioned himself as God in the world of humans (cf. the God of the Old Testament).

"To be able to reach God, there was only one problem: 'You are a human being with a soul. This soul must be activated or redeemed in order for you to be saved. Salvation gives you eternal life in God's kingdom.' Without understanding better at that point, humans accepted Anu's home-made law. Most of them still do. So it also came about that the Nature spirits retreated, step by step. The rest of it you already know."

"That was new history!" exclaimed Lydia, astonished.

"Is there no hope for us - I mean, humans?" I stammered, terrified.

"Now is the time when 11,000 years of captivity is heading towards its resolution!" Mother Earth smiled encouragingly. "We'll come back to this later, because now I think it's time for your next visit to the world of the Nature spirits. The more you know, the more you understand. This also includes magic, Nature's vertiginous, unfathomable, and boundless magic. I will let you jump over a gap, all the way to 30,000 years ago. There were also humans then, albeit primitive, however with a certain culture. Now then, off you go!"

10. Neanderthals, Native Americans, and Elementals 30,000 Years Ago

The magic door opened. Hand in hand, we floated out in a mist, where small shimmering light beams played tag with each other like guppies in an aquarium. When the mist had dispersed, we once again stood on a flowering meadow, a wonderfully colorful, fragrant meadow.

> *In the first singing winds of the summer*
> *I was shown a winding path*
> *in the middle of a meadow where veils of mist wrap*
> *dewy pearl jewelry around you and me!*

I sang and put my arm around Lydia's shoulders. This "game" started to be familiar by now, and the winding path was underneath our feet. Behind us, dark mountains with peaks of whipped cream brooded, and before us lay a hilly plain where the path led. The romantic atmosphere of the landscape, all the flowers that I didn't even know the names of, and the distant mountains that were reflected in the equally distant cornflower blue lakes, made me as exhilarated as a ten-year-old boy taken to the circus for the first time. Elementals floated like light bright clouds and performed their acrobatic somersaults and high jumps across the whole meadow, without pretending about us.

But our small group quickly moved forward towards the hilly plain, where humans moved between very simple oval huts, surrounded by stones.

"They may be Neanderthals," Lydia was panting in my ear, "or both Homo Sapiens and Neanderthals. It was about 30,000 years ago when the two species intermingled and the Neanderthals eventually became extinct. Then they built oval huts, with roofs made of tree branches and skins on the floor. They began to dress in hides and I see that many wear leather clothes. I wonder if they have any contact with the beings of Nature over there in the meadow."

We would soon find out in a more tangible way. When we came in sight of the villagers, we saw how they pointed at us and grouped themselves into defensive positions. Soon stones and stone arrows began to whiz towards us. Balthori stopped and raised his hand in a deprecative gesture. The stone-throwing ceased, but we still felt a pending threat from the villagers.

"I will walk over to them and talk to them in their own language," suggested Balt. Now we were close to the humans, perhaps only a few yards away from them. Their faces were dark and some looked ferocious, while others behaved more calmly. It seemed like there were two different races. The more ape-like ones, who, however, walked upright, were incredibly ugly. The others resembled humans of today; I would like to call them Native American-looking. They had proud postures and beautiful faces, with noble, curved noses. They were moving smoothly and easily, with almost dancing steps. They tried to calm down their ferocious brothers and prevent them from throwing more stones.

Balthori went smilingly towards them with calm steps and with one of his hands raised as a peace sign. One of the Native American-looking men detached himself from the crowd and came towards him. I held my breath. As usual, Lydia pinched me hard and I managed to suppress a yell. Behind the Native American-looking man walked one of the menacing natives. He was extremely ugly. He looked like an ape, but he walked upright with waddling gait and he carried stone weapons in both of his hands. His weapons looked like stone axes and I thought that I really didn't want to receive a blow of an axe by such a weapon.

The Native American-looking man was well-built, with straight black hair, flashing dark eyes, and a well-shaped, slightly curved nose. His mouth was plump and beautiful. He had tied feathers in his hair and he was wearing a leather cloth that covered one of his shoulders down to his knees. His second shoulder was bare. Around his waist he wore a belt of leather. He looked and behaved like some kind of Native American chief. He smiled gently at us.

"We are friends from another world," explained Balthori when the Native American-looking man stood in front of him. "We are here to find out what relationships you have with the Nature spirits. Are they your friends, and can you speak with them?"

The chief opened his mouth to say something, but the native behind him turned around and made a sign to his people, and so the stone war began all over again. Since we were invulnerable, the stone projectiles just bounced against us and we remained standing completely still. I tried to crouch, but Lydia motioned for me to stand straight. It was very uncomfortable in the stone rain, even though we didn't feel anything. The stones bounced close to the head, face, and body, and the worst, of course, were the bounces towards the head. It didn't hurt, but as it should have caused us a lot of pain and because we ought to lie bleeding on the ground by now, I felt a mixture of fear and wrath. Balt shouted something to the chief and he turned around and screamed at the troublemakers to immediately stop their stone war.

"At times we are friends with the Nature spirits," the chief told us after the wildings had calmed down. They sat on the ground and glared at us with unfriendly eyes, but those who resembled Native Americans approached us carefully and smiled.

"At times they become upset with some of the villagers. We are two species that have decided to live together and fight against the beasts that exist around here. We ourselves don't like killing indiscriminately. We hunt animals for food, not for any other reason. Our brethren here compete in the killing. They are afraid of the beings of Nature and would rather not have anything to do with them. Meanwhile, there are problems we need to solve together."

"What elementals do you have here besides those we have already seen in the meadows?" I asked.

"The entire forest is full of them," replied the chief. "We do not go into the forest; they have armies of war-desirous dwarves and other strange beings. We have accepted this, and thus we are located here on the plain. I warn you not to enter the forest. It can never lead to anything other than hostility, and wild animals are plentiful in there. We can only hunt those who graze on the plains around here." He pointed to the deer and other small animals who kept their distance from the village. "I would advise you to return whence you came, before the next shower of stones gives you new discomforts."

He smiled briefly, swung around, and wandered back to the huts. We got sneaky glances from the ape-like ones, and with a sigh of relief we took each other's hands. It was probably best for us to disappear. At least we had received an answer to our question.

11. The Girl and the Faun Show Us Around

"That was a quick visit," stated Mother Earth when we were back in her cave. We told her what had happened and she nodded seriously.

"I suspected that it would be a short trip this time, but it didn't cause you any harm," she continued. "You must get different points of view regarding the beings of Nature. As you can see, the Nature spirits are working independently of humans in all of Nature. They even defend themselves against mean-spirited villagers. The dwarves are real aces on waging war, but surely you already realized that when you visited Vrang's domain. Now there is someone else waiting for you in a completely different place. If you think it's strange that you understand what everyone you meet says, it is I who have arranged it. You can't find out things without understanding those you meet."

The transitions occurred in an instant. We surfed the waves of the wind through a fresh light green mist, and suddenly we sat down on our butts in a new landscape. Our butts said "tjong" and, laughing, we looked at each other and then all around us.

A small child was the first thing we saw, a cute little girl with dark skin and big brown eyes. Her hair coiled in jet-black curls far down her back. She was wearing a short shirt of unbleached linen. She held someone or something in her hand. It looked like a faun. Could it be a doll? No, it lived and moved. It was as bright as the girl was dark. A real live faun! It had cloven hooves, a tail, and small horns in its forehead, but apart from that, it looked like a human. The face was thin, the chin was pointed, and the ears ended in a small tuft of hair, but the impression was actually human-like. It must be a very young faun, I thought, actually a faun child.

The girl held a real live faun in her hand.

"Who are you?" asked the girl. We looked around. The only thing we saw was sand, some palm trees near us, and deep blue waters a little farther away. This must be some kind of beach, I thought. It was Thesa who answered the child.

"We are visitors from another world," she said with her big, beautiful smile. "We are kind; neither you nor your little brother need to be afraid of us."

"He's not my little brother," said the girl angrily. "He's my best friend, Sim."

"We have come here to visit fauns and other elementals," said Balthori. "Where are we, and where are they located?"

"They are at their homes, of course," said the child. "I live at my house over there!" She pointed over the fawn's shoulder, but all we saw was sand dunes.

"At what time have we arrived?" Lydia wondered. Now it was the child's turn to smile.

"It is NOW," she replied excitedly. "It is now, and you are welcome to visit my home. Come with us!" She turned around and started to run away towards a sand dune, along with the faun, who jumped in sort of gallop-like leaps at her side without letting go of her hand.

"At least we have a kid with an elemental here," I commented. "Don't you think we should follow them in order to understand what time we have arrived at and where we are located?"

The girl was already far ahead of us, so we got moving across the dunes. Her hair and linen fluttered while she occasionally turned around to check if we followed them. Palm trees grew there, in the beginning rather sparse, but later on denser, which made them form a grove, where the little girl disappeared, still hand in hand with the faun. He turned around before they dove in among the palm trees and his smile went from ear to ear. At least his smile wasn't unkind, I thought, as we dove after them at the position where we believed this strange couple had disappeared.

A glimpse of the bright shirt flapped near a spring that suddenly appeared. We must have been close to a settlement, because the palm trees and other vegetation thinned out.

When we arrived at the spring, the faun stood there, but the girl was gone. His broad smile and his little waving hand told us where to go. After only a few minutes we found ourselves in a village. A different village.

The houses were built together and formed long rows that stood close together, separated by a narrow road. They were built of some kind of stone, reddish in color. All had round, low chimneys, and from some of them a bluish smoke welled out. The faun waved and smiled, and suddenly we were surrounded by elementals that looked pretty much like him.

"Are you the ones living here?" asked Lydia. The faun shook his head so violently that his white-green hairs blew around by their own storm. Apparently, this was the dark-eyed girl's village. She stood in the low doorway of one of the houses and waved at us with both her hands.

"Binbin want you look at her house," explained the faun, still smiling broadly. "Then you look at elementals' house." He had a slight accent, but spoke clearly. He flew away to the girl and hooked up his hand with hers again. We followed close behind him, and a long tail of elementals followed us. They stopped outside the house and we crouched to get through the doorway. We came to an astonished halt inside the door.

We had entered a large room. In fact, it was a very large room, and literally everything was in there. The ceiling was high, with a hole in the middle. A pipe that appeared to be a chimney pipe because it came from the open fireplace was led up through the hole. The fireplace was in turn "made-up" with flat stones, which were placed in a ring. That was probably where the food was cooked.

There were at least ten beds, or rather sleeping places, along the first wall. A table with benches ran along the other wall. We stood on a hard-packed clay floor, covered with leaves and moss. It was soft to walk on and it smelled like forest. Binbin gestured wildly for us to sit at the long wooden table, and she herself sat with the faun opposite us. Just as I was going to start asking a bunch of questions about where we were, at what time we had arrived, and how everything worked here, Binbin put a finger to her mouth and made it clear that we must be silent.

Through the door came what probably was her family. First entered two adults, tall, slender, beautiful, and happy, and then lots of kids that resembled Binbin. Finally, an elderly couple with a venerable appearance stepped inside. Everyone carried flowers in their arms and placed them in a beautiful pattern on the long table. No romping, no fighting, just quiet, smiling faces.

A young man who I assumed was Binbin's father took out a peculiar instrument that seemed to be a cross between a violin and a harp, as strange as it might sound. He began to play with a short, relatively thick string, presumably made of a tree branch. Half the instrument was apparently intended for the fiddle bow and the other half consisted of strings that he occasionally tweedled. He played, and the music was enchanting. It sang its own song, which first slowly, in staccato, climbed up the bare walls. Then, after it had reached halfway up the wall, it floated out in harp-like tones.

The melody escalated and became a song, a cry, a completely, unbearably beautiful cascade of tones, that somehow formed a tapestry around the whole ceiling that slowly thickened and turned into a sparkling smoke that swam out through the chimney. When every tone had disappeared - and this took a considerable time - the company around the table burst into cheers. We visitors sat paralyzed. Lydia and I had never experienced anything like this, apparently not the elves, either.

"Nice, huh?" Binbin asked merrily, and thereafter the hugs began. She and the faun started, and then came all the others. We couldn't get up nor do a single thing, except for allowing us to be hugged. I could hear Lydia's delighted giggle while I found myself in the midst of the embrace of several small children who laughed, patted me on the cheeks, and kissed me on the nose. I was curious to see Balthori's response. How did he react to this treatment? When the crowd of kids thinned out to make room for the older couple, I noticed that Balt looked really exhilarated. Then I was pressed adjacent to a somewhat more voluminous bosom than the previous one and I looked into a pair of remarkable eyes and a beautiful old face, framed by silver-white hair.

"Strangers!" whispered the woman halfway through our hug. Then she turned to our little group. "You are welcome to the fragment that remains of the world's oldest and highest culture after the last ice age. We have created our prosperity in collective love and care. This country is called Russia and the place Siberia in the time you are coming from. Your arrival has been announced to us."

"So ... so now we are shortly after the last ice age?" stammered Lydia, astonished. The woman nodded, with a soft smile on her lips.

"Yes, we haven't progressed further in purely practical terms," she replied. "But even if our lodging has changed, we have preserved many of the ancient secrets that the humans of your time will be so covetous of. These secrets will come to the fore when the evil grip on humanity is released. My husband and I have created this village as a model of how life in the simplest external forms can grow to an enormous inner strength and wisdom. Our ancestral palaces are not so important to us anymore. We only need our inner temples in this village."

"But ... but," I stammered, "how is your relationship with the beings of Nature? Do you tolerate each other? Are you friends? Do you collaborate?"

"Although we live in different villages and in different ways, we are very good friends and collaborate with them all the time. Our children are always together - indeed, you saw all the small children of Nature outside, didn't you?" Binbin and the faun Sim flew up from the bench and motioned for us to follow them. Slightly dazed, the four of us rose and went after the children.

"We serve food when you come back," shouted the young woman, who I assumed was Binbin's mother.

"You have lots of siblings," said Thesa to Binbin when we walked together into the forest.

"Most of them the child bringers have brought here," the girl replied. "The child bringers - well, you know them, don't you?"

We produced a collective "no." Binbin and the faun looked at each other and grinned delightedly.

"Child bringers bring children," cried the faun, and then howled with laughter.

"They are sent out from our village to look for lonely children everywhere. Sometimes they take the boat and search on the islands, sometimes they look for them on garbage heaps in other strange villages," explained Binbin in a wise tone. "There are people who throw away children. Then we find them. Not all of them, but as many as we can get hold of."

I knew very well that such horridness occurred throughout the ages. Hitherto I had only been horrified over it without taking any deeper notice than any other news, but suddenly I saw the tremendous implications of this. I saw that Lydia looked frightened, and a tear fell down her cheek. The elves walked ahead of us. Certainly they didn't behave as badly as humans, surely there was not such evil among their people. Their children were their treasures, Thesa told us later.

My thoughts fell silent, like gentle streams that flow into a non-cloudy well. We faced our little faun's village. It was teeming with people I would prefer to call "the fairy-tale people."

12.   Scary Stone Images
Beneath the Library

Dome-shaped buildings shimmered like glass - but they were not made of glass. They had no windows, but they must have been transparent, as we could see both the inside and the outside at the same time. I counted fifteen buildings, but there were also other tubular constructions towering here and there between the round ones. The ground was covered with flowers of many colors. Because of the translucent character of the construction material, everything became sort of illuminated. It was truly a fairy-tale village, as if cut out of the Arabian Nights. Everywhere beings of Nature were flowing around, large and small, and all had friendly smiles and cheerful greetings for us. Some were transparent, others were more solid, some supernaturally beautiful, others subterraneously abominable.

"Well, I'll welcome you here, then!" a familiar voice was heard. When we turned around - since the voice was heard behind us - Vrang was standing there. Our old acquaintance Vrang, as pyramid-shaped, green-clad, and physical as when we last saw him in the mountain halls, but with the difference that his grumpy face now was gone and he gave us a brilliant smile that bared his dazzlingly white, pointy little teeth.

"This is a good place," he continued, unfolding his hands in a welcoming gesture. "I made sure that you arrived here to show you that the perfect balance can exist between humans and elementals. You see, it takes a certain sort of humans to make friends with the Nature spirits. That sort of humans isn't still there in your time; it hasn't been around in a very long time. However, there are still occasional humans currently living on Earth who dream about us. But there aren't many, and they dare not speak about us, because then they are ostracized and regarded as absolutely crazy."

"Thank you for meeting up with us, Vrang," said Balthori, and he hugged the master smith. "We would be honored if you'd like to show us around here." The dwarf went up to each of us and took us solemnly in hand.

"Mother Earth has asked me to take care of you when necessary," he admitted. "That is probably needed, since you are going to embark on many adventures where I can be useful." Then he motioned for us to follow him. I started thinking about whether he was a sort of guardian angel for angels. His rather hefty, pear-shaped, shimmering green exterior otherwise gave the impression of an earthy natural phenomenon. He radiated a strange, compelling, authoritative power, which I would later understand was pure, unblended magic. A pleasant scent of pine needles surrounded him.

When we got into the village - what a modest word for this strange, radiating collection of houses - we discovered that the round houses lay in a circle, surrounded by plantings. Everywhere there were fountains and small ponds, with waterfalls that did somersaults over pearlescent boulders. Fairies and other elementals danced and played at the top of the bubbly water jets of the fountains. They allowed themselves to be brought down, thereafter driven up by the power of water, and then they slipped down a bit again. Others went sliding down the waterfalls. They had fun and so did we. Here and there we saw humans, probably from Binbin's village. They seemed to be busy with various matters and were running around with firm steps. When Vrang saw that I looked questioningly at them, he said:

"We'll go into a house, but we will manage just one. We take the library!"

Lydia and I looked at each other. The library! In a time that ought to be primitive, and certainly was in other places, there was a library. Thesa and Balt turned around and winked at us. For them this couldn't be as remarkable as it was for us. In the middle of a glass dome there was a spiral staircase. The entire round building was divided into different book floors. From top to bottom, circular floor ledges extended, full of handwritten books and parchment-like rolls. They were able to be viewed and studied with the help of walkways equipped with railings that ran out from and around the spiral staircase. We stood down there and stared until it spun around in our poor heads. Such a culture in the middle of Siberia's primeval forests? Now it was Balt who answered our wonderings:

"These are books and writings that have been preserved in a secret location during the Earth's catastrophes," he told us. "They are never loaned out, but both elementals and humans can come here and read them. We have something similar in our world; they are also relics of a departed era."

On the floor there were low tables and chairs with cushions and stools. Upon closer examination, I saw that both humans and beings of the strangest kinds were sitting there, engaged in their studies. I was seized by an irrepressible desire to read in any of the ancient documents and learn something new about the Earth I had left. I wasn't allowed to. Vrang showed with a determined nod where the limit was. So far and no farther.

I had no desire to leave this fascinating place, and I saw that Lydia thought the same thing. How about attempting a coup? We read each other's thoughts and took each other's hands. We went last in our little entourage, with Vrang in the lead. He was engaged in a conversation with Balt and Thesa. He turned, nodded, and smiled gently at us. Then the three of them continued talking while we took a chance.

In a round room there are no sharp corners or other crannies to hide in. Quick as thought, I tested if we could make ourselves invisible. It went well. Then we just had to escape down one of the many descending stairs - where it led, we didn't know. But we soon found out in a less pleasant way.

Lydia stumbled. The staircase was very narrow, and we went backwards because there were no banisters. Since she stumbled in front of me and my feet were close to hers, I followed her example before I could think the matter over. In one single messy stack, we both rolled down the remainder of the stairs and ended up lying dizzy at their end. Or at least we supposed it was their end. Moaning and hissing, Lydia tried to free herself from the angel colossus Jan, who had landed on top of her. Under ordinary human indecent circumstances I would have been very amused by the situation, but now it was unfortunately not the case.

"Did I hurt you?" I panted to the soft, warm angel under my legs.

"No, but look around you!" Lydia moaned, as she tried to free herself from our intertwined conveyances. I hadn't thought about that. I had only looked at the stairs and at the angelic creation beneath me. Thus I looked around. It resembled a mausoleum, and it certainly was one, too. I saw stone images everywhere, floating, lying, sitting, standing ... stone images with cold unseeing eyes and distorted mouths. So beneath the library was a gravesite, that much I understood. But it didn't look like an ordinary gravesite, that was for sure. It was scary down there. In some gruesome way, all these stone figures appeared alive, despite their immobility. It seemed as if their distorted lips spoke or screamed with quiet words, quiet sounds, quiet lament.

There was no order among the stone statues. They stood, lay, sat, and flew close to each other like a heavy army, and the air was heavy with their weight. The air was thick, dense, and muggy. We began to feel ill, and I pulled Lydia's arm to get her up the stairs again. She appeared dazed and I wasn't surprised; the odor down here was disgusting. I put my arm around her waist and supported her. Probably I would have to carry her up the stairs. I stared at the whole spooky army of statues, and it seemed like it came closer. I could sense steps .

"What are you doing down here?" asked an angry voice. "Leave immediately, or else I can't answer for what might happen!"

It was a man who spoke, or rather an old man. He was thin and scraggy, almost transparent, and his back was curved as if under a huge burden. His head was bald and a few thin wisps of white hair hung from his chin. He was a hideous sight, just as if raised from the grave, with his big empty eye sockets directed towards us. Of course they were not empty, a pair of pale, almost white eyes glistened in there.

"Here are the abodes of death, and I am the guardian of the dead," he continued, with his hollow, crackly voice. "You are bothering us. If you go any farther in here, you will never return ... "

When I, far too late, happened to look at my ring, a fiery red warning beam flashed from it that I shouldn't have missed. Hastily I looked at Lydia's pendant and the same thing happened to it. A flame flashed just like a warning lamp.

But now Vrang's clear voice was heard from above the stairs.

"Lydia and Jan, are you down there? Come up immediately, the air down there is toxic. Hurry up!"

We hurried up without any hesitation. We stumbled up the stairs, me first, with a firm grip on one of Lydia's hands.

"What were you doing down there?" Vrang's surprised voice asked when we, flashing and flickering, came up in the daylight. It was Lydia who replied:

"Actually, nothing at all. We were simply curious and wanted to see some more of this amazing building."

"Then you could have asked me," Vrang snapped. "It's good to be curious at the right places. However, this place is not one of them. I'm responsible for you now. Ensure that you accept this and turn to me when you are curious, then I will calm that feeling in one way or another. More challenges are coming up on this walk!"

13.   A Cool Experience

We held our tongues. We silently followed our odd guide. Actually, it felt good to be unaware of where we were going and what would happen. Balt turned around and winked at me while Thesa took Lydia's arm and chided her, with roguishness in the corner of her eye. We continued our rapid journey through the bright, lively village.

Suddenly Vrang halted so outright that his peaked green stocking cap swayed. We stood in front of a brilliantly white building that was unlike the other houses.

"You will get to meet and speak to Someone," he said obscurely. Binbin and her faun came running and joined us. My question got stuck on my lips; this was probably not the right moment for curiosity.

"Here I want to participate," the happy child exclaimed, while Vrang probably knit his brows, if he had any, because he held up a gnarled hand in warning. He stepped through the white archway and we trotted close behind him. What did we see? A great white archway that somehow was self-luminous. Within the archway it was so blue that you had to stop and rub your eyes. Archway, intense blue ... and then?

At first I couldn't discern anything, because the blue air was variable, opalescent, and therefore difficult to penetrate at first glance. Vrang made a circular motion with his hands, and suddenly the view was crystal clear. Doors and rooms usually appear within archways. Not here. We were standing on a sort of elevation. (One can't talk about rocks or cliffs indoors, right?) We were indoors, and yet it felt endless. This must be some kind of optical illusion or hallucination, I thought. Indoors became outdoors . or? However, what we saw, what we were facing, couldn't be a delusion.

A landscape appeared below us. Soft green and flourishing plants embraced a little waterfall, from where a merrily splashing brook was curling towards us and disappeared below an edge of our "mountain."

Swarms of animals were frisking on both sides of the brook, and silvery fish tails were making somersaults in the waterfall. I saw wolves and bears, wolverines, lynx, otters, beavers, foxes, and deer. I saw birds, large and small, which swung themselves around the man standing in the middle of the brook and laughingly trying to capture his flying friends.

He was a very tall man, fur dressed all the way up to his neck. His dark curls revealed two small horns on his forehead - very small, however, but still horns. His broad, smiling face showed a long row of regular white teeth. His dark, shifting eyes resembled fire sparks, but the whole man radiated Love. I've never before felt or experienced that much Love in one single being, but this Love was also associated with a tremendous strength and power, a certain severity, and incorruptible justice. His hands were human-like, his feet were hefty and lengthy as those of a chimpanzee.

Pan, the God of Nature, the guardian of the plants and the animals.

It was Pan. I've always wanted to meet Pan in his natural surroundings. I've always admired the God of Nature with his unparalleled, all-embracing task and gift: to preserve the wonderful Nature with its arabesque, diverse animal life that allegedly only exists on Earth. This laughing being who was seething with life and power looked exactly as I had imagined him. He motioned for us to come down to him. Suddenly, a green staircase appeared in front of us. I thought we'd look like ants next to him, but when we had gone down the stairs he was standing there, a little bit taller than me, a little bit taller than Balthori, maybe slightly more than six feet high. One by one, he took us in his arms. His embrace was warm and loving in a way that you could feel your whole body filled with vibrant energy.

"Friends from other worlds in my world!" he then cried out, and invited us to sit down on a collection of flat stones on the banks of the brook. "I know about your mission and I ask you to listen to some words from the Father's house."

"We are listening!" I dared to release my voice in front of this radiating, wonderful being. Balt looked at me and smiled. Perhaps I had been vacillating. That's probably what you do when you meet someone that you've been dreaming of all your life. "Which Father's house do you mean?"

"There's only one, Jan!" His facial expression was both grave and mischievous. "Basically, we belong to the same Father's house. The soil on Earth and everything that grows on it and the whole mixture of wild, tame, and incredible biota belongs to the Father's house, the residence of First Source. You are located on the border of another Universe, and in this second Universe lies the Father's house. When the Earth raises her consciousness, her boundaries are stretched, and we aim for them to reach all the way out there. So it is prophesied in the dawn of time, and so it shall be."

"If we don't destroy all our chances before we get that far," I muttered, since I knew that the Earth's current state was and is very gloomy. "Unless we already have managed to eradicate all animal species and poison the whole of humanity by then."

"It's not a day too soon that something extraordinary happen!" rumbled Pan, but the roguishness was still visible in his eyes. "You've messed up for yourselves on Earth. You have no idea how many watchful eyes are waiting for the final step indicating that now the time has come. You have ruined your chances - but not all of them. Previously you have seen that the elementals and the humans cooperated pretty well in the beginning of Earth's orbit. Then it went downhill, but there are intervening periods when we were accepted and could be visible to the human eye - at least to some."

"Those are the periods we are going to visit," interjected Thesa, smiling.

"Yes, the others are pointless to look at," added Balt. "But there are always humans who doubt. Doubt is the weak one's best support."

"I am going to send you to some known periods now," Pan told us. "When you have seen everything that Mother Earth has decided for you to see, we'll talk again. Jan will communicate this to the Earth in a present time that risks becoming ash and water. When brother stands against brother, father against son, mother against daughter, and faith against faith, it is time not only to think, but to act. This encompasses not only the outer environment, but at least as importantly, the inner environment. Come on, enough talking for now; we are in a hurry!"

Again Pan grew in height, and the brook became a river where the undines were dancing and hid everything with their veils of froth and mist. A veil wall, outside of which only the four of us remained, Balt, Thesa, Lydia, and me. All around us there was rumbling and hissing - but only for a short while. We continued our walk in history.

14.   The Irish Druids' Interaction with Nature Spirits

Gone were Pan and the undines. Ahead of us mighty oaks rose their leaf-rustling crowns towards a blue, cloudless sky. The roots of the oaks were as powerful protozoans that crept into the grassy ground, and the straight, vigorous trunks were like pillars. Between the trees a glade was formed, so solemn that it could have been a church hall. In a way it also was one: the church hall of the Druids.

A boulder of considerable size, oblong and flat on the upper side, apparently served as an altar. I shuddered slightly, because I had read somewhere that the Druids sacrificed humans, and this stone resembled a sacrificial altar.

"No, Janne, you're wrong. They sacrificed animals, flowers, and vegetables, but not humans. There were certainly human sacrifices among the Celts, but then the Irish Druids didn't participate. Celts and Druids often get mixed up." Of course it was Lydia, the historian, who showed her skills again.

Several men and a few women stood around the stone altar. On top of the altar a child was laid down. I stared dismayed. Was Lydia wrong? What were they going to do with the child? It was a three- or four-year-old boy, who appeared to be sleeping. One of the women, presumably the child's mother, bent over him and stroked his forehead. A tall man, dressed in the white robe and the peculiar headgear of the Druids, was holding a twig.

"This is a healing procedure," said Balt. "The man over there is holding a twig that is consecrated through a sacred procedure. It will make the child well."

"But what have Nature spirits to do with it?" I asked.

"The Druids use the knowledge of the Nature spirits in most of their rituals," said Balt, smiling. "You surely didn't know that, did you? We cooperated with the Druids until their knowledge and influence waned. They were kings' advisors and magicians with immense knowledge."

The child on top of the stone slab moved, opened his eyes, and whimpered. The mother put her hands together, lit up with joy, and was going to carry away her offspring. The tall man made a repelling motion and two of the white-dressed men standing there gently brought her away from the altar. Then strange things happened. Invisible, we stood there witnessing a miracle ... *or?*

The child had closed his eyes again. The tall man with the twig raised it above the child's head and made both circles and signs in the air.

"The twig is a verbena," whispered Lydia. I knew that verbena was a medicinal plant, but nothing more. "Therefore, vervain," whispered Lydia again. I don't know if you can be heard when you're invisible, but caution won't hurt. Exciting things were happening at the flat stone. A white light suddenly appeared around the tall Druid and the child on the stone. It was as if a giant torch had been lit and highlighted its target - but the light was soft and floating and seemed to live its own mysterious life. The tall Druid worked constantly with the verbena twig and the light flickered around them. It was as if a quite peculiar atmosphere had seized all us spectators, visible and invisible. It was like a devotion in the middle of this flourishing grove of oaks.

The white light shimmered, and visible waves and thin figures, barely discernible, were moving inside of it. The figures bent over the boy child, after which they disappeared and the light began to sizzle. The light took the form of a beam that dove down into the boy's stomach, after which it sizzled even more intensely and was launched like a rocket up towards the bluish-black dome of the nocturnal firmament. It was a remarkable sight. An even more remarkable sight was that the little boy on the altar opened his eyes, smiled, raised up on his elbow, and said loud and clear:

"Why am I here? Where's my mother?"

We saw the overjoyed mother rush forward and lift her son in her arms. The tall Druid withdraw quietly back into the shadows and the woman looked for him without finding him. She and the child were the only ones at the altar - and the four of us, of course. But we weren't visible.

"I thought the Druids did other things on the stone," I whispered.

"There were times when the Celtic Druids abused their gifts and sacrificed humans. The Irish Druids never did that," answered Balt. "We are in Ireland now."

"I have never read about this sort of healing," interrupted Lydia. "Everything can't be found in books."

"You saw the Nature spirits who participated in the light," Thesa said. "What happened was very secret and belongs to the magic that was inherited among some Druids and that wasn't talked about out loud. The boy was rescued from the jaws of death - because he was very close to death in a dangerous disease. You have seen something that nobody else has been allowed to see. But not long after this occurrence, things started to go wrong with respect to the cooperation between Druids and elementals. The Druid that followed the one you saw was very greedy for power and he began to use the secret powers on the wrong humans and in the wrong situations."

"The Nature spirits didn't want to be used in that way. The successor cured in order to receive economic prosperity and fame," continued Balt. "The secret knowledge was wiped out from the memories of the Druids and soon no one remembered that it had existed. Therefore, there is nothing written about it."

"And what is happening now?" I asked. Balt smiled, and the familiar mist surrounded us. After a moment, we stood in front of Mother Earth, inside her green cave. We told her about what had happened since the last time we were there and she listened, smiling.

"What kind of conclusions have you drawn from your excursions?" she asked when we fell silent.

"The beings of Nature actually existed in Ireland during the period of the Druids, but then we haven't gotten any further," I replied.

"There have been great leaps of time between our visits," added

Lydia. "There must have been intermediary periods when the Nature spirits remained invisible. Or perhaps they even have reigned alone on Earth?" Mother Earth nodded.

"I am going to send you to such a period," she said, and was I mistaken when I saw a mischievous glint in her eyes? "You are going to see some more of the dwarves, and Vrang will take good care of you."

She opened the door to the next peep-hole and we walked expectantly out in the mist. I turned around and saw Mother Earth still standing in the doorway, smiling a wide smile, on the verge of a laugh. What would actually happen? Lydia pulled me after her, close behind our dear elf couple.

15. The State of War Gets Its Dissolution in the Dwarf Kingdom

Suddenly it brightened and the mist cleared. We found ourselves on a hilly plain, overgrown with flowering heather. With outstretched arms Vrang stood there like a happy Christmas tree.

"This much heather is only found in Scotland!" Lydia exclaimed.

"Sure! Dear friends, welcome to Scotland!" our dwarf friend replied. "Or more correctly, what later became Scotland. If you're wondering what time we have arrived at, we are now in one of the time gaps when we, the dwarves, ruled parts of the Earth, and humans were few and existed elsewhere. We didn't ask for them and they didn't ask for us."

"Was it a completely visible, operational dwarf kingdom?" I asked.

"Yep, dear poet, that's exactly what it was, many kingdoms during several thousands of years. And if you stick with me now without making any ill-considered excursions on your own, you are going to experience a real dwarf war." Vrang made a face of great delight. Indeed, this wasn't an everyday occurrence for angels, or even for elves. He was inviting us to something unparalleled.

"Why did the dwarves make war?" Lydia asked. "What we got to see from the dwarves' activities in the mountains didn't indicate that they warred, only that they were skilled armorers."

"I actually know that the Earth was inhabited by dwarves during certain periods and that there were several dominions with different dwarf rulers," Balt said.

"Sure," Vrang interrupted eagerly, "and these were far too often at loggerheads. For example, this could be about some ruler who wanted land from his neighbor or that the neighborly relations had been disrupted for reasons the gentlemen easily could have sorted out among themselves. In a way, they liked to go to war. The dwarf kingdoms were becoming overcrowded."

"I thought there was prosperity in the dwarf kingdoms," Thesa objected. "You dwarves were knowledgeable of and skilled at finding out the gifts of Nature."

"Some kingdoms thrived," Vrang nodded. "Others were arguing. We'll have a look at a couple of countries that were busy trying to keep their peace. We may also have time to look at a fertile, peaceful kingdom. Come with me!"

To come with Vrang in this case meant to join hands and slide, as on long distance skates, over grass and tussocks. You really had to hang on to keep up! Lydia and I gave each other amused glances as we slid on through the turns. Meanwhile, the landscape changed. We left the huge plain where we had landed, and were now "travelling" towards a gray and steel blank city wall that suddenly prevented us from getting any farther. It actually looked menacing.

"I am not refused to come in, I have safe-conduct everywhere," Vrang proclaimed. "We need to get all of you in, and if I call you my relatives it will probably be fine." A gate in the wall, which I at first didn't recognize because it was hidden in the vertical stripe pattern of the wall, was opened when Vrang rang a small bell. A gruff dwarf poked out his long nose through the gate and inspected us closely. Vrang's face was haughty and determined and the dwarf opened the gate, allowing us to slip in - but no more. When I turned around I perceived a bunch of dwarf people who crowded behind us trying to sneak in. None of them succeeded. The long-nosed dwarf counted us as if we were sheep, and then he disappeared into a small guard cabin in the city wall.

We found ourselves on a cobblestone street. Small stone houses lined the street. There weren't many dwarves outdoors, but an occasional one rushed past us without even looking at us. Vrang seemed to find his way, and he led us with a firm and resolute face into a swarm of small streets until we finally stopped in front of a large house with towers. It resembled a medieval castle. There we entered.

A tall angel like me had difficulties walking through the doorways.

Certainly I could stand up straight in the rooms, but not more than that. It was easier for the rest of the group; none of them were like me, six feet, four inches in stocking feet. We passed through room after room, all lined with wood and with paintings or weapons on the walls and armor neatly hung in rows. Occasional dwarves were doing various chores, and we greeted them kindly. We only got sullen faces in return. Finally we stopped in front of a pair of double doors and I crouched expectantly.

"Here the ruler is living, or if you so prefer, the king," Vrang declared and opened the doors rapidly with a bang. The hall behind the doors was very large - well, quite enormously large, even from a human perspective. Its ceiling height was higher than the other rooms, so this must have been an extension. A long table was standing in the middle of the hall, and farthest away there was a dais with four thrones. A merry company sat eating and drinking at the short side of the table. There was chatting and singing and they toasted, bellowed, and yelled. We went over there.

An elderly dwarf with a gray beard all the way down to his knees flew up as if shot from a cannon when he saw Vrang. Our conical friend received a big hug and was almost suffocated by the gray beard encircling him. I supposed he was the king, because beneath his hair and beard glinted precious jewels, and the belt around his belly (I couldn't see any waist) was decorated with gemstones.

"Imagine having a visit from my oldest friend on a day like this!" sighed the dwarf with the long beard. "Nowadays, my son is king of our kingdom, and he has acted contrary to my will. Tomorrow morning we'll be at war as soon as our good sun has risen her nose over the mountain edge."

"Dear Alonsio, don't you rule this kingdom any longer?" Vrang asked, and worryingly tapped the old king on his shoulder. "I have brought with me two friends from the Angelic Realm and two friends from the Elf Kingdom. What do you say about that?"

Alonsio came up to us and pressed our hands cordially. I immediately liked the old king. He was majestic, but he had a good, friendly smile and he radiated wisdom and joviality. Bellowing was heard from the table, and a dwarf girl began to stomp and clomp in a frisky dance upon the table, so that goblets splashed around and wooden plates with food were spread over the floor. Alonsio sighed and shook his head.

"When I was roy of Ashamarra, things like that weren't allowed to occur," he said, distressed. "When my beloved queen died, I was about to perish of grief, and my son took over the rule. It was supposed to be only temporary, but he didn't let go of the reins, and forced me to resign. I've never gotten him in order; his mother took care of that. He has a whole army of cronies, and my grief has made me weak, so I can't defend myself. I'm still the rightful roy of this country." Apparently "roy" was the same as king in the country of Ashamarra, I thought.

"But surely you also must have many faithful friends around you, and all the people love you," Vrang objected, and put his arm around the king's shoulders.

"Not so many anymore," sighed the old king. "Some of them are jailed, even though they are innocent, and others have been murdered. Some have simply disappeared; I think they were deported against their will. Nothing is as it used to be, and yet it's not even a year since my beloved wife was buried. The people live in fear. They have been threatened in all possible ways. This is sheer terror."

"You need help," Vrang stated grimly. "You will get it, old friend, you will certainly get it. Both angels and elves are powerful, magical beings, and I'm sure we'll find something together!"

Now the messy group at the dinner table discovered the newly arrived guests. A young man, who was a head taller than Alonsio, quickly came up to us. It must be his son, I thought.

The young man stood in front of us. He put his hands on his sides and asked bluntly:

"Who are you? I can't recall that I have invited such odd people .."
He was definitely not sober, because he laughed to his heart's content and then he roughly grabbed the shoulder of his old father.

"If this man has invited you here, you can consider yourselves as enemies. My father is not only weak, he is also weak-minded, and he has nothing to say in the matter. He only drifts around. Well, what do you want?"

"You recognize me very well, Gilo," Vrang coldly replied. "When I last saw you, you were a happy and pleasant twelve-year-old boy. What has happened to you?"

"Well, I certainly know who you are." Gilo's tone was arrogant. "Your acquaintances have nothing to do here. Make sure to get them out of here. You may well drink a beer together with my father and talk about old times, but tomorrow morning we'll make war and then you must have left Ashamarra."

We'll certainly be more than one person to decide about that, I thought, and exchanged an understanding glance with Lydia. She had "shut down," as I called it. Then she stiffened, and her face was both cold and absent. The elf couple stood behind Vrang and their faces were quite determined. Determined for what, I thought, but we were probably in agreement that help was needed here. Then Balt raised his voice and it was pretty loud and clear.

"We shall leave your hospitable house, squire Gilo! Don't worry about us. But we'll bring Vrang and your father with us, which prevents your father from getting injured in your unnecessary war."

With a quick gesture, he wrapped something around all six of us and we disappeared in front of the astonished eyes of Gilo and his rabble. Like a gust of wind we were gone, and like a gust of wind we were moved to a tower in one corner of the city wall. Suddenly we all sat around a round table at the top of the tower. We had a view of large parts of the city, including the residence of the king. The old roy looked out through the window and exclaimed with a trembling voice:

"This tower I had built as an observation post for me and my family. My son confiscated it when my wife died and the tower was filled with guards. I have longed so much to come back here! How did you manage to accomplish this, Vrang?"

"We have driven away the guards, dear Alonsio. They are now at a wine tavern in the other end of the city, together with all of Gilo's commanders! None of them will be able to go to war tomorrow morning. Both their wine and their beer are enchanted. I'll meet the enemy shortly and cancel the war!" Vrang laughed so that his whole body was bobbing. "They don't want to make war; it's Gilo who has come up with a declaration of war. I will tell them that he has repented and that the old roy Alonsio soon will reclaim his throne. Then comes the duty of bringing order to this poor mismanaged country."

Vrang disappeared as quickly as we had just done. Now Alonsio was one big, wide smile.

"As soon as he comes back we will fix more things. My old friends who are still alive must gather here. I'll make a list of them. I am sure that all farmers and craftsmen of this country will support a revolution against my son, since he has commanded that all products of the people's work shall be transported directly to him. The need across the country is indescribable. A war would impoverish us completely, the suffering would be terrible, and soon Ashamarra would no longer exist. Then it would be easy for other countries to walk in here and conquer it all. I can't believe that my son doesn't realize this. He is power-hungry and has terribly bad advisers. He has always liked too much to live the happy days of life."

"Don't you believe there's a risk that a revolution against your son also would be very bloody?" asked Lydia. "One war isn't better than the other."

"I believe the residents here will get so excited when the war doesn't occur and I go out waving on my balcony like I've always done, that they simply will boo out my son. There will surely be no bloodbath, rather a renewal and cleansing bath," replied the roy. And in that moment, Vrang returned.

"The people greet you, Alonsio, and wish you welcome back to your rightful position. But if you don't immediately return as roy of the country, and your son continues his questionable governance, a war between the two of you can't be avoided. I would like to pass on a special warm greeting to you from your old friend Tubas, the roy of the neighboring kingdom. He will come to visit you in peaceful conditions when you have returned as roy. His daughter would be a suitable wife

10

for your son. She is strong and beautiful and doesn't allow herself to be stepped on. She would surely get him in order."

"Dear Tubas!" Alonsio chuckled contentedly. "It was a wedding and not a war we had planned, and so it will be with your help, dear friends!" He wound up his long, gray beard on one of his arms and sat comfortably down in a high chair, where he had an overview of the view. "Well, where do we begin?"

"We have already begun," Vrang replied. "I found one of your old friends on a street corner. He was standing there begging; your son has taken away from him everything he owns. I inquired whether there were any people faithful to the king left in the city and it turned out to be a considerable bunch that meet secretly and conspire against your son. They want nothing more than to get you back. Now I've also made sure that the wine and the beer in the residence contain sedatives, so tomorrow they will sleep late into the day. In the meantime, we'll meet your friends and inform them about what shall be accomplished."

I saw a large, round, and clear teardrop falling down the cheek of the old roy. He became very embarrassed, wiped it with a gold embroidered handkerchief, and took both of Vrang's hands.

"How am I going to reciprocate you and your friends for what you are doing for me?" he asked. Vrang laughed.

"Friends are supposed to help each other," he said, "and by the way, we haven't seen the end of this story yet. But we don't leave Ashamarra until after the wedding. Tubas, his daughter, and their royal court will arrive by horse tomorrow morning, and then there will be a wedding whether Gilo wants it or not."

"But ... but nothing is prepared," Alonsio stammered, terrified. "A wedding and additionally a royal such with the dwarves takes place with great pomp and ceremony."

"There will be no shortage of pomp and ceremony," Vrang assured. "Your old room inside this tower is prepared and there also awaits your royal accessories: the robe, the crown, the royal ring, etc. The only ones not being informed about this are your son and his cronies, who sleep sweetly on the floor in the throne hall."

"There's no way things could have happened this fast," the roy objected and stroked his brow. "How on Earth did you carry this out? We've been sitting here all the time."

Vrang smiled secretively and exchanged a glance with Balt and Thesa. Thereafter, he asked Lydia and me to follow him. Something had happened that had passed by our noses. We walked down the tower stairs and entered a guardroom. Two guards were sitting there, sleeping themselves sober. Vrang woke them up bluntly. They stood up, confused, and then Vrang told them in a commanding tone:

"The roy is sitting at the top floor. He shall be escorted to his room, and his wishes are your law. Who is your roy?"

"Roy Alonsio of Ashamarra!" replied both of the guards and saluted. I was amazed.

"The relay that Alonsio rules the country again, and that his son is going to marry the princess of the neighboring country, is spreading across Ashamarra as we speak, and the people rejoice!" Vrang explained. "You angels aren't as good as us dwarves and the elves in the art of magic, but we'll stay here and take part in the wedding tomorrow. I have booked two rooms at the inn next to the residence. They have to be rooms in human size for both angels and elves. When you are in your physical bodies, even you need to sleep."

"I agree with Alonsio, things have happened staggeringly fast," I said, and Lydia nodded in confirmation.

"I work with the power of thought at the speed of thought," Vrang replied. "The vitrigo has that ability and I've been using it here. While the sinners are sleeping, the whole kingdom awakens. Now go to sleep, even you, and we shall rejoice together tomorrow."

16. A Royal Dwarf Wedding with Pomp and Ceremony

Next morning - well, it must have been the next morning - the room was bathed in sunshine and Balt sat at my bedside, chuckling.

"This was the first time I've ever seen an angel sleep," he said excitedly. "The ladies are still sleeping, but now it's soon getting time for the wedding. Since I conjure so much here, I have conjured forth clothes for us in human sizes. Thesa provides the dresses for the women. As you know, the dwarves' fashion reminds you more of the dress code that existed during the medieval times on Earth, but I have created something different for us."

I looked at him. He wore white silk pants that closed tightly like close-fitting pantaloons at the bottom. His shirt was also made of white, patterned silk, with ruffles around his neck and arms. His jacket was green, with long tails, and embroidered with pearls. He had brought forth similar pants and shirt for me, but my jacket was blue. I had never before worn something so flashy and I crouched, delighted, in front of the low mirror.

There was a knock on the door. It was Thesa and Lydia who proceeded into the room. Yes, they proceeded, since both of them had long trains on their white silk dresses. They wore tight vests that were embroidered all over with pearls, Thesa in green and Lydia in blue. Balt examined them contentedly.

"Maybe I should change profession and become a tailor!" he exclaimed, and of course we laughed. There was excitement at the inn when we entered the taproom. Partly our size was a sensation, partly our outfit. But everyone had dressed up as elegantly as they were able to; all wanted to participate and get a glimpse of the festivities. The innkeeper offered us delicious bread and wine, but we asked him for something more soothing, so we were served a good soup instead.

The walk to the residence was very short - fortunately. Our outfit was a bit troublesome to walk with. When we entered the throne room, there were no traces of yesterday's orgies. The room was decorated with flowers and there were chairs in rows for the spectators. Vrang embraced us. He was wearing a white, gold-embroidered robe, just like the roy, who already had taken his seat on the throne. But Alonsio stepped down from the ornamented throne and embraced us, even he.

"Where are Gilo and the rest of his gang?" I asked.

"Oh, the groom should probably show up on time," Vrang grinned. "Soon roy Tubas and his daughter Mea will arrive. The groom is in good hands, namely with Alonsio's old friend, Til, who yesterday begged in the street. Today he got back his house and his fortune, and he's the one helping the groom get dressed."

"What if Gilo will protest?" I asked.

"He can't. He's no longer the roy of Ashamarra. He's now under a legal guardian, namely his father. His friends have been deported to the coal mines in the north of the country. If he disobeys, he will accompany them." Vrang's eyes beamed with roguishness and he couldn't suppress the triumph in his words.

Then the doors to the banquet hall opened, and Tubas marched in with his royal court. He held his white-dressed, pearl-glittering daughter in his hand. She was a beautiful dwarf girl, but she had a resolute mouth and chin, and stern, wise, light blue eyes. Now, however, she smiled kindly, and she and her father greeted all of us courteously. The two roys embraced each other.

And now Gilo and his companion entered. The companion was an old man who looked as if he had suffered a lot. Gilo was dressed like his father in white clothes, but he wore a red tunic embroidered with pearls. He looked pale and absent. He didn't seem to recognize his future bride, but he was certainly pleasantly surprised by her beauty, because he greeted her unexpectedly courteously, bowed, and then kissed both her hands. In the dwarf kingdoms there were neither priests nor religions. They were all under the protection of Pan. Alonsio would be the one marrying the young couple. I saw how relieved he was and what happiness he felt at having regained his throne - thanks to Vrang and Balt. I understood that Gilo in some way was hypnotized. Maybe it's not right to marry a man who is under the influence of hypnosis, but now it was necessary, I thought.

The hall became silent and Alonsio stood up and married the young couple in the manner of dwarves. They also practiced the custom of exchanging rings. Perhaps this custom of humans originates from the dwarves? Indeed, the ring has been a very important jewel link ever since ancient times. But among the dwarves, music was also important. Special wedding music was played that connected the married couple forever. It sounded very beautiful to my ears, but also stern. The music proclaimed a message that was irrevocable. It contained heavy, ancient chords from the Source of Wisdom that caused my stomach to tingle. Never again would I get to listen to such music.

Both the bride and the groom must have answered "yes," because suddenly the whole hall began to cheer. In the midst of the cheering, Vrang stood up in front of us four and whispered:

"Now we are going to leave the wedding. We have done our part, we have to go home. We know that humans and elementals weren't on good terms in this time. We'd better not stay too long."

I didn't even have time to feel disappointed before Balt had surrounded us with the veil that belongs to our invisible journeys. I was a little disappointed, though. We didn't get to know how things turned out and we weren't allowed to participate in the royal wedding dinner. This time I would have loved to stay a little longer. I felt Lydia's little hand in mine and heard her thought: "I also would have loved to stay!"

17. The Short-Toed Eagle Keeps Track in the Snake Village

I thought we would go back to Mother Earth. That was apparently not the case. When our "travel veil" disappeared, we were standing in a meadow. As we had seen many times before, elementals flew around among the flowers and the vegetation was abundant. But there was something more there. A group of horses was grazing a bit farther away.

"Horses!" I exclaimed. "Are we going for a ride?"

"Look closer, Jan!" said Lydia and pulled my sleeve. "They're not horses."

Now I saw. The animals had a horn in their forehead. They were unicorns.

"Unicorns don't exist on Earth!" I declared angrily. "It's an optical illusion. Or else we are standing in the middle of a fairy-tale." Vrang put his arm around my shoulder.

"Now, you have to stop being doubtful and believe in what you see," he admonished gently. "Unicorns have indeed existed on Earth, just like dragons and other 'strange' animals that you have bundled off to your imagination. Do you in real earnest believe that someone invented the unicorn thousands of years ago as a mythological animal? The same applies for dragons. Do you believe that this myth would have survived for millions of years if it wasn't based in reality? We haven't come here to experience fairy-tales that the angels can tell their angelic children. We have come here to examine the relationship between humans and Nature spirits. As you can see, the Nature spirits also exist here in a fully visible state."

"Are we still in the land of dwarves?" asked Lydia. Vrang shook his head.

"Dwarves exist here also, but they work in the mountains and their villages are located at high altitudes up in the north. But here humans and elementals exist and now we'll see what they are up to." He took up a small whistle and blew a signal. Immediately five of the grazing unicorns came galloping and stood before us as on command. They snorted expectantly. They were wonderfully beautiful, shimmering, shiny, white, gray, beige, and speckled, and the one who stood at the front scratched his hoof impatiently in the ground. I wondered for a moment whether we were materialized. I looked at Lydia. We were!

Vrang rode in the lead. He looked wondrously small upon his unicorn, despite the fact that it was quite small. Unicorns are not large, stout horses; they are lithe as thoroughbreds and more slender in their structure. We rode without saddle and reins, and strangely enough, it went well. I remembered when I rode on a donkey in Palestine and fell off. I also remembered when I was riding an ordinary horse on my journey through France to England with the Grail. But this was riding in a completely different way. We sat straight and confident on unicorn backs that merged with our bodies. We held on to the silky soft manes. It was truly an experience. The ride went quickly and I wasn't able to register many elementals, but they were there all the way.

The village was situated in the sunshine like a giant wooden building. It was the strangest village I've ever seen - and I've seen many. A great many trees grew there and they were the prerequisite for that kind of building construction. Tree branches were stretched between the tree trunks as support for houses, which also were built of branches that hung about half a yard above the ground. The roofs were completely flat, made of thinner branches. They were cleverly spliced - how, I couldn't figure out. Neither did I have time to reflect more on that problem. We slipped off our steeds, who scampered off - somewhere. I was hoping that they would be within our reach for the return trip. The village didn't look particularly hospitable and I didn't see any Nature spirits inside it.

The people who lived here were reddish-brown. Their skin color resembled that of some of the Native American tribes. Most of the men were quite tall, while the women were shorter, often stocky and roundish. The village was crowded. A kind of square was situated in between the wooden buildings. Several braziers were placed at different locations. The braziers looked as if they were made of clay; they were round and approximately half a yard in diameter. Many of them had fires lit, but I couldn't determine what kind of fuel they used.

The humans wore very colorful clothes. They were apparently skilled weavers. Many of them were redheaded, but most of them had black, shiny hair. They seemed completely unconcerned by the fact that five unicorns galloped into their village and unloaded five strangers. They looked at us quickly, nodded a short greeting, and pointed at the timber house in the middle. On the roof there was a picture of a large, remarkable bird, with a sharp, wide beak and a colorful comb on its head, and with yard-long thin feathers on both its head and tail. The bird's body was also colorful, with long, shiny plumage. It was sitting perfectly still and looked at us with sharp, yellow eyes. Was it alive or was it a cleverly made sculpture? That was still to be found out, so we headed for the door below it.

"Why are the houses hanging between logs?" I asked Vrang.

"Because of the snakes," he replied. "There are many sorts of dangerous snakes here that hunt at night. The bird on the roof is a paradisiacal short-toed eagle, which only exists here, and it's alive."

We knocked on the wide door by hammering with an iron rod that hung beside it. The door was opened and we stepped into a large timbered room, which was full of people of both genders. We had to make our way through the crowd with pushes and shoves until we reached the far end of the room, where it seemed to be a bit less crowded. Two men and a woman were sitting at a small table. Vrang stepped up to them. He greeted them by putting his hands crossed over his chest and then bowed shortly, which more resembled a nod. The three persons did the same without standing up. I looked at my three companions and then we also did the same greeting.

"And what do you wish?" asked the older of the two men. It was hard to hear his question because of the buzz - not to call it chatter - in the room behind us.

"We only wish to know how you cooperate with the Nature spirits that we have seen everywhere here," replied Vrang. The man asked why we wanted to know this and then Balt stepped forward and explained who we were and where we came from. We smiled as friendly as we could towards the three commanders, but who were they, really?

"I am a vitrigo!" Vrang said, loud and clear. Then there was a different tone of voice from the three. It started as a murmur. They looked at each other and then they got up and repeated the same bowing again with crossed hands towards our dear dwarf - not towards us.

"Now it is a different tune!" I whispered to Lydia. She nodded, but I saw a kind of fear in her eyes. Something wasn't right.

The two men at the table were tall and rather stout. The older man had a round face with scarred skin, walleyes, a black beard, and a broad, fleshy mouth. The younger one looked a little bit nicer; he was redheaded and very freckled. He frowned all the time. The woman was also older, small, and pretty plump. She had large, slightly protruding brown eyes, a small nose, and a big mouth, with which she made deprecative faces.

"A vitrigo is always welcome to us," said the older man and pulled his mouth into a half smile. "You are a very wise man from the dwarves' tribe. Concerning the other four, we know that there are elves, but not here. Angels are totally unknown to us."

"You will go to heaven when you die and then you become an angel," I tried, just to explain us in a simple way. It was of course not entirely true, but you could always try.

"Heaven is the ceiling up there, above the rooftop," the younger man pointed. "You can't go there, it's just too far away. When you die you go to the Exercise Yard. Some become warriors, others become servants. The Exercise Yard is for men. The women come together in the Spinning Mill. We don't know more than that, because no one has ever come from the Exercise Yard or the Spinning Mill and told us how it is there. We only know that there are snakes there too, snakes acting as guardians."

"I have heard that there are different departments in the Spinning Mill, and the highest woman there is called the Spinner," the woman told us. "I've never heard about angels. It sounds like something you eat."

I dared not look at Lydia, because I knew she was fully occupied with trying to control her amusement. These people were really different.

"Thus the Nature spirits that are outside the village don't work together with you?" Balt asked.

"Sometimes," the young man replied distractedly. "When there are too many snakes here they help us send them away. If someone gets snake-bitten and dies, we bring him to the Forecourt. There he will be lying until we see if he becomes alright again or if he stiffens in spasms. In that case, he becomes snake food. It happens quite often."

"The Nature spirits also often help us make people well again after a snake bite," added the woman.

"Can't you get rid of the snakes in some way?" I wondered. "Kill them or carry them off to a faraway location ... ?"

The three speakers rose up again quickly and stared at me with horrified disgust. Obviously, I shouldn't have said that. Vrang shook his head at me and put a finger to his mouth. Balthori stood next to me and whispered:

"The snakes are their gods. They don't know of any other god. You have offended them deeply." I cleared my throat and knelt in front of the table.

"I ask for forgiveness," I moaned. "I didn't know that you put such a value on the snakes, since they kill you. I didn't understand that you love them."

"We revere them," corrected the older man. "You're forgiven this time, but you now have to undergo a test. Follow my son."

The younger man grabbed me pretty hard and led me out of the crowd. Balt followed us. He swiftly pulled on his invisibility cloak. The three ones at the table prevented Vrang, Thesa, and Lydia from coming along with us, but they didn't notice that Balt disappeared.

It was nice to get away from the congestion and to come out in the fresh air. There weren't many people left in the square, but the snake bird glared at us with his yellow eyes, and for a moment I thought he moved his head. We took a narrow path between the houses that led into the forest. I felt the invisible Balt walking close to me and that was reassuring, since my terrible forebodings came true very soon.

We stood at a snake pit. This was a huge pit. All kinds of snakes were crawling on trees with lots of branches that lay in the pit. Every branch had a snake entwined; some slept, and others were staring desirously at us with their stinging eyes. The sun shone relentlessly on the terrible collection.

"The snakes sleep here in the daytime," said the young man. "At nights they go out and bite whoever happens to step on them. Therefore, we are seldom out at night. Now let's see if you get bitten."

With a rapid grip, and without me having a chance to prevent him, he pushed me down among the snakes. It was a slippery, twisting surface I had under my feet. But the man hadn't reckoned with Balt, who he didn't think was still there. Just as fast as I went down into the pit, I came up. Then Balt provided me with an invisibility cloak and we took a flight with Olympic leaps. The young man's face was totally perplexed. I've never seen someone so confused before. I gave a laugh, which made him even more perplexed, but Balt grabbed me.

"We must hurry back and pick up the others. Vrang can make himself invisible; I will help the women."

Since Vrang was a venerable person in these people's eyes, the situation wasn't dangerous for him. In our invisible bodies we squeezed in among the people in the great hall and arrived at the table with the young man's father and probably also his mother. Presumably, they ruled over this village. Balt threw invisibility cloaks over our women and hissed at Vrang, "See you out there at the unicorns!"

Then all four of us ran out of the house. Two yellow eyes had seen us. Maybe the ability to see the invisible belonged to the magical short-toed eagle on the roof. In any case, his eyes glittered dangerously as he flew on his enormous rainbow wings above our heads. Balt found the unicorns near the village. They grazed in a meadow and were surrounded by elementals. When we took off our invisibility cloaks, the short-toed eagle sat down a short distance away and examined us carefully. To my amazement, Thesa walked over to it. She turned around and a sunny smile played on her lips.

"I can talk to animals, especially birds," she said. Then she bowed down before the short-toed eagle and sat down in front of him in the grass. A lot of small, sweet elementals flocked around them, curious to see what would happen.

"What do you want from us?" Thesa asked. "We mean you no harm, and I love all birds. Does your chief want you to keep an eye on us, mighty bird?"

The short-toed eagle bowed his great head and his yellow eyes glittered.

"Does the chief want us to leave?" she asked, and again he bowed his head in agreement.

"We are going to ride up in the mountains and visit the dwarves there," she explained. "Do you mind that? Are there a lot of snakes along the way?"

Now a small fairy detached herself from the flock and sat upon Thesa's outstretched hand.

"The short-toed eagle is not dangerous here and now," she squeaked with her bright bell voice. "The villagers have him on their roof in order to keep track of the inhabitants. There is much division and strife in the snake village. Furthermore, the eagle lives on snakes, and there are plenty of them there. I believe the short-toed eagle wants to show you the way. Greet our friends up there in the mountains and tell them that we will soon come to them with honey."

"How do you socialize with the villagers?" we asked the fairy. She laughed and excitedly shook her bright curls.

"Not much!" she replied. "They let us work here in peace. We usually don't have any contact with each other, except occasionally when they need help. We make ourselves invisible if any villager happens to come this way. But they rarely do. However, we have contact with the short-toed eagle; he clears off the snakes so we don't suffer because of them. And now he protects you, as you can see." She waved cheerfully around with her little hand and disappeared among her friends in the colorful, fragrant arms of the meadow.

18. Visiting the Mountain Dwarves

The huge bird clattered with his beak and flew up in the air. We quickly stepped up on our "horses" and rode in the same direction it was flying. The least we had expected was to have such a powerful protector and guide. But since he only ate snakes, we could hardly attract him to delicious pieces of food, I thought. Lydia giggled by my side.

"Hardly," she said. "I am trying to keep up with your unicorn so we can have a little chat. I was scared up there in the village. Certainly dead people can't die again, but you could have gotten furiously unpleasant bites from the snakes, since we are materialized. It was fortunate that Balt helped you, and invisibility cloaks are the best things that have ever been invented."

"On Earth they haven't been invented yet," I said, smiling. "Where are we going now? Is there a mountain village with dwarves? Are they physical?"

"Certainly they are," Lydia replied. "Actually, they are a kind of pygmy. I don't know whether they are benevolent, but a vitrigo is welcome everywhere; he has all the power we need for these journeys. The power of the elves is also unrestricted, as you have experienced."

The scenery was monotonous. Indeed, the unicorns were galloping enormously fast after our colorful guide, but we had time to look at the rocky road we rode upon, which the hooves of the unicorns barely touched. The road ran along mountain after mountain, and from time to time we whizzed over precipices on narrow suspension bridges. It was creepy, but at the same time fascinating. The blue ceiling of heaven hung like a lamp globe above us and we were getting closer to it. The mountains around us sparkled raggedy and their lower sides were covered with green vegetation. So far this vegetation surrounded us, but it was becoming increasingly low growing. Somewhere down there in the valleys a river was flowing - well, I actually saw several rivers glint between the heights. Waterfalls whirled down in sparkling veils, and just when we arrived at such a waterfall, the unicorns stopped as on command. Maybe it was on command of our large bird guide, because he stopped abruptly in front of the five of us.

"Shall we dismount?" Thesa shouted, and the bird nodded. We had no reins, and the unicorns started off behind a rock wall without us. The short-toed eagle remained sitting. I was thinking of his wingspan; it must have been several yards. We walked up to him and bowed. I wondered if the bird could be a cross between an eagle and a dragon, but of course he had no scales. He was as tall as an ostrich, his neck was thin when he stretched it, and right now he had his wings folded back, trailing his long, gorgeous feathers on the ground. Now it was Thesa who pleaded our cause.

"We are standing between a rock wall and a waterfall," she said. "The road continues up towards the heights. How should we go?"

The short-toed eagle nodded towards the rock wall that traversed another rock wall, which didn't look inviting. Between the rock walls was a crevice that barely allowed a human to pass, but where the unicorns actually had slipped through. There were no other options than to get started with the mountain march. The yellow eyes of the short-toed eagle glittered with delight when he rose in the air and quickly disappeared above the high mountain edge.

When we had squeezed ourselves through the crevice we couldn't refrain from making an exclamation of delight, all five of us at once. A panoramic view that was among the most beautiful we had ever seen opened up in front of our eyes. Our Lord really must have joked with us on our way here, when we passed the monotonous, grayish landscape. It's really hard to describe the enormous difference we experienced.

Actually, it was a valley that lay before us, as a staircase led down from the ledge where we stood. The strange thing was that the valley stretched as far as we could see. It should have been limited by cliffs, but it wasn't. Below the stairs awaited our short-toed eagle, and if he could laugh, he surely did when he saw our faces. Our unicorns were grazing peacefully in grass that was greener than green in this meadow of the emeralds.

A white road went straight across the meadow to a village - or a city. It was hard to tell. The houses were not high, but that's not required for the dwarves. They were shimmering white, probably built of stone. It was difficult to see, since all the houses were overgrown by flowers of different colors. Low trees grew everywhere and gave pleasant shade in this fairy-tale landscape. The houses were either square, rectangular, or round. One house rose higher than the others; it was probably the high seat of the village.

Around the city was immense vegetation with several fountains, and farthest away a lake glittered azure-blue, while sails in different colors were moved by a light breeze that swept across the water. Farther away we couldn't see, because it was just green, green that lost itself in the distance. Behind us were the mountains, a gray, rough, and cloudy boundary that you rather wanted to forget.

When we got closer, we saw the humans who lived in the village. They were about as big as a two- or three-year-old child. I can only describe their appearance like this: they resembled humans. Men and women were completely different than each other - different hair colors, different shapes, thick and thin, happy and grumpy. Everyone had quite a brownish skin. Their heads were slightly too large for the rest of their slender body, but yet they seemed graceful.

If they didn't notice us, they at least detected the short-toed eagle. They had been wandering around, seemingly on different matters, but at the sight of the mighty bird, they ran to the side like perplexed chickens. Some merged their hands, some howled, some fell on their knees. Some became terrified, some were very delighted. We didn't see any elementals, unless all of them were such. We kept closely behind the colorful tail feathers when we all walked into the village.

The short-toed eagle gravely went towards the only tower. One could catch a glimpse of the outlines of a door beneath the climbing tendrils. The short-toed eagle rose slowly on his wide wings and sat down on the roof, where he sat perfectly still, staring at us with his yellow glittering eyes. The only one of us who was somewhat the same size as the inhabitants of this village was Vrang. The rest of us felt like giants.

Vrang pounded on the door and it opened immediately. He entered and we crept after him. We crawled through a passage that had lamps on both sides. The floor was made of wood, so it wasn't that painful for the knees. But suddenly the passage widened into a large room, so we all could stand straight. It was a marble hall. It had marble floors, and the lower half of the walls was of marble, while the upper part was made of wood. The ceiling was also a mixture, but mostly it was made of carved wood. The hall was filled with small, round tables and chairs, as in a cafe. Here and there, dwarves sat and drank some kind of beer or mead in mugs of porphyry. (How do I know this? Well, I asked a dwarf who was running around serving! The drink was some kind of beer or mead.) In one corner, several dwarves sat around a round table. There were both men and women, and they waved at us. Would we have to go through the same unpleasant scrutiny as by the snake people?

"All strangers come here first," said an old man with a very wrinkled face and white spiky hair. "Of course, we have to know who have found their way here and how. It has been reported that you arrived on unicorns, and since you had the short-toed eagle as your guide, I assume that you have visited the snake people. Who are you, and how did your visit there turn out?"

It was Vrang who had to answer both of the questions. The seven people at the round table listened. When Vrang had fallen silent, the old man got up again and took us all in hand.

"Good that you came here," he said. "The short-toed eagle doesn't usually come with enemies. He is our observer of the snake people."

We looked at each other and I saw the cheeriness bursting out in Lydia's beautiful face. She held Thesa's hand tightly. It was just the opposite, we thought. If the bird was a spy for the snake people, he apparently was it for the mountain dwarves, too.

"My people were certainly both frightened and happy to see the short-toed eagle arrive with you. We live so isolated here, which means that foreign faces cause sensation. But you bring the proud vitrigo of the dwarf kingdom, and we thank you for that. He - and even you - are warmly welcome to our small mountain city named Bluona."

Now I couldn't remain silent any longer.

"It's so incredibly beautiful here!" I exclaimed. "How have you managed to get this place so fertile and cozy amidst the mountains?"

"Hard work, my boy, hard work!" replied the old dwarf. "We are many, and we have good help from our magic. Without it, this still would have been a barren mountain landscape. But we've been doing this for four thousand years. We dwarves become very old, and I've been involved from the beginning. And so have the short-toed eagles, and your bird out there is a sapling from the first of them. We call ourselves herculeans."

"Hercules was a giant," I pointed out timidly.

"That's right, my boy, that's right. We are giants, too, in our own way. You can be a giant inwardly, even if you are small outwardly. Therefore we live here, isolated from the rest of the world and due to our big secrets."

"We can do things and we know things that would amaze you!" said an old woman by the old man's side.

"What kind of things?" Vrang asked.

"Please, sit down by my side and we'll have a chat," said the old venerable man. We obeyed him immediately. The others who were sitting at the table left it at once, except for the old woman.

"Tonight we'll have the great Fire Night celebration," she told us and smiled a surprisingly dazzling smile with all white, even teeth intact. "If you want to, you are welcome to participate. Njamon here is our leader and I am his wife, Njanja. If you need to sleep after the celebration, there are beds for you in our house. You see, the Fire Night is a form of awakening - consequently, the inhabitants in our village don't sleep then."

"The salamanders, the fire spirits, are with us then. The celebration is in honor of them and their wisdom," Njamon added.

I felt a tingling of excitement rushing through my body.

Something like this was exactly what we had longed for, and finally we encountered it.

"Furthermore, we are just as much human beings as you are, or have been," the old man continued. "We are only a different race, just as there are many different races on Earth. And we live very isolated, but that we have chosen ourselves. The wisdom we have is divine, but it can also kill if it's used in the wrong way."

"We know all about that on Earth," I muttered. "There's a lot there that is used incorrectly and with fatal effect."

"It is good that you understand us," Njamon nodded. "Then you can safely participate this evening. We have a particular site on the outskirts of this city that is sacred. You will soon get something to eat, for you cannot participate in such a celebration with an empty stomach."

Njanja had been away for a few minutes. Now she returned with a pot containing something that steamed. She also brought plates and cups and cutlery for us - even though they were quite small, of course.

"You may take food several times with these small plates, but I believe we have bigger cups." She laughed and picked up five cups of normal size for us. They were filled with some kind of delicious mead. The steaming hotchpotch in the pot tasted divine. Since we were materialized, we could eat and enjoy ourselves. How these things were for Vrang I didn't know, but anyway he was eating with relish. Njanja gave us bread, and I've never tasted such delicious bread before. Fluffy and light, it melted on our tongues, leaving a lovely aftertaste of spices. After the meal, it was time to wander to the sacred site through groves of roses and other fragrant, colorful flowers.

19. The Fire Night Celebration

It wasn't a long walk. Rows of inhabitants wandered slowly towards their destination. They were all dressed in cloaks of different colors, depending on age and wisdom, as Vrang put it. The site was circular, and in the middle was, of course, a fire. It was an exciting place, not quite what I had expected. I thought it would be some kind of square. Instead it was a rather giant amphitheater. At the edge of the circle ran a shelf with reliefs that was supported by beautiful pillars. The fire burned on a podium down in the middle of the arena, with marble stairs surrounding it. The seats in this remarkable place ran along the entire circumference in close rows. Lydia expressed my thoughts by whispering:

"What a giant circus with these little people! How do they accomplish this?" We were soon to find out. The "amphitheater" was quickly filled by villagers, who were many more than we ever would have imagined. Where did all of them come from?

Njamon forced his way through the crowd down to the first bench that encircled the fire. He waved at us to keep ourselves close behind him. We noticed that we attracted interest, but also fear. Njanja walked last in line, so as to mark that we were guests of the leader. Soon we sat huddled in the front row seats. The fire burned calmly in front of us and the buzz from all the little people was deafening.

I heard swishing wingbeats in the air. Above us sailed the short-toed eagle, and for a moment I thought his yellow eyes winked at us. Somehow it felt good that he was in our vicinity. All along he had been kind to us. In case something unpleasant would happen, I thought. As if he could read my thoughts, Vrang turned to me and whispered:

"We are among friends, Jan. If we are hit by something, so will all who sit here."

"How come there are so many dwarves? This place is packed!" I whispered back.

"You have only seen our city. There are many villages around it. This is a huge area that stretches for miles into the mountains."

"Creepy," I thought. My feeling was something like watching a scary detective movie.

Lydia squeezed my hand. Of course she read my thoughts like an open book and we actually could talk to each other without using any words. I asked her by using my thought: "What do you think will happen here? Sitting and staring at a fire is surely nothing fancy. At least we sang at Walpurgis Night back home!"

Hardly had I finished thinking my thought when a large number of dwarves came walking in pairs, dressed in glittering costumes, and they sang! Their mighty song rose up towards the dancing fire. How come? The fire was actually dancing! Lydia whispered: "Don't you see the salamanders?"

The lengthy choir, consisting of forty dwarves, encircled the fire and continued to sing. The higher they sang, the more intense the fire danced, and small, fully visible figures were jumping and twisting in the flames, dancing, gamboling, flowing around, and getting the fire to adopt various shapes. Sometimes it was a tree, sometimes a burning bush, sometimes a tall, scrawny figure with arms, legs, and a head, where its hair became snakes in the flames of fire. It was extremely fascinating to behold. The fire took the shape of all sorts of animals: bears, wolves, deer, otter, fox, lynx, and then lion, tiger, and elephant ... How did this come about? Njamon looked contentedly at us when he noticed our interest.

"This is just the beginning!" he said and leaned forward towards us. "The fire is looking for a character that it can use tonight. It still hasn't found anything permanent."

What did he mean by "permanent?" A fire is a fire, and it can't become a body. This I told Lydia and she put her finger on her mouth and pointed at the large fire right in front of us. It had taken the shape of a giant-like man, dressed in a gown with a hood. You only saw

126

his glowing eyes that threw sparks as he slowly turned around and scrutinized the audience.

"That one will probably be permanent," Vrang whispered to us. "We don't know if it's good or evil; it can be anything."

A very tall fire figure among all the small human dwarves! He must understand - if he had any understanding - that he already was a winner. But what could he do? Then I remembered that fire consumes. He could consume. Consume the audience? A shudder went through me. If he was good, then what could he do? My reflections were interrupted by the short-toed eagle circling above our heads. It had its yellow eyes firmly fixed on the fire-man's sparkling red eyes. In truth, the Fire Night had begun!

The forty dwarf singers managed with difficulty to drown out the crackling from the fire-man. He spoke, and his voice was like a roar.

"Strangers are here this evening! Alien blood is here, in front of my eyes."

The eyes of the fire-man shone straight at me. There was no doubt. I stood up and replied:

"Two elves, two angels, and a noble dwarf, a vitrigo, greet you! We are invited here by Njamon and Njanja. We only have good intentions." I felt Lydia's hand in mine and Balt held her other hand and the hand of his wife. Vrang was sitting on the other side of Njamon, but I felt that he focused his thoughts on us. Together we were strong. I wasn't sure whether the giant figure in the flaming gown was good.

"I have found the permanent one!" rumbled the fire gown and pointed at ... Lydia! My heart jumped up in my throat. I saw Balthori whisper something to Lydia and then she detached her hands from us and stood in front of the fire gown.

"I'm ready," rang her angelic voice. "You cannot destroy me, not even burn me up, so what do you want from me?"

"If you are invulnerable, you must stay here!" rumbled the gigantic one. "At every Fire Night celebration, a being must either stay with me or be consumed by the fire. When you are consumed by the fire you become one with me, and together we can rule the salamanders in the Fire Kingdom. Well, what do you choose?"

At a given sign from Balt, we placed ourselves behind Lydia. Vrang stepped forward and stood in front of us.

"I choose that you are consumed by your own fire if you want to do us any harm, and that you become an ordinary fire that heats and lights up if you're good," Lydia said, and the rest of us grabbed each other and concentrated on the shrinkage of the fire. The audience behind us apparently held their breath, because they were dead silent.

I don't know how long we stood there, but the fire gown, who at first stood with folded fire arms, his fire eyes shining under the hood of the gown, started to shrink infinitely slowly. When an ordinary fire was burning on the podium, we returned to our seats beside Njamon and Njanja. Both of them embraced us (as best as they could; they were so small). Then Njamon took the floor:

"This was a test, dear friends. I didn't know it at first, but I realized that the fire-man exposed you to tough challenges. Any harm to Lydia would never have been allowed, because then I would have intervened, but I understand that you are strong in yourselves. We haven't seen a fire-man in several years; the fire creates such different characters all the time. But the fire-men can be dangerous when they invoke the permanence, which means death for the one they choose. The rest of this fire spectacle will be very beautiful, dancing and singing, sparkling fire rains, and lovely music. Many have probably drawn a sigh of relief that we got away so lightly this time. Would you like to hear about our history?"

"Previously you talked about secrets," I remarked. Njamon nodded but didn't answer.

Once we had seen the dance and listened to the song, we went back to our friends' palace. We sat comfortably at a table in the main hall and Njamon began to tell their history. Njanja served a delicious wine in very small glasses!

"Believe me or not," was Njamon's beginning of the story. Of course we believed him. "Actually we are ordinary, large, real humans, like those Jan and Lydia were on Earth. It's also the shape you have adopted here. A few thousand years ago we looked like you."

"Though more beautiful," Njanja interjected teasingly and smiled her beautiful smile. "Far more beautiful."

"Now I understand that you wonder how we have shrunk in this way," nodded the leader of the dwarves, and Vrang frowned.

"We dwarves have always been dwarves," he said seriously.

"But I assure you that we haven't," Njamon objected. "Rather, most of us were very tall. We weren't that many back then, but we were an incredibly warlike people, always ready to kill both people and animals. Our killing became a desire, a compulsion that we put on ourselves and on each other. Our women suffered. They were also exposed. We had an evil leader, and executions on both women and men were always close at hand. In this way the population of our tribe was reduced rapidly and inescapably.

"The location where we lived then was actually here, though a little farther away in the direction of the lake. We were skilled boat builders and we fished a lot. But no one was safe from the other's homemade weapons. Knives were common, as well as a kind of nastily sharp, poisonous spear. The women were forced to boil poison, even though they never knew if their own family would be afflicted with someone's anger, a relative's or a friend's. It must have been a terrible climate to live in. No one's life was safe."

"Then a young girl gave birth to a dwarf, a boy. She had been down to the lake for laundering, and there she had met a dwarf. Even in those days, interaction between humans and elementals was prohibited, as no elementals could thrive among such warlike types like we were. The dwarf was out hiking and had gone astray. The girl got scared, despite the unimpressive size of the dwarf. He started to talk to her in a friendly way, because he wanted to know where he had ended up. So one thing led to another. The women in our former village were accustomed to making love with those who demanded it. If they denied any man lovemaking, they were killed.

"At first the men here were going to kill the newborn, small-sized baby, but the mother hid him and told them that the baby had died. The girl lived together with her widowed mother and they helped each other raise the dwarf boy. Their cottage was located on the outskirts of the village, near the forest on one side and the lake on the other. After a civil war, there were only a few women and children left; all men were dead, even their evil leader. They simply killed each other in a terrible bloodbath.

"The dwarf who had fertilized the girl returned to see what had become of her. He arrived to a dying village. He got to meet his child and the surviving women. He saw a nicely situated village and a beautiful landscape, so he returned to his own people and suggested that they should move from the mound of stones where they lived to the human village. So it was. The surviving women in the village intermingled with dwarves and more dwarf children were born. I call them dwarf children because of their small growth. Instead I should say that a new race was born, the one that you see here. The extremely tall ones became extremely short. It certainly is remarkable, don't you think?

"We had to hide up here in the mountains and we found this huge valley between the cliffs, near a lake. With the skill and patience of the dwarves and the ingenuity and shrewdness of the humans, Bluona came into existence during thousands of years of work. There you have our history."

"You really are herculeans!" I exclaimed admiringly. "But, how about the secrets?"

"They are stored in our secret archives that shall remain secret," Njanja smiled. "However, one secret we will let you know: We have mixed our daily work and our everyday lives with magic. Therefore, we are such a happy province with harmonious inhabitants."

We slept in very comfortable quarters for the night, a hall in the big house of Njamon and Njanja. All five of us slept well on soft cushions and woke up well-rested. We pondered if we could stay longer, but realized that we had to seek more connections between Nature spirits and humans. No matter how much Njanja assured us that the residents of Bluona were humans, we still thought that their tribe was a kind of

Nature spirits of flesh and blood. Their history was very strange, but they were open, cheerful beings and we got on well with them.

"It's time for us to move on," Vrang said to our amiable host couple, "before we eat you out of your house. Moreover, we have more visits to do with humans or with Nature spirits. We travel in time, and Mother Earth is our leader. We must not disappoint her."

We bid a loving farewell to our new friends, and the yellow-eyed short-toed eagle immediately appeared outside their house. Vrang could talk with him. He leaned forward with his peaked head near the bird's wide beak.

"The short-toed eagle wants to show us something," he said. "He flies above us and shows us the way. Our unicorns are waiting off the mountain, in the meadow, where we left them."

I almost felt a little disappointed, because I had hoped that we would enter into the usual mist that would bring us to Mother Earth's cave. That was obviously not the case. What could the short-toed eagle show us? The bird apparently understood our mission in this dimension, so we'd better just follow him. The unicorns grazed quietly, and they seemed almost happy when we arrived. They snorted and whinnied in a friendly way and stood absolutely still when we climbed onto their backs. Off we went on a new adventure.

20.   Visiting the Anasazi Tribe

I was both fascinated and a little afraid of the short-toed eagle. Surely he was brilliantly beautiful to look at, but could you trust him?

"Jan, do you trust me?" It was Vrang riding by my side who asked the question.

"Of course, as in God the Father himself," I snorted. I felt a bit embarrassed. Obviously Vrang tracked our thoughts, at least now. It would have been more natural if Lydia had read my thoughts, but she was engaged in a conversation with Thesa. The women almost hung along the horsebacks, so it must have been something important they discussed.

"We are not going to cross the boundaries of our mission," Vrang continued. "We are going to visit a contemporary tribe on another part of the Earth, and you can trust the short-toed eagle. He leaves us when he wants to. He has decided to protect us. And as long as there are snakes on the ground, he surely will keep up with us."

"So we're actually on Earth?" I exclaimed, astonished. I couldn't keep track of all these different epochs we visited, whether they were earthly or not.

"We are currently investigating the relationship between the humans and the Nature spirits on Earth," Vrang replied dryly. "Not on some other planet. But the area of the Earth's surface wasn't less in prehistoric ages compared to what it is now. It was more or less sparsely inhabited during certain periods of its development, but there were humans present almost all the time and elementals, more or less visible. However, the Earth was born in collaboration with elemental spirits - how else would it have come into existence? The basic types of elemental spirits that you have met, earth spirits, undines, salamanders, and sylphs, existed long before the Earth came into being. We have lived on other planets and in other solar systems, but we have been around, be sure of that!"

"I believe you," I assured him, astonished at this lecture on horseback. "That explains a lot."

"There are also the Spirits of Motion, Time, Form, Wisdom, and Will; they're also called thrones," Vrang continued severely. "You probably don't know much about that. We ought to have a lesson on spiritual beings in connection with elementals when the opportunity arises. Now we have to ride into the cloud you see over there. It will bring both us and our unicorns to the place we are going to visit."

I hadn't learned about any spiritual beings whatsoever at school and I contemplated if it wouldn't be a good idea to let the kids learn such knowledge. Wouldn't the Earth look different if we started to spend time together with elementals and spirits? In fact, these things are terribly exciting. But now I had to look around. We rode along a fairly narrow ledge. On our right side there appeared to be a deep, grassy ditch, or maybe it was a slope without an end. I saw no precipice. I saw fairy-like elementals that flew back and forth in the grass and among the low, tiny flowers growing here. They could be mistaken for bumblebees or butterflies; only on closer inspection you saw their thin, almost translucent bodies in miniature that were humanlike.

A little farther on there was a bluish cloud, which stood still and shimmered. That was probably where we were heading. How nice that we were allowed to bring the unicorns with us, I thought. Puff, now I was riding as the last man behind the others into the cloud, and there my steed stopped with his nose close to the animal in front of him. I saw nothing but a milky mist surrounding me, so I leaned my face towards the soft mane of the unicorn and caressed his neck smoothly. He responded with a friendly neigh.

Did I fall asleep? I don't know. I was awakened by a scent, a scent that I recognized, but couldn't recall. It was a pleasant scent.

"Sage!" a familiar voice whispered in my ear. "Now jump off, Janne, we are in an exciting place!"

The first thing I saw was a great waterfall some distance away. The water was flowing down into a river and the river flowed through a broad valley. On one side, where I stood, there was an open landscape with settlements of huts, on the other side there were mountains. It was from the huts the pleasant scent of sage swept over me like a welcoming cloud. I saw my unicorn disappear together with the other equines beyond the village, where there probably were pastures. I saw the short-toed eagle sit on the roof of the nearest hut, with his flaming yellow eyes fixed on the odd group consisting of two angels, two elves, and a dwarf.

Outside the hut sat an old woman binding baskets. A man came out of the hut and spoke kindly to her. I've never before seen a Native American in real life, but many in pictures and in movies. I could swear that the old woman and the young man were Native Americans. Of course, the answer came from my trusty Lydia, who once again stood by my side with her eyes sparkling.

"Surely we are visiting the Native Americans now," she whispered. "We are at a tribe called Anasazi, who were the ancestors of the Mayan Indians. The short-toed eagle just took off with our unicorns, since such animals are unlikely to exist in the time we are currently visiting. Certainly we will need the unicorns again, so they are probably hiding in the forest over there."

The Native Americans were moving back and forth in the small village, which was located close to mountains, water, and lush forest. Probably we were invisible, because no one seemed to take notice of us. It was a good opportunity to study the inhabitants of the village.

The women were, in my opinion, very beautiful, and the men were handsome and muscular. I can't explain why this Native American tribe felt so special. Maybe it was because their smiles were so open, because the younger man showed such love and consideration for the old woman, because the kids played so light-heartedly .... The women wore colorful long pieces of clothing or covers of thin, smooth skin wrapped around their hips and bare breasts. The men wore tight leather pants or thin leather pieces from their waist to their knees. Both men and women were tattooed, the men to a greater extent than the women.

Or perhaps all their tattoos were painted on their bodies. They were all so well-made that it was hard to tell. Their hair color was mostly black, but I saw occasional individuals with dark brown hair.

Suddenly Vrang stood in front of the hut where the old woman manufactured baskets. He bowed deeply to her and she looked at him with a smile and uttered a few words. I understood that we were visible now. The villagers paid attention to us, and it wasn't long until they flocked around all four of us. Vrang had gone into the hut, together with the old woman, but he quickly came out again and waved at us. We bowed, crouched, and stepped into a room that was dimly lit by a fire. There were both children and adults, and certainly the sage scent originated from here, since it smelled very strongly from the fire. An older man came towards us, and to our surprise, we understood what he said. But then I remembered that Mother Earth had given us the ability to speak and understand the languages we met on our journeys.

"Welcome to Anasazi." The older man reached out his hands towards us, then crossed them over his chest and bowed his head. "Please sit down by the fire, the food will arrive shortly."

A young woman put a large, round bowl on the table. I looked at Balt and he nodded with a smile. Thus we were humans again who could digest food and drink. I liked that. Here the use of goblets was out of the question; instead, you let the bowl go around. Another bowl arrived on the table, and it was full of some kind of very delicate grilled meat in small pieces. My temporary stomach had grown accustomed to it, and certainly Lydia's, too. The older man took the floor again:

"My name is Leehan the Deer Hunter, and I'm the chief of this tribe. We are aware of the reason why you have come here. When you have finished eating and drinking, my son will show you around here so that you will see our cooperation with the beings of Nature. We have prepared them so they will be visible. They can appear or prefer not to appear at will."

"I would like to find out a little more about your culture," said the curious Lydia, who always wanted to know as much as possible about history and culture.

136

"The tribe has a female shaman who is a goddess to us," Leehan replied. "I'll ask her if she wants to show herself to you and tell you about us. She lives in her own abode inside the mountain. She is very old and very wise, and she leads the destiny of the Anasazis."

I could hardly wait for this meeting, I knew that it was important for us, and I wanted to get there immediately. I stood up, but Vrang gave me a warning glance. Later, as we walked around in the village, greeting the villagers, he repeated several times:

"Everything has its own time, everything has its own time. Bide with patience, bide with patience!"

I understood that I had to wait, but I also knew that the meeting with the female shaman would be incredibly important and powerful. Now at least we had the opportunity to meet a great many elementals. Vrang seemed to be very delighted at meeting his own kind: dwarves. We saw dwarves at the edge of the forest, where they cleared land for any purpose. In the distance we saw undines dancing in the waterfall, and the son of Leehan, Karyo, explained that they kept track of the water, preventing it from seething over its banks, which otherwise could easily happen.

The Anasazis grew their own food; they were amazing cultivators and they had help from the earth spirits. There was much to look at, and my human body was getting pretty tired when darkness fell. We hardly saw each other's faces when the old chief Leehan the Deer Hunter came walking out of the shadows with a torch in his hand.

"Now the time has come!" he declared. "Our shaman is ready to accept your visit."

My temporary heart jumped up in my throat. I didn't know how I would feel or if I was scared - but an angel never gets scared. I was probably a slightly odd angel, who could even think that way! Expectant I was, of course.

Somewhat below the village, a suspension bridge crossed the river. We were brought across it with help from the torches of the chief and his son. To be honest, I don't like suspension bridges at all. We walked close together and it was so dark that we didn't see much of the glistening black water beneath the bridge. The walk wasn't long, either. Very soon we were standing in front of the entrance to a cave, but it was a wide entrance and it was shining brightly from within. We immediately entered a large cave room.

The furnishings I can't remember or talk about, because all my attention was concentrated on the luminous apparition in front of us. Probably this was the case for all five of us. The chief and his son bowed deeply, and so did we. An unusual but very pleasant scent of spices met us. It was dark in the other parts of the room, but an inexplicable light radiated around the shaman. She stood there smiling and stretched out her arms towards us, as if she was Love itself.

The chief had told us she was an old woman, but in my eyes she seemed young. Mature, but young! Her hair was dark brown, with stripes of silver - very thin, subtly shimmering stripes. Her face was oval, with large, dark, sparkling eyes, a straight nose, and a generous mouth. Her skin color resembled bronze - the entire tribe was of that color. She was possibly somewhat brighter than the rest. She was dressed in a sort of dress made of very thin and pale, almost-white skin, perhaps from a deer. It was low-necked, because around her neck a remarkable stone hung, as sparkling as her eyes.

"Welcome to the Bearer of the Golden Stone," she greeted us. "You can also call me Liihai. It's an honor for me to meet two real angels from another dimension, and the same, of course, goes for the elves and a revered vitrigo! My wisdom is yours, and your wisdom is mine!"

She motioned for us to sit down in a semicircle in front of her. There were soft cushions everywhere.

"Can you explain your name?" Lydia asked. The shaman nodded and smiled.

"The golden stone is hanging around my neck," she answered. "I'll tell you how it ended up with me. I wasn't living inside this mountain when I was younger. I lived in a hut, together with my family, like everyone else in my tribe. One night when I was twelve years old I had a strange dream - if it really was a dream. Three beings were standing in front of me. They were intensely blue luminescent and I couldn't tell whether they were male or female. They told me that when I found the golden stone I would always have to wear it. Its wisdom would penetrate me and turn me into the medicine woman of our tribe.

"When I asked them how I would find the stone, they gave me no proper answer. The first one told me the stone was buried on the ocean floor, the second one said the stone was inside the Earth, and the third one claimed it was flying around in the air. The dream ended with the three of them crying out all at once, 'Your heart will find the golden stone when you least expect it.'

"Whether it was a dream or not, I still don't know, but their last words came true. I didn't forget the dream, but it faded over the years that followed. At the age of fourteen, my parents decided that I should marry one of the boys in our tribe. I had nothing against it, since I liked him a lot. In our tribe we have the custom that some time before the wedding the bride must stay in a hut with two other girls, without meeting anyone else from the tribe. This would be a kind of preparation for the marriage, and all three of us had certain tasks.

"In the evening the night before the wedding, we strung the last pearls on the wedding jewelry. In the daytime we had collected the herbs that I would be lubricated with and blended them together into a powder, which thereafter was moistened with fragrant plant oil. One of the girls discovered that one herb in the mixture was missing, and that particular one was important. I decided to go looking for it; I knew where the bushes grew. I brought a torch and walked the short distance to get there. I arrived there and started to pick the herb when I suddenly stumbled and almost fell. I held the torch high and regained my balance. Something glittered at one of my feet, probably the object that I had stumbled upon. I bent down and picked it up. It was an irregularly-shaped stone. At first it looked grayish on the ground, but when I took it in my hand it started to glow. I understood that this was the three blue beings' wedding gift to me. I hadn't found the stone, it had found me! One of the men in the tribe quickly drilled a hole in it so I could wear it during the ceremony. Since then it has never left me."

"And then you became a shaman woman?" Thesa asked. The woman nodded.

"I became more than that. The stone possesses supernatural powers and has brought me out on odd journeys. It has been my teacher. Without it I would have been one of the women in the tribe; now I live outside of it. I was given a new name. Liihai means 'the stone from heaven.'"

"What about your husband? How was the wedding?" Lydia asked eagerly.

"There was no wedding. Our chief had gotten a message via a dream that I would become the shaman of the tribe. We had a very old man who was our medicine man at that point, and he was dying. I wasn't allowed to marry, according to the message, and my prospective husband had to put up with another girl in the tribe. I have never regretted this. I have learned about the worlds that exist around us, other planets, and much more. I have experienced incredible, amazing adventures, and there's still more to come. Now we finally come to the question: Why did you want to meet me?" It was Balt who answered:

"As a shaman for my own tribe of elves, who are humanlike beings with our own kingdom and our own history, nowadays relocated to another planet, I want to answer that question. In the past we lived on Earth, but it has changed in such a way that we don't want to be there anymore. However, our love for it still remains in our hearts, and we don't want to see it perish. Not only the environment is being destroyed, but also many humans have changed in a negative way, i.e., being enslaved under the minions of evil, and performing errands for the dark.

"This goes on in this moment - we need all the help we can get to save the Earth. It is said that it's the most beautiful planet in this universe. The angels here have gotten the idea that the beings of Nature should be able to assist with this. We hope the same. What else would we do with the good ones, the pure ones, the loving ones? There are many such left on Tellus."

"There are also hidden elementals in many places," Vrang added.

"They dare not come forward, due to their fear of being poisoned or abused by religious, fanatic humans, who don't believe in Nature spirits, even when they see them."

"Trying to get a modern human being to believe that the beings of Nature are for real is an impossibility," I interjected.

"The trend in the world is to eat or be eaten, to kill or be killed, to serve or be served. Power and money, preferably without any effort, is the most prestigious employment, and our politicians in all countries are fighting and intriguing about this. Empathy, cosmic love - what is that? We who believe in such things are considered weird. The only things that are socially accepted are science fiction and fantasy. Not because anyone believes in them, but because they bring excitement. The kids of today are allowed to see TV shows and movies with blood, shooting, hate, sex, and violence. How do the brain and the heart of a child cope with seeing continually repeated violence?"

"Some cope with it better than you might think, my angel friend," Liihai smiled. "I also travel in time, and I have visited the future many times to create experiences that can help my people. Therefore, the Anasazi tribe lives in peace and cooperation with other tribes. But how am I going to help you in an upcoming time that is filled with both good and bad inventions and that must go beyond the normal and ethical to satisfy the people? If you want advice, you must penetrate behind the veil of what is happening. I can help you with that. However, whether that can put the problems right is uncertain."

"What do you mean by 'penetrating behind the veil?'" I asked. I didn't understand what she meant. It is difficult to demand advice which can be applied to practical deeds in a world of billions of people. Should you write in the firmament, thunder in the sky, or dance around with the big corporations and all the political leaders?

"Neither part, angel!" Liihai answered happily. I had forgotten her ability concerning the reading of thoughts.

"If you wish, you may follow me on a little excursion, or rather an incursion, here in the cave." She rose up agilely and elegantly from her cushion on the floor, and the rest of us followed her example.

21. On Dragon Wings to the Spirits' Palace in the Flower Kingdom

As in many caves, there were passages leading in different directions. One passage was narrow and winding, with a sharp downward incline. Liihai chose that one and we stumbled after her. Next to her walked little Vrang, who had an incredibly contented expression on his dwarf face. I accidentally slipped, and happened to slide alongside him. He stretched out his surprisingly strong, short arm and supported me.

"To be sure, I told you that I would continue initiating you in the activities of spirits," he laughed. "Now it will occur in the company of this odd woman!" He bowed his head towards Liihai, who was in the lead. "I'm not really sure what's on her mind right now, but anyway, this will be exciting. Her thoughts are not as easy to read as yours!" His laughter widened into a roar, and I actually joined in. We had reached the bottom of the steep cave passage and we entered a cavity with a wide exit, resembling a portal. There our charming guide stopped:

"From this portal you can reach almost whoever, whatever, or wherever you want!" she called out to us. "We can visit other dimensions, parallel worlds, other planets, and other star systems. I will be the one to decide, because I understand what situations you are able to handle or not handle and because you have a definite objective. Not even I can handle certain parts of the secrets in space. Since it's elementals you're looking for, you will get it!"

We took each other's hands in a long row and threw ourselves out through the portal, with Liihai at the front. Thereafter we floated. This was nothing new to Lydia and me; we were used to being transported around in the most peculiar ways. That is one of the advantages of being an angel. The eventual fear of heights from my Earth life is gone, even if, for example, the memory of rope suspension bridges still is uneasy, in spite of the fact that you walk on them with air feet. But scared? No, I wasn't this time, either. The only thing required was to sail calmly.

We stopped, and as usual, the ground quaked for a little while. As usual, we found ourselves in a haze at first. As usual, we didn't let go of each other's hands until the haze lifted and a landscape appeared. As usual, I didn't know if I was an angel or a human here, or something else.

The landscape was rather bleak, at least initially. We were standing on a ledge, and all around us were just cliffs. It was gray and gloomy, as a rather icy wind penetrated us and brought moisture beads that flew in the air. Our lovely guide stood in our midst and smiled happily, as if this was the most stunning place in the world.

"We are not there yet," she declared, "but almost. It's just that we can't travel farther on our own, so we are waiting for our transport."

There were no flights in those days, I thought, and then I gave a laugh. At what time? I neither knew where nor when we found ourselves in this gray environment. At the same instant, a swish was heard, as of heavy wingbeats. When I looked up, Lydia grabbed my arm.

"Janne, don't you see? A dragon! It's a dragon!"

It was a dragon. Such animals don't exist, but this must be the fabulous dragon animal. Vrang tiptoed up to me and grabbed my other arm.

"You truly are stubborn!" he grinned. "First you don't believe in the short-toed eagle that was together with us for so long, and then you don't believe in unicorns, which you have ridden on and which are waiting for us at the Anasazi people. And now you don't believe in the dragon that is landing here in this very moment! I would like to inform you that dragons certainly have existed in the great mountains of Earth, and that even well-preserved skeletons originating from them have been found in the Ural Mountains, and thereby it has been discovered that they indeed spit fire, as the tales tell us. Now you'd better accept the dragon, since you will ride on it!"

The panting of the dragon behind me was deafening, as I took a look at him. Both Vrang and Liihai walked up to his huge nose and talked to his large head with its small ears. The dragon showed no tendencies of anger or attack. He kindly laid his head on the ground and I saw how smoke came out of his wide-open nostrils. I looked a little closer at his scaly body. It resembled a giant lizard, green with bluish tints, and a bright red spot on the underside of his nose, extending down along the neck, fading into yellow-red. His narrow feet had long razor-sharp claws. But to really ride on him?

Our beautiful priestess caressed the nose of the dragon and then she easily swung herself up on his neck behind his small ears. She waved to us to do the same and Vrang boarded the long neck with her help. Thereafter, Balt and Thesa climbed up, even they without apparent difficulties. Now it was Lydia's turn, and finally mine, and it went surprisingly well. It was like sliding upwards instead of downwards. Magic was probably in play.

Surely we could sit up there on his back; it wasn't really uncomfortable and his scales weren't slippery. But how would we be able to remain there? The answer came instantly. Liihai made some magical signs in the air and we felt how we were tied up both to each other and to the dragon. We were fixed so firmly that we couldn't move our bodies; only our hands were loose. When this magic was accomplished, the magnificent animal fanned his wings. In an instant he was up in the air.

An odd flight commenced. Far above the clouds we went ahead, and since we couldn't bend our bodies or even our heads, we didn't see what existed underneath us. I had decided that this would be an unpleasant flight, but actually it wasn't. I heard Lydia's low, warm laughter in front of me. I was a bit ashamed, because she felt like a protection to me in all this. It should have been the other way around. I have no idea how long we were flying. To be sure, time didn't exist at these latitudes. Anyway, when the dragon dove down through a dense cloud mass, it felt good. He landed as elegant as an airplane - well, in fact, even more elegant. The leap from the gray, cool cliffs was shocking.

Our magical guide made a similar maneuver with her hands as

when she locked us on the back of the dragon. Now we slid down very easily and found ourselves on flourishing ground - so flourishing that it took our breath away.

Liihai caressed the nose of the dragon and whispered a few words in the animal's ear, whereupon he disappeared as quickly as he had appeared. While we were rubbing our eyes in front of the beauty of our new sight, the shaman woman took command of us again. We found ourselves outside a temple. Well, what else should I call it? There were flowers everywhere, and certainly the temple pillars were made of solid material, but the rest were flowers, flowering trees, and flowering bushes. The balsamic scent, the birdsong, the beautiful insects, all contributed to a brand new, distinctive atmosphere. What was this? We didn't see any human beings. Not any Nature spirits, either. Only flowers in tasteful groups, with very narrow aisles in between.

"Are we in the Flower Kingdom?" Lydia asked loudly.

"We find ourselves in one of the Spirits' palaces, those spirits who are not accepted or don't even exist, according to the humans on Earth," Liihai replied. "I have summoned them, so you will meet them in a while. Let's enter one of the flower halls."

The word "flower hall" alone must give the reader an idea of how it looked. We followed our guide and Vrang in between the pillars, and after a short while we entered a large room. The floors in this remarkable palace felt velvety. I believe they were made of tightly compacted plants. The room had flowery walls and high windows, of course without glass. There was a long table and several chairs, and Liihai motioned for us to sit down. The table was made of wood, with an outstanding, shiny, polished surface, and the chairs, with their high backs, were perhaps also of wood beneath their soft, moss-like covering.

"Are we human now?" I asked, and Vrang shook his head.

"You are what you are, my angels," he replied, "and fully visible."

Now music was heard, as to complete the lovely picture that all this gave us. Four beings entered through the flowering doorway and stood at one end of the table. Liihai stood up and proclaimed:

"May I introduce the Spirit of Will, associated with the thrones, the Spirit of Form, associated with the exusiai, the Spirit of Motion associated, with dynamis, and finally the Spirit of Wisdom, associated with kyriotetes, related to the Nature spirits. We thank you for letting us enter into these flourishing chambers."

I scrutinized the four spirits that seemed very different. It's difficult to determine the gender of spirits, but their radiation can either be masculine or feminine. The Spirit of Will definitely had a masculine radiation. He was tall and lean, with rather sharp facial features and a determined look, but that is indeed understandable for a strong-willed person. He was wearing a long blue dress.

The Spirit of Form seemed very young in her movements. She was soft and looked very friendly and happy. Her dress was yellow, as was her hair. She moved her hands gracefully in a warm gesture towards us. The Spirit of Motion mostly resembled a dancer. She swayed, made pirouettes, and made different movements all the time. She was dressed in white, but when she spun around, her costume became multicolored.

Finally I looked at the Spirit of Wisdom, and he was a very old man. He made a majestic impression with his long white hair and beard and his light gray costume, embroidered with silver.

"I don't understand this!" I exclaimed. "You are four spirits who represent four talents or properties - it's so hard to define. Why have we been brought here?"

The Spirit of Will smiled gently, and then his stern face lit up and became alive and beautiful.

"You want to be confronted with the spirits of Nature and know more about their collaboration with humans," he said. "We are a kind of foundation pillars. Human beings were created with free will, and that shackles me. For example, I can't influence them to think positively; they have to decide that for themselves. Yet I still rule the elementals on your Earth and other places where they are operating. Our wills are in constant contact, and this Flower Kingdom is always open for those who have been chased away from their natural origin. Here is a sanctuary. It's my task to protect it."

"I am a creative power!" It was the Spirit of Form that spoke.

"I have been operating on Earth for thousands of years and a lot more, but now I have drawn back because the forms that are created on Earth have largely become the minions of fear. The lovely muse who was my closest cooperator lies weeping between the worlds. Her power has been weakened, and her cooperation with the beings of Nature can never be completed, since they are fleeing the Earth."

"I haven't lost my hope yet!" The beautiful little Spirit of Motion smiled at me. "Perpetual motion! You just have to change the world of motions into a beautiful world of constant evolution. To radiate good motion in an evil world can produce good results."

"You have to be wise in all that you undertake." The Spirit of Wisdom spoke with the deepest seriousness. "You have to be thoughtful, and above all, to emanate Love. Without Love, wisdom is worth nothing. When combined with Love, wisdom can accomplish miracles. However, wars, violence, and evil don't contribute to this, but complicate my work. We, the spirits here, also need help in order to help the Earth."

"But if assistance is required to help the Earth that we all want, from where do we get the aid?" I asked, and Lydia added:

"We angels don't live on Earth. The Nature spirits are on their way from Earth. The climate of Earth is changing. It's obvious that you have abandoned us."

"No one has abandoned you!" There was resentment in the voice of Wisdom. "Don't think along those lines! Each day we deliberate on what kind of help we can give you, and believe me, the help has already started. It may take time, but the beautiful planet Earth will continue to flourish after the disasters. However, we can't tell you what we are doing. We can only instill hope in you!"

He beckoned us to follow him, and we left the flourishing hall to walk out in the blossoming garden. The Spirit of Wisdom led us through a narrow passage to a spot that was completely empty. It was a round spot of gravel about one yard in diameter. Here he stopped.

"Here is the visual proof that something is going on," the old man explained. "Each time we succeed with any kind of help to the Earth, our flowers disappear here and this kind of gravel circle emerges."

148

"What if your whole garden becomes a gravel circle!" Lydia exclaimed, delighted. "What will you do then?"

The Spirit of Wisdom smiled.

"Then we plant new flowers," he replied.

"As long as there are invisible elementals on Earth, they will work with their tasks, and even if they are not seen, their work is giving results. There are probably still humans who want to grow crops without toxins and humans who want to help to improve the environment. Put your trust in them and widen their circle with your thoughts." It was Liihai who spoke.

"You should also rest assured that we exist, both we and many more beings who are trying to help the Earth," the Spirit of Wisdom assured us. "We have to work in our way and at our pace. Return to the Anasazi tribe and discover their hidden magic, based on our knowledge and our knowing." He made a slight bow, and thereafter the four spirits disappeared. So must we do, because our shaman woman led us out of the flower garden, back to the flourishing meadow. There our dragon was waiting.

22. To Anasazi and From Anasazi

Leehan the Deer Hunter, the chief of Anasazi, and his son Karyo waited for us in the chief 's residence. There a generous meal also waited and we told them what we had experienced. The magnificent shaman woman Liihai had stayed in her cave after taking a loving farewell of us and wished us welcome back. She was regarded as a kind of goddess by the tribe, and goddesses don't sit down eating and drinking with common people. So I thought, and Lydia winked at me. Vrang waited until I had told my version, and Balthori his, of the visit to the high spirits; thereafter it was his turn to speak:

"My four friends here are making desperate attempts to find out how they would be able to help the Earth. Somehow, I think they expect us Nature spirits to intervene. Even if almost two thousand years are between the time of the Anasazis and the present time on Earth, I don't think you can do that much at present. Indeed, you heard that the spirits of the Flower Kingdom firmly stated that they already have started a rescue action on Tellus. I suggest that we continue our journey to different cultures and find out who have worked together with the beings of Nature. To be sure, that is your primary task."

Of course, he was right. We had to leave this gorgeous place and continue our search. Outside the chief 's residence, the short-toed eagle was waiting. I hadn't seen him since our arrival to Anasazi and I was really happy to see him. Certainly he was also a guide. Vrang talked to the bird and it also felt good. None of us except him knew where this journey would take us. But it was with confidence that we saw our unicorns again and sat down on their bare backs.

As usual, we took off into a haze, and as usual, I dozed. I woke up when the unicorns stopped with a joint stamp and Vrang was crying something. The landscape seemed familiar, but yet not. We stood in a forest, though it was sparser than Swedish forests and with much more hardwood. For some reason it felt good, but I didn't know why. I dismounted my unicorn, which disappeared along with the other four equines. A fairly broad forest road led to a glade.

"We are in England," Lydia exclaimed.

She was absolutely right.

England is full of elementals, at least if you believe in what Shakespeare claimed. However, he wrote "A Midsummer Night's Dream," which has become widely renowned. Did he believe in elementals? That was still to be found out, I thought, full of laughter. England, how cozy! I really felt it, too. I jumped rather than walked towards the bright glade.

Something moved beside me. I looked in both directions, but only a little laughter, or rather a giggle, was heard.

"Don't be silly, Lydia," I said sternly. But then I discovered that Lydia was walking a good distance in front of me, arm in arm with Thesa. The giggle was heard again. A quick motion behind a tree and a glimpse of green cloth behind another tree made me understand that it was elementals who were pulling my leg. I constituted the rear guard, since Vrang and Balthori walked together and talked. I hurried forward to catch up with them, when I heard the low laughter again. Now a being appeared between the tree trunks. It was a faun.

"You don't need to hide from me," I said kindly. "I am used to seeing elementals and I am an angel, not a human."

Cautiously the faun approached me. He looked exactly like the pictures I've seen and like the fauns who had surrounded Pan when we met him. Two small horns were sticking up out of his brown fuzzy hair, two green, sparkling eyes looked at me, and a pointed nose and a smiling mouth were positioned above a tiny pointed beard. He was about as large as a ten-year-old.

"Hello!" he squeaked with a clear, but very tiny, voice. "What are you doing in our forest?"

"Looking for the beings of Nature." I laughed. Now the others had stopped and walked back towards me. "And here we apparently have one. Who are you, at what time have we arrived, and where in England are we?"

"In Wales," he replied. "Here we are allowed to be at peace. The humans here accept us. Nature here is so special, and it suits us. Early 1800s, according to your counting, is what it is. Time doesn't matter; we stay here on a timeless level."

"Do you cooperate with the humans?" I asked.

"Sometimes," he answered. "With those who see us. It's easier that way."

"Aren't you resisted at all? Isn't there any who doubt your existence?" Lydia asked. Now the whole company stood around me. Vrang went up to the faun and gave him a cordial hug.

"I can see that you have brought a kindred friend to us with you." The faun smiled and showed his small, white, pointed teeth. "There are so many who don't believe in us and who are afraid of us, so we keep ourselves away from the doubting ones."

"Do you live in the forest?" I continued to ask.

"Yes, we are forest beings. We look after all the trees in the forest, the ground that you walk on, and all other vegetation here. Other elementals take over when you get out in the meadows and among the mountains. We get on well together and cooperate with each other. When humans cut down the trees, we are always there. We understand that they need wood to build with, and as long as they don't cut down unnecessarily, we are friends. We make sure that the tree falls the way it should, without harming animals or humans, and that its deva, its spirit being, is taken care of."

"We are also related to you," Balthori said, smiling. "We are a kind of cross between humans and elementals; we are elves. We are also related to the fairy people, but we are a more physical branch of the large group of elementals. We don't happen to have any sympathizers left here?"

"Ooh yes, you have," the faun replied, delighted. "There are elves who have settled down on an island outside Wales and on other islands off the Scottish coast. One of them is called Iona. I think some also are on a headland in Ireland. Where do you come from?"

153

"From another planet, where we moved when we no longer could dwell on Earth." Balt's voice sounded sad. "We are fine, but we are only making a guest appearance in this company. We are also trying to find out the cooperation between the elementals and the humans. We know when it began, but not when it ended."

"It starts to run out now," the faun sighed. "We can't show ourselves, in any event; only when it's necessary. We pull back more and more and we all wonder how it will end. Some of us are actually afraid of humans. We believe that the power of money has exceeded the common sense of humans."

"There you are right," I agreed. "And you have told us exactly what we wanted to know."

"We will move on," Vrang decided. "We'll have a look at Scotland and maybe at Ireland before we continue to the next era and culture."

We said goodbye to the friendly faun, and sat up on the unicorns. The whole United Kingdom seemed to be populated by elementals; we met them everywhere. Most of them were overwhelmingly friendly, cheerful, and good humored, but there were also darker types. We didn't talk to them; we only glimpsed them as small shadowy figures hiding among the trees. We concluded that all these beings were prepared for more difficult times. They didn't plan to abandon their country, but rather to disappear from the eyes of humans and hide beneath the cloak of invisibility. That process began in the early 1800s and has continued ever since.

23.   Visiting an Old Icelandic Magician

When the usual procedure with unicorns and riding through the haze was over and done with, we landed on, for me, very unusual ground. It was hard ground, no soft grass wrapped around my feet. I thought it felt more like a rough floor. But it was definitely ground.

"Ground on Iceland," said Lydia, who read my thoughts as usual. The unicorns had disappeared, and our whole group was standing on the ground. A flat dropping silica terrace lay before us: This was Hveravellir, I later learned.

"We are standing on the other side of the dangerous country, on Kerlingarfjoll," Vrang told us. He seemed to enjoy the stripped terrain. Since I saw neither trees nor plants, it was stripped to me. But it was an impressive view, with the white smoke that slowly fluttered by from close-lying bodies of water.

"Here are glacier rivers, quagmires, and a lot of sulfur springs," he continued. "I wonder if we will encounter some leprechauns here; there are those who are accustomed to the barren terrain. They are not aware of anything else, they were born into this. Look over there!"

Surely it was a leprechaun who was curiously staring at us from behind a boulder. Then came another one and another, until Vrang waved to them to appear. Maybe they saw that we weren't ordinary humans, because they crept cautiously closer to us. Finally the first leprechaun came slowly striding, with both his small hands to his mouth. Either he kept himself from laughing or he was afraid that we smelled bad. We stood completely still. Vrang made his usual greeting with his hands crossed over his chest, followed by a slight bow. To my astonishment, the leprechaun answered the greeting by doing exactly the same. Vrang took a step towards the leprechaun while I intensely observed this new amusing being. He didn't resemble the others I had seen - in case it was a he.

His face was round, with a pointed chin. His eyes were large and somewhat protruding, and his nose actually aimed upwards, as tiny as it was. His mouth was wide, with narrow lips. His hair only seemed to be a bright, greenish down and he wore a funny little bowl-shaped cap. His body was thin, with long arms and legs, but he was probably slightly more than half a yard tall. His clothes were like a tight bright green casing, but behind him I saw a being that might be a she. Her cover was a little longer, from her neck to her knees, and her hair was certainly also like green down, but bushier and longer.

Vrang explained to the leprechaun about who we were, and the little being first looked relieved, and then he started to talk. He was talking eagerly with Vrang, who probably had some difficulties keeping up with him, because he wiped the sweat from his forehead. Then Vrang turned to us, while the leprechauns flocked around the first one, and they observed us as carefully as we stared at them.

"This is the sort of Nature spirits that dwell here in the mountains and around the springs," Vrang told us. "They say that the Icelandic people in general are friendly towards the beings of Nature and try to protect them in every way. Apparently there are several kinds of elementals here; they divide themselves into rotations. This relates to different groups with different tribal symbols. They claim that the Nature spirits have small villages here and there and that many humans know about it and respect it. They say that when the Icelanders build roads, they make allowances for the leprechauns. There are many in this country that can see us and speak with us, says this young man named Pyll.

"He also wonders if we want to see any of their villages. He gladly offers to be our guide." Of course we wanted that. Since Pyll was small even in comparison with Vrang, our new guide sat down on Vrang's shoulder. Then we took off for slightly more civilized areas, just outside of Reykjavik.

Now we got the opportunity to behold "real" houses, inhabited by entirely human Icelanders. The houses were special. I had never seen that kind of dwelling before. I got stuck in front of a house made of stone and covered with turf and grass. It was a low gable house, with its roof running along with the ground and with its windows extending their amazed panes from an embedded place in the middle of the roof wall. I actually fell into a trance of happiness due to this remarkable dwelling until Lydia pulled hard in my sleeve.

"Stop being a tourist!" she whispered. "It's not human dwellings we are supposed to look at." We followed Vrang and Pyll. Some distance from the houses, there was short green grass on the ground and a low, white-painted fence. Behind the fence was the leprechaun village that Pyll was talking about. Now we weren't allowed to walk upright anymore. Vrang motioned for us to go down on our knees and crawl after him. Soon we found ourselves in a new world.

We had entered the lowest village I've ever seen. No houses were higher than about one yard. Nevertheless, it was an absolutely delightful village. The houses were painted in different colors and resembled a Swiss village, with gingerbread work everywhere. Small plots surrounded every building. Low flowers in cheerful colors adorned the tiny, cozy gardens, all of which were equipped with benches and tables. In the middle of the village was a street, the only road that was possible for us to crawl on. Not a single being was out in the village, but we saw the inhabitants moving around in their gardens or staring at us through their windows.

Pyll had slithered down from Vrang's shoulder and ran around, waving and greeting. He was a bit too tall to really fit in, but everyone seemed to know him. We continued to crawl until we reached the other end of the village. There we had to continue our crawling for a short while more, and then we finally could stand up and brush off the dust from our knees.

"Now we are going to visit an old Icelandic magician!" Vrang proclaimed. "Pyll has told me about him. The magic here on this island is a matter of course, no matter what time we would have ended up in. So our little guide continues to show us the way. But now we have to sit up on our unicorns again." »

He blew his little whistle and the unicorns came running at the speed of the wind. Pyll sat in front of Vrang in the lead. The leprechaun really looked content. Perhaps it wasn't that often he experienced adventures like this.

I wasn't sure whether the unicorns were running extra fast or if we simply were flying. As soon as we sat up, we were told to close our eyes and keep a firm hold on the mane. Therefore we didn't know anything until we "landed," this time rather abruptly. My butt jumped high in the air, and if I hadn't been that light I would have fallen off. Obviously we weren't in our human bodies now, but rather in our dear old angelic bodies. Maybe it was better that way, because we had come to a dreadfully barren and inhospitable mountain landscape, which absolutely wasn't created for human feet.

All around us were high peaked mountain tops. We were certainly standing in a valley, but it was covered with rough rocks that didn't invite any walks. We had ended up in a cauldron and it was a cold one, because the cold penetrated into our bodies, although we were angels.

"You are a little in between now," Vrang laughed when he saw that we were shivering. Pyll grimaced on his shoulder; it seemed like he was making fun of us. Thesa and Balt looked untouched, but to be sure, that was something they were good at. Everything was grayer than gray, and Lydia's red fur-lined jacket contrasted sharply with the surroundings. From where did she get all her clothes? I thought irritably. She read my thought and giggled happily. Angels can create in their own ways, an ability that I evidently had forgotten. Immediately I thought of a padded homespun jacket - and presto, I was wearing one.

The valley was wide, and almost a desert. There was a house right in the middle of the mountains. I call it a house, because it was some kind of dwelling. Since it was also gray, it matched the mountains, and therefore you didn't take notice of it immediately. At first it appeared to be without windows, but upon closer examination there was gray turf that reached down to the ground and small windows were embedded in it. There were three chimneys on the roof and smoke was coming from the middle one. Somewhere there had to be a door, so we started walking around the house. When I turned around, I didn't see any unicorns. They had a habit of disappearing all the time.

The door was located at the gable. It was just high enough that I could enter through it when I bowed my head and stretched my neck. I was last in line, as usual. The others had already grouped themselves around a man who was sitting amidst a large room full of strange objects. In one corner was a huge fireplace where the fire crackled and cast long shadows on the walls. The man sat in a leather-covered chair in front of the fire. A long, wide table cluttered with books and writings was by his side. I looked at the man.

His old wrinkled face was currently facing Vrang, who was speaking eagerly with him. The old man's eyes were very strongly observing, close-set and light blue, with a strange pupil that changed its form all the time. His nose was large and curved. His mouth was just a line in the spider web of wrinkles. He was beardless, but had long white hair, and he was dressed in a kind of dark brown cowl. Eventually he signed for Vrang to be quiet and said with a powerful voice, more powerful than you would have expected to come from his frail, crooked body:

"Welcome to Jotna Vultir, the volcanic mountains in the heart of my beautiful island. I have named them myself; they are mine and I am watching over them. No strangers come here, yet I am today visited by a vitrigo, together with a son of our Icelandic little people on his shoulder, two elves, and two angels. Apparently it takes such a combination to penetrate my walls." He suppressed a rusty laugh.

"Great magician, we have come to express our admiration for you and to humbly make a request," Vrang spoke squiggly. The old sorcerer bowed his head and made a welcoming gesture with his slender hands. His hands were beautiful, the most beautiful hands I've ever seen. Strangely enough, they weren't wrinkled; the skin was bright and smooth and they were exquisitely well shaped, with long, well groomed nails. He had angelic hands, I sent to Lydia, who apparently heard my thought and eagerly nodded.

"The Earth is suffering," Vrang continued. "It is feared that the twenty-first century will be the end of the world. What do you say about that?"

The old man stretched across the table and dug out a glass sphere, about the size of a fist. He took it with both his hands and stared into it. We all saw how something started to move in the sphere. There was a breathless silence in the room, not even our hearts seemed to beat. After a long while the sorcerer said:

"Our Earth is in trouble, but not just the Earth. The atmosphere, outer space, and the nearest stars and planets are already affected. You are not the only ones who are concerned. I work daily with this. There have to be changes, and if humans don't achieve them, Nature must intervene. I have talked to my mountains and my volcanoes. They are in readiness, together with their sympathizers all over Tellus. I can't encourage you with any happy news. What is happening must happen in order for mankind to change.

"You must look upon the downfall as a transition. The very Earth you walk on will not be lost or destroyed. It will only change for the better. Lakes, maybe oceans, will rise and flood the land that is destitute and destroyed. We sorcerers have a big task ahead of us. Soon I have to step out of my mountainous landscape to help out, with the powers I have at my disposal."

He fell silent as he turned towards the fire and stared into it. Then he continued:

"For dust thou art, etc. - as the priests say - is completely untrue. From the Sacred Source you are, and that's where you shall return to be purified and to get a new assignment. That's what humans ought to hear. What else do you want to know?"

"We elves, as well as our relatives, can no longer live on Earth," Balthori said, and he put his arm around Thesa. "We now live on a planet which isn't nearly as beauteous as our Earth. Will we ever be able to come back?"

"Yes, so it is written," the old man replied with a soft smile. "You belong to the Earth and you will come back. You were involved in the creation of the Earth and you have been forced to flee from your creation. That's not right. There must be a change, and there will be. When you return, you will be visible to the Earth humans. The dragons will also return. They have existed for a long time on other planets.

160

If they are treated well, they are an asset. The terrible war material of various kinds that Earth now possesses, and develops more and more, must be destroyed. Weapons must be destroyed. So it is written."

"How will this be accomplished?" I asked. "Then these things will be invented again by some other 'Gyro Gearloose.' If war material and weapons of all kinds are destroyed, the memory of them and their construction must also be destroyed. Otherwise, hatred only finds new paths."

"Oh, young fool," the magician answered, "you have forgotten that I'm not the only sorcerer in the world. We are quite numerous. We have all the power we need to destroy all weapons."

"Then why haven't you done that already?" I asked, a little bit grouchy at being called a fool.

"Because each day has its own path, my son. The path of today doesn't consist of doing such a thing. Some things must first find an outlet before we can purify the world. So it is written." The old man looked patiently at me, smiling, and I couldn't do anything but smile back.

"But how can you live like this without having any food available? You must be very lonely," Lydia said.

The old man looked at her and then burst out laughing. He clapped his hands three times. From all directions came several men and women who looked very humanlike, walking with their hands full of different foods. A banquet table was laid out in no time in front of our astonished eyes.

"Who are these? Is it a hologram?" Lydia asked with wide eyes.

"They are my students," the old man answered quietly. "I have a school here for aspiring magicians from different countries and from different parts of the world. There are humans who are equally concerned about the Earth as you and I, and I am delighted that so many cultures come together under my roof. Please, help yourselves, my friends. Food is not an issue here, and everything originates from our farm, which is located in the far end of the ravine. The food is vegetarian and I promise you that it tastes good!"

"And I will be merciful," Vrang cried out. "Lydia and Jan, take your physical stature and enjoy the food. Bon Appetite!" I felt as if I was filled with matter, and probably Lydia felt the same. And I can promise you that the food was delicious! Even little Pyll, who had behaved very still and quiet until now, ate with gusto.

When we had gotten both spiritual and bodily food, it was time to return. Return to where? I asked Vrang, and Pyll responded by sticking out his tongue at me. I would never have imagined that leprechauns could be so ill-behaved!

"Here, cooperation between humans and elementals has prevailed since ancient times," Vrang answered. "We are aware of that. Maybe we should try the Native Americans and hear what they have to say."

"Native Americans also have an ancient idea of Nature and its inhabitants," Lydia said. She had now set the tone of the historian, so I feared a longer exposition.

"That's right," Vrang interrupted. "Now I know where we will go, but actually not to the Native Americans."

We said goodbye to the Icelandic magician, who nodded and smiled, making his net of wrinkles smooth out and his strange eyes send mild flashes.

"You have visited me to learn about the fate of the Earth. I have passed on what I know to you with joy, because so it was written."

Thereafter his net of wrinkles returned and he leaned his head against the backrest of his chair in front of the fire. He looked like he was sleeping and we drew reverently back.

Vrang summoned the unicorns and we rode towards our next goal.

24. At the Maori in New Zealand

We returned Pyll to his home on Kerlingarfjoll. The farewell was very swift and unsentimental, as Pyll immediately went to his dwelling behind the boulders. We rode off on our unicorns again. I praised Vrang for having arranged such nice trips with amazing guides and pleasant treatment - mostly, at least. However, I felt like an eternity passed by before we landed again, this time on soft ground.

"Where has the short-toed eagle gone?" I asked and looked around. "I haven't seen him in a long time."

"He has returned to his snakes," replied Vrang. "He is dependent on his diet. If he feels like it, he will show up again. Now tell me, where do you think we are?"

On one side there was a mountainous landscape, with grass and a few thickets. On the other side there was a forest, sparse in the edges, but thick inside. Our happy trotters immediately started grazing. Between these extremes a river ran, or what you might rather call a wide creek. Some brown-skinned humans bathed and a few others collected water in large buckets. Some children danced around on the narrow mudflat and sang. Others waded in the shallow waters. Their dwellings must have been located in the forest, because when they saw us they rushed right in between the trees.

"Aborigines!" I exclaimed. "Are we in Australia?"

"Close enough!" Vrang replied with a smile. "We are in New Zealand. We're visiting the natives there, those with the oldest culture. Those aren't Aborigines, they are Maori."

"Which year is it?" our historian Lydia, who always wanted facts, asked. Vrang's smile got even broader.

"It's an ancient time," he replied, "very old, long before so-called civilization. It's sometime in the first thousand years AD. That's when the first Maori came here. The reason why I wanted to come here is that the origin of the Maori is unknown, even in what we call the modern age. It is a mystery, just like with other peoples. The Maori came here with their culture from some unknown place on Earth, or ..."

"Are they extraterrestrials?" I excitedly exclaimed. Vrang shook his head.

"No, but many of them came from Atlantis."

"That's impossible," objected Lydia. "Atlantis went down about 10,000 BC. You said this was in the first thousand years AD. Additionally, it's not like it would be close for the Atlanteans to cross South America."

"I'm talking about descendants of the Atlanteans," Vrang continued. "The Atlanteans had access to what you call flying saucers. They had friendly connections with extraterrestrials. The culture of Atlantis was much more advanced than you can imagine, and that also became their downfall."

"I agree," said Balthori, and he put his arm around Vrang's shoulders. "Our dear vitrigo knows things that your science hasn't yet understood. During Atlantis' last hundred years there was a frightening ongoing development, much due to the part of their extraterrestrial friends, where all didn't belong to the good ranks. The evidence of this is on the bottom of the ocean. Maybe a future diver will find them some day. But the evil power managed to cause enough misery."

"Stop with the fairy-tales," growled Lydia. "History is history, and the Maori came to New Zealand from different South Sea islands, so there." But I was thinking about what Mother Earth told us about King Anu and what he gotten up to on Atlantis. I hoped that we soon would get to hear more about that.

It was time to visit the Maori people and find out how much they knew about their own origin. We waded across the creek and climbed out of it towards the forest in the direction where the children had run off. Pretty soon we found a gathering of somewhat primitive huts, and around them there was a lot of activity.

The Maori were dressed in simple home-woven cloths that were held together by a belt. Their faces were fairly broad, round and with high cheekbones. Their eyes were dark, their noses short and stubby, and their mouths fairly large. They smiled friendly towards us and instantly I felt that this wasn't a tribe that would cause us any problems. Everyone smiled and bowed, and they got all excited when Vrang started talking to them in their own language. We sat down on some rocks that I guess were the outside furniture of that time. The natives kept their distance from us, but they waved friendly and kept smiling the whole time.

"They come from a green island where there lived a lot of people," said Vrang when he came back to us. "One day their tribe departed from there to seek for better accommodations.

"They had a long canoe trip, and many lives were lost before they found this island, which was completely desolate and uninhabited. They settled down and walked a long ways to see if there were any other inhabitants, but the island was completely empty of humans. However, it was lush and rich with food sources, so they settled down for good. They have no religion besides Nature and all that exists there.

"When I implied that someone must have created Nature, they looked surprised at me, laughed, and assured me that everything was all right. But they had contact with the beings of Nature, and that was enough for them. They said that there are beings for all plants, for earth, sky, sea, and storm. All these were their friends and a kind of equals. More is not needed in their lives, and I would believe they've lived here for about a hundred years. They don't know themselves; they just reply 'Long time!' if you ask how long they've lived on this island."

"Oh well, so we can't get more out of this visit," said Balt and waved at us. "I think that once we're done with the Maori it's time to go to the Aborigines in Australia. Maybe we'll find out more there."

Vrang agreed, and he whistled for the unicorns. We noticed quite a commotion when the beautiful animals galloped on the other side of the beach. Surely the natives wouldn't have had anything against a unicorn, but we'd better get moving. Just in case, a misty cloud was prepared for us by the vanguard. We heard screams and clatter from the other side of the creek, but then we had already departed.

25. The Naked Nomadic People
in Australia

We were standing in a clearing. In front of us, men and women were moving who were totally naked. Lydia pinched my arm and I pinched hers. I looked at Thesa and Balthori, who stood next to us, and their faces were also very amazed. Vrang was already on his way over to the group of naked humans in the clearing of a sparsely forested area. A stately man, with a medium brown body color and a face painted with white streaks, talked vividly with our dear vitrigo. The aboriginal looked very harsh.

Vrang gesticulated, turned around, and pointed to the four of us and one of the unicorns, who had lingered at a patch of grass. Not until he saw the unicorn did the man smile. He made a special signal or whistle with his hand to his mouth, and immediately all five unicorns came running. A woman handed him what looked like pieces of bark and he invited our riding animals to feast on them. They seemed to appreciate this enormously - they whinnied (as unicorns whinny, a little lighter sound than horses) and shook their magnificent manes. The man and woman fed our animals for a long time; thereafter the unicorns ran into the forest. Vrang waved at us to come join him.

We had learned to greet with our hands crossed over our chest and with a short bow; it was a greeting that apparently worked everywhere in the ancient cultures. We didn't see any Nature spirits, but there was a very special atmosphere in the clearing. One of the men was about to make a fire. We saw water gleaming between the tree trunks and realized that there was a watercourse nearby. We saw no houses or huts of any kind, only several "mattresses" of large leaves, lying on the ground along a border of trees.

"The Aborigines are nomads," Vrang explained. "We may accompany them tomorrow when they continue their walk. Do you want to? I'm not sure I want to. Elementals are unknown here, but the chief will tell you more himself. Now they have a sort of break-up party, and we're offered to attend it."

The party consisted of a barbecued kangaroo on an open fire, and served with it was a salad of all sorts of wild grasses and fruits. When we were materialized we got to eat, but only vegetarian food. For the most part we were treated with a lot of vegetarian food, wonderful breads, nuts and nut loaves, root vegetables, and fruits. Here, we had to explain in detail why we didn't want to taste the highlight of the feast. In the end the chief - if he indeed was chief - told us he understood our reasoning and was satisfied with our explanation.

Meanwhile, I observed the Aborigines, this endangered people. Threatened by us, the white people, who believe we are lords of the carriers of dark skin in every country. It is a disgrace and terribly wrong, the way that we behave.

Lydia read my thoughts and put her little hand over mine. This was a tribe that had not yet been caught in the nets of civilization and probably had been hiding for years in forests and deserts where few humans ventured. I found that the Aborigines were beautiful. Their round, or perhaps a bit square, faces were illuminated by wisdom and cleverness. Their eyes were big and beautiful, mostly brown, but often with shades of green and gold, and even blue-gray. Their hair was mostly cut short and was dark and curly. Then came the expected question:

"Are you in contact with the beings of Nature?" Vrang asked the chief. He flashed his smooth white teeth in a wide smile and threw both hands up in the air so that the grease whirled from the fried piece of meat in his hand.

"The spirits, you mean?" was his counter question. "The spirits of our ancestors and the animal spirits are our protectors and our friends. We are one with Nature. We pay back what Nature gives us, and the smallest feather or flap of skin is put to use by us. So yes, we have constant contact with the animal spirits."

Vrang was speechless. This was another part of the whole, of the gifts of the universe. Balthori answered for him:

"My wife and I are half human, half elemental," he said. "By elemental, we mean that all of Nature is alive, that stones, plants, and animals have their special representatives in the form of, to humans, invisible beings. The kangaroo that you eat now had its elemental, which has now been returned to its origin. Vrang sitting next to you is an elemental! You talk about spirits, we talk about living beings that can no longer live among the humans because they are being persecuted and scorned. We are elves, and we have had to leave the Earth. There is a thing that is called 'magic' in human language. I reckon that you know it, at least you have some sort of knowledge of magic, but we master it fully. The beings of Nature are knowledgeable in such things, both the lowest and the highest."

The chief had listened intently. He looked very serious. After a while, when silence had settled around the fire where we sat, he began to speak:

"When you came here, there was a very small and strange human who first spoke to me. I didn't doubt for a moment that he was a human being and that you all were humans. He mentioned something about angels and I thought it was the same thing as the spirits of our ancestors." He looked at Lydia and me. "I didn't think they looked like this. I thought you belonged to some particular human tribe that we didn't know of. Unfortunately, we don't mean quite the same thing when we think of spirits and elementals. I respect your views, like I understand that you respect ours. We understand that you don't want to wander with us, as we first thought. We live to help each other and others, we work together with Nature in its visible form, and our gratitude to the Great Spirit who created all of it is unlimited."

"You're going the right way," said Balt and nodded. "We admire you and are happy that we got to meet you. Now we need to take off, so we say goodbye."

There was mutual hugging and laughing, and the Aborigines

were singing at our departure. They sang when the unicorns were gathered together and when we sat up on them. The last thing we heard when we blew away right out of the wilderness was the song of the Aborigines.

26.   At the Drumming Sami
Wisdom Teacher

When I opened my eyes I stood inside Mother Earth's cave. How we got there was a mystery, but both Vrang and Balthori were good at solving mysteries. Balt supported my back so that I wouldn't fall backward, and Lydia kept a firm grasp on both my hands. Apparently I was the last one to wake up, because Vrang already was standing, talking to Mother Earth, together with Thesa. As soon as she saw that I looked up, Mother Earth hurried over to me and embraced me. Were our journeys over now?

We sat down in the moss-green, sparkling hall and our lovely hostess asked us how it had been. Had we found many human tribes that cooperated with the beings of Nature? It was Balt who answered:

"We have found a few, and they are generally from a very long time ago. If we were to search in modern times, we wouldn't know where, since so many different religions are about to eat up the old knowledge. It is devoured, and there is nothing we can do about it."

"You must continue," Mother Earth decided. "I think you need to rest for a while, and my cave is best suited for that. Next dawn you will have new tasks."

I went out like a light in the arms of the moss, and the same probably happened to my traveling companions. When I woke up I felt very strong and happy and I woke up Lydia, who slept in the moss by my side. Our bodies were transparent and rather angel-like. On our next trip we would probably be invisible.

"Unfortunately, you have no unicorns anymore," Mother Earth said when we had gathered around her to get new directives. "You're going up north, and they don't fit into that picture. Now you'll have to trust Balt's magic. You will land on Swedish earth - or rather snow. Therefore, you must keep your angel- and elf-bodies. If it's necessary for you to materialize, we'll provide you with warm clothing. Vrang will stay with me this time, even though he doesn't want to. It will be Balthori who leads you to the cold Sami kingdom."

Through the opening in the cave room, the four of us traveled tightly together. A swirl enclosed us and in an instant - or an eternity - we traveled up to the cold. Insensitive to physical influence, we put down our feet in the snow. And snow was what our eyes saw through a dense curtain of snowflakes.

When our eyes had become a bit more accustomed to the shallow light and the white environment, we saw that we were standing in a village. It was a village of Lapp cots - probably we found ourselves in Lapland. Reindeer stood stomping in the snow, a gray smoke was coming out from the top of the cots, and we heard dogs barking. Apparently it was dawn, because the darkness was beginning to disappear and the camp seemed to be asleep.

But we didn't have to wait long. Loud yawns could be heard and a lad of about ten years came crawling out from a cot and was in a hurry to run behind it. He was accompanied by a grown man with a pointed face, narrow eyes like slits, and a narrow mouth. One after another came out of the cots to take care of morning's needs. We stood there invisible and wondered where the beings of Nature could be found in this treeless, snow-covered area.

Since we were invisible, we were able to take an unseen peek into the huts. We saw the fire in the middle of the dwelling, and we saw women rocking their babies in strange cradles that hung from the ceiling. We saw food being cooked on the fire and old women who were humming for the little ones. But we had not come to spy on the Sami people; we wanted to know about their understanding of the beings of Nature. Therefore it was necessary for Balthori to materialize.

Tall and stately, our elf suddenly stood in the middle of the yard in the snow. He had gotten his boots on and was wrapped in a fur-like garment. When the Sami people saw him, they gathered around him.

The dogs could certainly see us invisibles too, since they behaved a bit strangely. They sniffed around us, and one of them howled. We heard a monotonous drumming from a cot. Balt said something in the Sami language, and the ten-year-old that we had seen before pointed to a particular cot.

"Follow me!" Balt said. Whether he said it out loud or our raised consciousnesses picked it up, I don't know. We followed him to the cot. The ten-year-old came with us and Balt kindly tried to get him out. It didn't work.

"That's my grandson's grandson," said a crackly voice. "He is welcome here."

A tremendously old man sat by the fire, with a drum in his lap. The little boy curled up close to him. We had seen many extremely old persons during our travels, but this old man broke all records. One couldn't guess his age, but he must have been well over one hundred years old.

"I am the shaman, or 'najd,' of this tribe," the old man continued. "I knew that strangers would show up here and I picked up my drum from boassjo." (The space in the cot where sacred things were kept.)

"Do you see others than me?" Balthori was surprised.

"I see two women and a man under the veil of invisibility," replied the shaman. "You're not coming from Earth, but from other spheres, and you have an important question to ask, don't you?" We were all amazed, and Balt made us visible to the old man. We reverently greeted the shaman and then we sat at his fire.

"Do the Sami people have contact with Nature spirits?" I asked. "And in that case, do you cooperate with them?"

"I answer yes to both of your questions." The old shaman smiled a bright, friendly smile. "We are in contact with many kinds of spirits, including the Nature spirits, of course. We call on them in our work with the reindeer, but also in everyday life inside our cots and in all the places we visit. We are a wandering people; we need blessing and help wherever we settle down, and we give the same in return. We often need to sacrifice to our gods, and then we ask the beings of Nature to help us find victims from their world. We call the beings of Nature advisers.

Each of the advisers is watching over their own species of animals or plants. If we go against them, things will go badly for us, so we treasure them very much."

"Thank you," Balt said and got up. "We have found what we were looking for and we wish you and your tribe happiness and joy in the future."

"I won't let you slip away that easily," the old man objected. "It's not common that we get visits by your kind, and therefore I ask you to stay a little longer. I want to drum you into the dreamtime and give you some beautiful images to take along on your journey."

He began drumming, and we sat riveted around the fire. Images appeared that first flew around in the ceiling of the cot like large flakes of soot, but which then unfurled into colorful stills that gradually came to life. In front of each of us was such an image. I stared fascinated at mine. It depicted my childhood home, the red cottage in the arms of the forest where we toiled and lived in the shadow of the great estate owner. But the image also shimmered of happiness and contentment. I saw myself, a boy in ragged breeches who walked in the flower meadows together with sheep and goats. I sang, I whistled, and I dreamed of a bright future.

Then the image became dark and I found myself in the big city, a lost poet. Somehow, a veil rested over the image that was partly shimmering with light and partly shone in dark, muffled tones without showing any details. However, what finished the image was a fantastic light, the same as I had seen when I passed over from my Earth life to my present one. I felt how it enveloped me and how I became who I am now and probably will remain.

We had all experienced the large soot flakes that turned into slideshows. We had all seen fragments from our childhood and youth, and we were all deeply moved. The old shaman looked very content.

"I wanted to give you a glimpse of the human- and elf-life that you have left," he said. "I wanted to give you the opportunity to weigh your present life on a golden scale and give you insight. All ego values are gone, and yet you have a fantastic ethereal life and outstanding discoveries ahead of you. The end, which is not an end, is just a beginning. You can't relive your life, but you can develop it and make it meaningful to others. You are now faced with an important discovery: the truth about humans. Do not dismiss it out of fear or reluctance; that's what you will work with in the future. It is the most important thing of all."

"But we, of course, return to our planet where the elves live," objected Thesa. "That surely applies only for the former humans, right?" The old man shook his head.

"It applies to you, too. You have once and for all received the task of helping the humans, and that you must do when it's time - and preferably before. The life you are living on the new planet is not something permanent. However, you are permanent in a more multifaceted way than you now can imagine. The Earth is about to enter a new phase. If the world is suffering, then you will suffer as well, because you are created to belong to the Earth. This is the Truth."

He closed his eyes and rocked back and forth. The little boy stood up.

"Now you must go," he said. "Great-great-grandfather has fallen asleep and he wants the hut to be empty. Thanks for the visit."

He bowed at us and laughed cheerfully. We bowed our heads and got out through the narrow slit in the cot. It felt like a dream. We didn't know if we were visible or not, but Balthori rushed to put his arms around us and form a mist. We floated away, back to Mother Earth's cave. There awaited us a bored Vrang, who graciously accepted our hugs. We told him what we had experienced at the old drumming shaman.

"Could there be a connection between what he said and what you told us about Anu?" Lydia asked. Mother Earth nodded.

"Most certainly," she answered. "The cooperation between all who know the Truth is enormous. We'll come back to it soon - I promise."

"At least I've had time to figure out where we are heading next," Vrang said, when we had told him that the Sami people had contact with the beings of Nature. Now he was in charge again, and he certainly enjoyed it.

27. Lydia and Thesa Become
Abducted by Kahunas

"I think you're going to like the next peep-hole," Mother Earth said, smiling. "This will be a surprise; we won't tell you where you're going. But Vrang is delighted to once again become your guide. We don't think you'll be disappointed and we hope you will find new Nature spirits. Unfortunately, I can't give you unicorns this time, either."

Curious as I am, I was a bit disappointed to not immediately get to know everything about this new place. Mother Earth gave us nourishment and energy in a way that we could receive, and we had to wait for our departure until we felt well-rested. We got to listen to wonderful music and see beautiful imagery, but I still felt quite impatient. Where would we be going?

Finally we were driven out in the blessed mist, and the homely buzzing was heard in our heads. The mist lifted and Vrang called an order of command. I was suddenly wide awake. We swayed on the waves, probably somewhere on our Earth, and we were inshore heading towards a beach. The boat we were sitting in had sail and oars, but right now it was gliding into a small bay entirely on its own. It was a lush bay, but not lush in a Scandinavian way. Lots of palm trees and exotic bushes with flowers in beautiful colors were growing there. The air felt lukewarm and the sand was shining white on the beach.

We stepped out of the boat, and the water reached to our ankles. Lydia held up her skirts while she gave out delighted cries: "Wow, how cute, yes so pretty, oh so beautiful ..." She bent down and picked up a large shell that she held up to her ear. "It sings, do you hear, it sings!"

"Welcome to Hawaii!" exclaimed Vrang. "I chose to disembark in a quiet place; here there are lots of people everywhere. After all, we aren't actually tourists. Mother Earth and I prepared this visit in detail while you were visiting the Sami. I know exactly how we should proceed."

Were we humans or were we spirits? Vrang immediately called out the answer:

"You are not invisible here. Remember that!"

I felt content and I saw Lydia's freed smile. Again we would enjoy ourselves for a while, but as always, you never knew how long it would last. Surely the elf couple was just as happy. As usual, they wandered behind Vrang. I looked around.

All around us the vegetation was very lush, but the greenery stopped abruptly and turned into a mountainous landscape, which in turn had a high volcano in the background. We followed no road, since there wasn't any. We trudged after Vrang, who apparently found the way, even without roads. I heard a strange sound above me and raised my eyes. What did I see? The short-toed eagle that we hadn't seen for such a long time was soaring right above us and looked as if he was counting us. His magnificent colors were sparkling in the sun and I felt a great joy, as if I had met an old friend. It was certainly the same for all of us. Balthori and Thesa looked just as surprised as Lydia and I, and as if on cue, we all waved to our huge bird friend. He clattered loudly with his beak in reply, even though a well-fed snake was dangling in his mouth, waiting to be swallowed.

There was a strange house in the middle of the landscape. Another strange house stood some distance away. Several more just as strange houses appeared before us. A village of strange houses and again more lush vegetation. The houses were built of a grayish wood, and somehow looked thin. They weren't resting on the ground, but were rather built on poles. A pin stairway led up to the door opening.

"I really wonder if there are any elementals here," I muttered. Lydia looked smilingly at me.

"I think so," she said. "Someone has to take care of the volcanoes on this island. There are several. Just see what magnificent vegetation! If the fairy people don't take care of this, then my name isn't Lydia!"

When we arrived in the village we heard singing and music.

We went closer and then we saw dancing humans with shiny brown bodies and with flower wreaths on their heads and around their necks. Everyone laughed and sang, and when they saw us they rushed up to us and put wreaths on us before we even had time to think. They took our hands and brought us dancing inside among the others, about fifty adults and children. We skipped along the best we could. As usual, Vrang seemed to feel at home when it came to new people; he sang and gesticulated all he could.

A very fat woman sat somewhat in the background and smiled with her entire face. She was fitted all over with jewelry made from shells, pearls, and flowers. She had a huge bust, covered in decorations, and the rest of her was just as huge. I won't go into details. The strange thing was that her face was beautiful. Very beautiful. She had shining eyes with long, dense eye lashes, a small nose, and a beautiful mouth. Lots of pearls were interspersed in patterns in her black, shiny hair. Despite her massive fatness, she had a peculiar radiance. Somehow we were drawn to her, as if she called on us and we obeyed.

"You are not humans!" she stated. "Do you belong to the beings of Nature?"

We introduced ourselves. She listened attentively and asked us to sit down next to her.

She whispered a few words into Vrang's ear. He looked at us with astonishment and explained that she was a goddess.

"At least she claims to be," he said quietly. "She is the goddess Shimantse, who rules over this volcano village. She says that she rules over the powers of weather and the vegetation of the land. The beings of Nature are her minions."

The goddess snapped her fingers and bright, transparent characters detached themselves from bushes and trees and hurried to us. They were undoubtedly elementals. She made a soft gesture with her arms and they started to dance. Then she made another gesture and they disappeared.

"Do you believe me now?" she asked. "The beings of Nature are always in my vicinity and we are constantly collaborating. You saw a few of them because I wanted to show that they exist here. They adopt physical bodies when I so wish; otherwise they are mostly used to operate invisible to human eyes. There will come a day when they can work openly with the humans again, but for now they are being persecuted. Not by my people, but by the tourists visiting our islands."

Thesa and Lydia had disappeared. They just were gone all of a sudden, while we were speaking to the goddess. Balthori had also noticed it, and we grabbed Vrang's scratchy arm. He had not turned around, but had started a new conversation with the goddess.

"What is it?" he snubbed. "Don't you realize I'm getting information?"

We told him about our ladies' disappearance. He forwarded this information to the goddess. She yawned slightly and made an averting gesture.

"It might be Akua Lapo," she said. "They are spirits who aren't exactly nice and who want to frighten you. Sometimes they go along with the Nature spirits when they dance; they like to abduct people. They probably believe that your ladies are humans."

"What is happening to Thesa and Lydia?" I asked angrily. A goddess surely should be able to keep evil spirits at a distance. "We want them back immediately."

"It's not that simple," the goddess said and smiled mildly. "Here we are of the opinion that a Nature spirit always should accompany a human. Everyone has their own elemental. Such is our belief. Your ladies had no such elementals, so Akua Lapo probably wants to find out why. We need a Makaula, a magician."

"Kahuna isn't an easy language," Vrang remarked. "We'll probably soon face a bunch of strange phrases."

That was exactly what happened. The goddess babbled and made gestures, and with difficulty she got up and performed a number of incantations. Her entire big body swung, and flames shot out of her eyes. All of a sudden, a man was standing in front of her. I have no idea where he came from. He was gauntly thin, and covered in a black cape with a hood. He looked more like a wandering skeleton than a human, but probably he was human, since he bowed deeply before the goddess.

180

"I know what has happened!" The black-dressed magician spoke with a powerful voice. "Two women were brought to a place where Akua Lapo are. They steal life force, mana, from humans if given the opportunity. They believe that these women are humans. The two women are very uncomfortably affected and are trying to get back here. I can help them."

"Thesa can probably help the two of them," objected Balthori, who didn't really like the countenance of the black magician. Perhaps his magic was as black as his cape, I thought. But the magician was already gone and the fat beauty smiled encouragingly.

"Angels aren't that dumb either," I interjected. In my own mind I wondered what that magician was up to. He looked as if he could suck the life force out of anyone, he too. But the goddess probably read my thoughts.

"My magician is skillful," she said. "You will have your ladies here at any moment."

She was right. In only a couple of minutes our ladies threw themselves around our necks, and even Vrang got his fair share. The black magician stood by the goddess' side.

"We were actually prisoners over there, in another dimension," said Lydia. "Horrible kinds of spirits were watching us, so it was hard to get away from there, even if we could have. I knew what they wanted; I've read a lot about Kahuna magic. Luckily, we couldn't offer them any human energy, but it took a while before they realized that."

"And when they did realize it, they became terribly angry," Thesa filled in with a laugh. "They looked as if they planned to give us some kind of punishment. They had not been able to hurt Lydia, but I'm of course half human. Evil has no laws, I know that too."

"The Kahuna magician wants his reward now," the goddess exclaimed. "He has saved your women from the servants of evil. Now he wants to get paid."

"And what have you promised him?" Balthori asked.

"Gold," the fat woman replied delightedly. "Both he and I want gold. We need gold for our village. If you don't have any gold you will have to stay here as our guests until you have found a way to repay us."

Our beloved vitrigo looked at her with great contempt. Thereafter, he walked up to a tree and stood closely adjacent to it, with his back turned to us. We neither saw nor heard anything unusual, but suddenly the trunk opened up before our astonished eyes. Something gleamed inside. He nodded towards Balt and me to come over, and we hurried over there. Inside the tree trunk were loads of gold bars. We helped each other to stack ten of the bars on top of each other on the ground before the goddess. Both she and the magician gaped in amazement.

Vrang walked back to the tree and closed up the trunk. Meanwhile, we stood together and called for the short-toed eagle. He immediately emerged before us, and we quickly climbed upon his broad wings. He rose before the goddess and the magician had time to open their eyes. He probably had foreboded that this task awaited him: the guardian angel of the angels! Moreover, a long journey lay before us, even though I wasn't aware of it at that point.

I thought the Kahuna people would be kind. My thought was immediately met by Lydia's. She stated to me by thought that in Hawaii, like everywhere else in the world, there were both good and evil. We had tasted both.

Goodbye, Hawaii!

28. At the Hunza People in Tibet

"We go directly, without any stopover," cried Vrang. "We are going to Tibet, where it's summer now. Hold on tightly, we fly the straight route over the highest mountains in the world. I will bind you with invisible threads on the short-toed eagle. Close your eyes!"

Tibet, I thought. What on Earth are we supposed to do there? The Tibetans were Buddhists, and perhaps their faith allowed elementals, but surely I seemed to remember that it mostly was all about lots of gods, small and large, controlled by Buddha. Furthermore, Tibet was occupied by the Chinese, but perhaps we were going there in a time before the occupation. Anyway, rather exiting! Maybe this journey wouldn't be so long. The by now well-known haze enclosed us rather soon, and a cool breeze awaited us on the other side of it. Soon we were allowed to open our eyes.

"We may conjure forth some warm clothes," muttered Vrang when the great bird descended towards the mountain tops. We could see a variety of peaks around a valley that seemed long and wide. I came to think of James Hilton's book *The Blue Moon,* where he tells about a lovely wonderland, Shangri-la.

"Are we going to land in Shangri-la?" I cried, when a flourishing valley was approaching us. Vrang nodded.

"Not far from there," he cried back. "We will visit the Hunza people."

The Hunza people! Hunza was a completely new word for me, a new concept, and a new experience. My geographical knowledge has never been outstanding, but still quite normal. However, Hunza wasn't part of it. I saw Balthori's and Thesa's delighted faces, Lydia's aha-countenance, and Vrang's happy look when he declared:

"You must get the opportunity to meet the inhabitants of a

kingdom where neither evil nor abuse of power exists and where the inhabitants' age may extend up to 150 years."

"You've got to be kidding!" I exclaimed. "Not for real, right?"

"Yes, for real," replied Lydia, while our bird Felix was flying with smooth turns above the blossoming valley to find a good landing site. "I have read about the Hunza people. I've always wanted to meet them in real life. It's a kingdom where the love of Nature and the love for each other have formed the foundation for the existence of all the inhabitants." Indeed, she was an inexhaustible historical well!

The short-toed eagle softly landed on a grassy slope, which later proved to be the lowermost terrace of one of the plantations belonging to the Hunza people. Almost all mountain faces were covered by terraces, where maize, millet, wheat, and vegetables of all kinds flourished in utmost prosperity. A river was running straight through the plantations. The Nature was so lavish that I never before had seen anything quite like it. The air was warm, with a cool breeze, and full of fragrances. A short distance from us we saw the gable of a house. It was a rather square, whitewashed stone house. There we wended our way.

A man and a woman sat outside the house, which had two floors. The roof appeared to be some kind of porch.

"We are visible!" whispered Thesa, "and that always makes me happy. I wanted to enjoy this wonderful landscape; I wanted to know more about the inhabitants living here."

"Welcome!" exclaimed the man and his wife simultaneously in such a warm and cordial way that we really did feel welcome. Vrang explained who we were and the couple fell on their knees with their foreheads towards the ground to express their reverence. Even if Lydia and I were angels, we weren't used to this kind of reverence.

"You have arrived in Baltit, the capital of the Hunza kingdom," said the man. "We are growers and live in the outskirts of the capital."

I looked at him. He had a weather-beaten but beautiful face and it was impossible to tell his age. He moved like a young man and the woman seemed slim and gracious. Her face was also beautiful and her hair was medium brown. She wore a little round, embroidered pill

184

box as a cap on her head, and on top of it she had draped a thin veil.

"We took a short break from our work," explained the man, "and then you arrived. We would love to show you around here. Probably the Mir wishes to meet you as well. He's the one who rules this kingdom. Follow us, and we will lead you to his palace."

Oh, I thought, they have a ruler who lives in a palace. That sounds like a regular royalty who isolates himself from his minions and lives the life of Riley in the palace at their expense. But I was completely wrong, which I soon would experience.

The Mir of Hunza was a very pleasant acquaintance. His palace was admittedly large and beautifully decorated, but it had been so for generations and the history of the Hunza people has had its fair share of blood. Now the door to his palace stood open for the entire kingdom. Poor farmers who wanted to discuss something were welcomed there and were invited to stay over, too. We were immediately offered rooms in the palace, but we declined the invitation because we were there only for a short visit. The Mir was just as hospitable towards the farmer couple who came with us. He told us that the farmer was 112 years old and his wife was almost 90 years old. We were astonished; this was truly a remarkable paradise on Earth.

There were no police, no banks, and no shops. All lived on farming and by growing fruits and vegetables. Raw food was their daily diet. They baked an ancient type of bread called chapati, which tasted very good. They made wine from their juicy grapes, but it never led to any abuse. Apricot trees were growing everywhere; they ate apricots and rubbed their bodies with the delicious fruits. Perhaps these particular practices contributed to the fresh look of the inhabitants.

In short, this was the ideal kingdom. If more countries in the world had lived like this, peace and serenity would have spread out in a completely different way. Their philosophy was to love life and to take care of all the good that exists in Nature, but also in all of us. The inevitable question regarding elementals came from Vrang, who was closest to it, since he was one. The Mir smiled in a secretive way. Then he unfolded his arms.

"How else do you think our crops would look like this? You see how everything is thriving here. The humans converse with the beings of Nature when they work in the plantations. Each plant has its own spiritual being, who responds to our prayers, our joy, our love, and our care. We don't speak about it, since it's a matter of course, and at the same time a symbiosis."

We had gotten the answer we needed, and it was time to move on. The Mir and his beautiful wife asked us to return; we had lots to talk about. We promised to try, a vague promise that we would gladly have met. I couldn't help but wonder if the kingdom of the Hunza people was as undisturbed and wonderful when the Earth entered into its twenty-first century.

I later found out that tourism unfortunately had gotten there and managed to destroy the immediate, the pristine, and the spontaneous. Nowadays, the collaboration with the Nature spirits is going on partly in secret and partly as a myth.

This time it was difficult to leave this incomparable kingdom, this only real paradise on Earth, located in Tibet and isolated from the outside world by a rim of high, snow-covered mountains. But we had to move on, always move on.

29.   The Monastery of the Seven Rays
at Lake Titicaca

Was it an ocean that lay before us? Water, water, water, and an amazing sunrise. We were standing on a beach, as we had done so many times before, and the thin waves glittered as if they were scoops full of diamonds. Tiny pebbles rolled unevenly gray under our feet. Behind us was surely a village. I turned around and I saw it. It lay there, just as expected. After all, it was humans we were looking for, humans in Nature.

"Lake Titicaca," Vrang said hesitantly. He dragged the words on as if it was something dangerous or uncertain. Then he danced around; his entire pyramid-shaped body whirled like green lightning. When he finally stopped, he grinned a relieved smile and swept out his arms towards us. The short-toed eagle had followed his dancing with its gold glimmering eyes.

"That was a dance of thanks to our friend and flyer, the short-toed eagle," he explained. "He leaves us now and wants to bid us farewell."

The short-toed eagle bowed his colorful plumaged head towards us and looked at each one of us with his shining golden eyes. Thereafter he rose and disappeared like a torch over the waters of Titicaca and up towards the heavens. We followed him with our eyes until he was no longer visible.

Lake Titicaca! Mountains, high mountains! The Andes, this mountain range that is a tale, an ancient tale as full of aspects as a clear crystal contains. A shimmering, snow-covered mountain range so full of mystery that just the knowledge of its existence can give you goose bumps and bewildered, expectant dreams. And Machu Picchu, the ruined city, where advanced wisdom has been mixed with human sacrifice. Where did the beings of Nature exist here?

"Everywhere," Balthori answered in reply to my thought. "They have other names here, but they are the same beings. The old Indians weaved them into their magic. Here they are more magical than at home, and there are both good and evil ones."

"Thanks, we just got a taste of the evil ones!" Thesa shuddered. "Please find the good ones for us here, so we'll know what they're occupied with."

"That's exactly what we're going to do!" Vrang exclaimed. I was amazed by how happy he looked. What had he planned for us this time?

"We've arrived here at the highest situated lake in the world, Titicaca, for a very definite reason," Vrang continued, and he exchanged a glance of agreement with Balthori. "We're going to visit an ancient monastery - how old, no one knows. It's a monastery for monks. The interesting thing about the Monastery of the Seven Rays is that there is a legend about a golden sun disc. This golden sun is supposedly hidden deep under the grounds of the monastery. It was hidden there when the Spaniards came; before that it was located in Cuzco. It has some very special properties, but it won't come forward until a new and better era is dawning. We will now find out if the monks know anything about the beings of Nature. The monastery is said to be known for its incomparable farming."

Once again we were carried away, as in a cocoon of mist. The monastery was situated in a valley surrounded by high mountains. We often visited unique places such as valleys surrounded by high mountains, I thought. Maybe it had something to do with good protection. There are numerous mountain ranges on Earth and most of them have a story or two to tell, and many of them have a mystical, often well hidden, valley.

There was no doubt that this monastery was as old as time. It was built from huge stone blocks, which themselves surely could tell remarkable stories. It looked more like an old castle than a monastery. It was impressive, unique, and mysterious. We all stood still in reverent awe before the gray shifting stone walls.

Where we stood there was a door. It wasn't that impressive, made from thick, unpainted wood, worn down, scratched, and unbeautiful. It opened as if we had knocked, but we hadn't. Maybe they have some sort of radar in there, I thought meanly. Maybe it's all just set pieces. Does it really exist?

"You bet it does," Lydia chirped and grabbed my hand. "Now let's go inside with the others, and you will soon see that it's physical. I don't know if we are, but I hope so."

A somewhat plump little monk waved at us to follow him. He had a yellow habit, with a rope around his belly. On the rope a number of keys were dangling. He was apparently a key person, I punned with myself. I had decided to be a little critical until the opposite was proven. I get these ideas sometimes, and I am of the opinion that monasteries are some kind of voluntary prison. This was indeed an old monastery, but there are plenty of those. Was it Catholic or Protestant? There was no way of telling.

"The Monastery of the Seven Rays is neither Catholic nor Protestant," Balt replied, even though my question had been silent. But I started getting used to our common thought stream, so I just had to think about it!

"Buddhist?" I thought.

"No," was the answer said out loud. "Jan, this is the monastery of the high Masters."

"Do you mean the Masters of the Great White Brotherhood?" I asked breathlessly. Balt nodded. Maybe I should avoid being so critical. It suddenly became reverent and somehow sacred inside and outside of me.

We had entered a big hall. It bore witness to ancient festival and strong sacredness. I can only use the word sacredness, because that's how it felt. Not like when you enter a church, but much stronger. The stone walls were as in a hall of knights, festooned with colorful woven tapestries; in some parts they were tattered and frayed, and in other parts hung mighty paintings with interwoven gold threads. Along the walls were short shelves with books and scriptures. In the middle of the hall was the longest table I've ever seen, a light green table made out of shimmering gemstones. Exquisite bowls and candelabra of the same material somehow grew out of the table top. I had never seen anything like it, so I stood still, just staring. Twelve high chairs were placed around the table.

"I thought you said there were seven Masters?" I whispered to Balt.

"This is the grand hall, where the entire council meets," Balt whispered back. The little fat monk had disappeared. We were alone in this impressive hall. I couldn't help but caress the wonderful table top.

"Do you think this is malachite, amazonite, or agate?" I asked Lydia, who stood right by my side and who, like me, admired the table.

"Jade," said a powerful voice behind us. A tall man entered the hall. "That table top is of jade, but it is not created from earthly gemstone. It is very, very old, and was brought here from another dimension. For certain, such jade does not exist on Earth. But may I now greet all five of you and welcome you to the Brotherhood of the Seven Rays. Not many find their way here, so you will be our very special guests."

We introduced ourselves one at a time, and the tall one had a warm and welcoming smile for every one of us. He looked good, but there was something foreign and different about him. It was an odd radiance. He was bright. Hair, skin, clothes - everything was bright, even his bright blue eyes. He didn't carry a cloak, but was covered in a white jacket with golden embroidery on the neck and arms. His trousers were of silk and covered his knees as in eighteenth century fashion. When he noticed our wonderment he laughed.

"No, I am not one of the seven Masters," he exclaimed, "only their representative. My name is Eliel. Please be seated by our jade table. Brother Bun will serve you something to eat and drink. We have our own farms here, and our food is completely vegetarian. May I ask if the angels can ingest any food?"

Balthori made a sign which made Lydia and me realize we'd been quite transparent. We then got physical bodies again, and it felt nice. The little monk came over with plate after plate, filled with delicious treats from their own farms. And then came the inevitable question, but this time it was first asked by Eliel.

"May I ask for what purpose you are here? I hardly think you came to our secret valley without any purpose or task."

We explained, and he immediately answered our eager questions.

"The beings of Nature are our friends. The beings of Nature are so many that we can't count them all, but the most common ones that we have the most contact with are Apus, the mountain spirits, the earth spirits, and the water spirits. There are, of course, also lots of little ones in and on the earth, helping us with our farming and being our friends. We talk daily with the beings of Nature. Without them we would be nothing. They have been involved in the origins and built the Earth and they deserve our eternal gratitude. There are many names of these beings, but I don't think you get much from me listing all of them."

"I don't know at which time we've arrived," said Balthori. "You live entirely protected here from the worries and the pain of the Earth. Do you have any idea what will happen on Earth after the year of AD 2011?"

"We aren't that far from that time and we have technicians and inventors of different kinds, both machines and humans," Eliel replied. "We are a tremendously vast team spread across the entire Earth; many of us are in unknown places like this one. All of us wait for what will happen with Earth during the time when humanity is doing its best to destroy it. We are far more powers watching over the Earth than you can imagine. From what I understand, the vitrigo, the mastersmith Vrang, is the only one of you living and working on Earth at the moment. He is the one who can spread our message."

"I don't live in the sight of humanity," Vrang objected, "but if I must spread a message, I must. Otherwise, I am the guide of these friends of mine."

I held up my hand and Eliel smiled towards me and nodded.

"I'm indeed an angel," I said, "but I communicate certain things to an earthly medium, who writes books about what I experience."

"Then I continue!" Eliel sounded really excited. "We want to communicate the message of the White Apus, the bright spirits, the joyful and compassionate devas of Nature. We want that message to fly on invisible wings around the Earth. Can you help us with that?"

"Actually it's not a part of our mission, but we have certainly come here to do so," answered Lydia. "We are listening!"

"We know that darkness prevails on Earth right now. We know that this darkness may wipe out Earth or destroy its beauteous surface. We know who the advocates of darkness are, and they are many. But let me give you a parable.

"A girl is sitting alone on her bed, staring out into the dark night. She doesn't see the mild moonshine or the flashing network of the stars. She only sees her own demons. She is afraid. Her whole body is shaking. She doesn't know what the only right thing for her to do is, even though the solution is near. It is to look the fear of the demon right in the eyes and embrace it. In other words, she should take her own fear in her arms and give it Love. She should send Love and embrace the unknown, which scares her.

"Do you understand? It doesn't help to sit still with a beating heart and wait for the evil. It only helps to embrace the evil and give it Love and thus disarm it. That goes for all kinds of fear. It might sound a little bit hearty and too simple, but try it, you humans on Earth. Try it and see what happens."

We sat quietly and sipped on the tasty, fresh drink that was being offered. Eliel had in some way managed to build us into a net of light and joy; we felt a shimmering vibration through the whole grand hall, and a little hope for Earth was lit in all of our eyes. "We know that the largest part of the humans doesn't listen," continued our bright host. "We know that only catastrophes can make them do that, and sometimes even that doesn't help. There must be a cleansing, even if it sounds harsh, and we know that it's ongoing. The word 'love' is becoming worn out. Something different, even more powerful, must be invented. God is also on the decline. That word contains too much conflict. The inner God must be discovered and used instead of the outer.

192

"Meditation is good, but how many can meditate in these times of self-centeredness? Meditation is dedicated to the ego. We don't recommend an extinction of the ego, which many teach. The ego might be good to have in certain situations, but then in a nuanced and conscious way. I'm speaking about the timeless wisdom of the elders, but on the other side of these mountains there is no timelessness. There it's the year 2009."

Lydia and I jumped high, while the others remained unmoved. I cleared my throat and held up my hand. Eliel nodded, smiling.

"Energies!" I exclaimed. "Can't you conceive energies in this context? That is something that humans know about. Can't you create some kind of energy which changes humans for the better, which removes negative thoughts and influences? That removes the wars!"

"Good thought!" Eliel sighed. "Unfortunately, it's not that simple, and it would take time. A long time. It's a matter of getting the energies, or the love radiation as we call it, into reluctant souls with free will. We can't afford a long time anymore. We must act quickly."

"My medium won't be happy to hear that," I sighed. "Free will is surely good, but not always. Can't you manufacture a little chip with positive powers and put it into the necks of humans while they are asleep?" Everyone laughed.

"We have considered many approaches," continued Eliel. "We will most likely find a solution soon; many of us are working on it. Where are you going to travel after this visit?"

"We have Africa left to visit, but there are too many cultures that sometimes interfere with each other, and the beings of Nature are mostly spirits of other kinds, many evil and fewer good ones. Most Native American tribes also have spirits to worship, usually the spirits of their ancestors," answered Vrang. "Our detailed classification of the Nature spirits largely occurs in Europe, but also in the USA and Australia. We are looking for original elementals, those who have always been here and helped to build the Earth. These are the ones who feel contaminated and frustrated.

"Millions of years are about to go to waste, and they can't do anything about it with their own power. As long as humans can't see them, they don't exist. That's how Earth humans are reasoning in general, but thankfully not everyone."

"Not until they find themselves in the vortex of a devastating catastrophe will they understand what they are doing. But then it's too late," said Lydia. Eliel stood up.

"You are welcome to wander around the monastery with brother Bun. We have many treasures, and other interesting things to communicate. Now you have received some material for your earthly book, Jan. It's about time that humans also learn that the Masters exist physically, until further notice in hidden places, and working to help Mother Earth!" He smiled and left us with a short bow.

We decided to continue, and we told this to brother Bun. He showed us out the same way we had entered.

30 Back to All Beings in the Nordic Summer Meadow

Something that we had been longing for was now grazing peacefully outside the monastery. It was our beloved unicorns, probably summoned by Vrang. I wouldn't call myself an enthusiastic rider, but right now it felt good to get up on my unicorn's secure and quite broad back and to grasp her wild, shiny mane. To ride into the mist and then to emerge from it somewhere else on the planet, now that was amazing, I thought.

And that's exactly what happened.

A mountain, a lake, a forest, a meadow!

We rode out on a Nordic meadow, full of old-fashioned and lush midsummer flowers, poppies, cornflowers, forget-me-nots, clovers, buttercups, daisies, birdsfoot trefoils ... and much, much more. We'd experienced this at the beginning of our journey. It was a large meadow, a mighty and colorful meadow, and yet unlike the first one we'd seen. To our left a deep blue lake was shimmering, with small white geese cruising along the waves. Swans were swimming there, together with ducks and other waterfowl. To the right of the meadow, a dim and green forest rustled with a mix of trees which you no longer see nowadays, with an equal variety of deciduous and coniferous trees.

At the far end, beyond the lake, there were tall mountains towering so high that some of them had their tops covered in snow. Everything I love in one single breath, I thought, and sighed happily. I could stay here forever. Next to me, Lydia sighed in agreement. Balthori stood on my other side, and Thesa's unicorn took its place next to Lydia. The journey towards the beings of Nature began on a Swedish summer's meadow, and maybe it would end in the same way, the thought flew through my mind. Now Vrang rode forth and stood before us.

"Remain seated on your unicorns!" he shouted. "I don't think that we should visit any more countries. Instead, we will experience that thing which we have met for. Whatever happens, don't dismount your unicorns until I give you the go-ahead to do so!"

What did he mean? Was this the end of all the fun? This was a nice outdoor experience that had included all the things that we appreciated the most and truly enjoyed, and I was grateful that it was repeated. Yet, Vrang remained seated on his mount in front of us and he raised his arms and began to sing in a very peculiar language. In a moment it grew dark, as if the sun went hiding in the clouds and a storm was approaching. However, there was no rumbling - it was quiet, a sacred silence. For a short moment, maybe just for a few seconds, the darkness grew thicker. Then it was torn in two, just like the curtains in a theater. The sun shone again on the summer meadow and the chirping of birds could be heard from all around. But the scene had changed, it had changed a whole lot, and I now understood why we were told to remain seated on our unicorns, who stood as still as statues.

Everywhere I looked, I saw elementals. I had experienced something similar before and I would love to be a part of it again. Again, I would like to describe Nature's wonderful, invisible inhabitants, and I will begin from below, from the ground, to sort things out. I must describe the Invisible People once more, so that they become imprinted in the brains of my readers. In the beginning of our journey we got to see many of them - now it seemed as if we saw all!

The Earth spirits, malignant elves, little gnomes, and goblins crawled or ran around on the ground among the flowers. They were about as tall as a hand; some were very dark, almost like small, black, turbulent shadows. Others looked like my perception of gnomes, clad in green, happy, and with a somewhat mischievous countenance. Then there were others who didn't look like any that I'd seen previously on our strange journey. They were also small and fair-skinned ones, with long pointy noses, green hair, and claw-like hands. In some places they were thronging around each other and in others they were fighting. It didn't seem like it was any serious fights, though, just acts of will, maybe some minor exercises of power. I'm not entirely sure what exactly it was that they were up to, but their tasks probably accounted for keeping the earth clean and protecting it, since some of the beings popped up and dove down into the earth as if it was a lake.

On and around all the plants, the fairy people flew, danced, and floated. I saw them very clearly this time. There were both older ones, younger ones, and children, thus whole families. They were light, beautiful, and lithe and very small, like my thumb and even smaller. I saw veils in pastel colors that fit together and formed sheer clouds, and out of them peered cute little faces. I saw the fluttering of wings, but it could possibly have been the butterflies, because some of the fairies rode on the bigger butterflies, and others rode on sturdy bumblebees. The air was full of sounds, some melodious, like tiny bells that rang with a brittle sound, and others were voices in all kinds of pitches; not high like the humans', but more like animal chirps. It's hard to explain, because it was a cacophony that quivered and vibrated in the air. However, it sounded pleasant, not messy or noisy.

In the air, yes! There also floated some fairy beings. They sailed above us, dancing and singing, pirouetting and twisting around gracefully. My gazes were drawn towards the forest. Another kind of Nature spirit was looming there. The devas of the trees looked up from the tree trunks. They all looked very different; some were slender and beautiful, some heavier and thicker and more troll-like. And, speaking of trolls, sure enough, small peering eyes could be seen staring from underneath matted tufts of hair, with broad noses striving upwards and with wide surprised mouths. They were all at different heights; giants, big trolls, and small trolls - surely they existed, indeed! I remembered the stone troll that nearly scared me to death on our first meadow. Now they didn't scare me anymore.

Maybe we were in the world of fairy-tales, maybe in a myth or a dream! Had the unreal become real? We had seen fauns many times before, but here they were wandering about with their eyes focused on a specific point in the distance, and they seemed very resolute.

You could no longer just see the waterfowl on the lake. I didn't see the Water Sprite because I've never believed in him, but I did see women and men with fish tails. They were not dense, but light and transparent. They were skipping and diving and bobbing on the waves. I now got to see them in their proper element. It was the fairy people of the water, the undines. They seemed to be having a great time. Their silver laughter tore through the entire rumble and sounded like pearls rolling over crystal. However, a different kind of voice reached through all of this. It was Vrang, our own elemental, that was speaking:

"My friends, Balthori, Thesa, Lydia, and Jan!" he shouted. "I'm showing you how Nature truly looks if you have your complete vision. This swarm of Nature spirits can be found almost anywhere on Earth, at least in places that are fairly calm and harmonious. Yet soon they will disappear; the evacuation of elementals to another planet has already begun.

"The group souls of elementals that have been formed during the last hundred years within the different plants is not what I'm showing you here. These are the original Nature spirits. All the beings you see here have indeed been living invisible to the humans, but they have done so for a peaceful and helpful purpose. Some of them have preferred to hide deep inside forests and mountains, but all the others have existed here in a fairly mutual harmony. Their disputes are never particularly long lasting or serious. However, I'm wondering how the Earth will do when all the Nature spirits have left it. What do you think?"

We looked at each other, terrified. What we experienced from our high positions on our unicorn backs was an incredibly complex and developed undertaking that the humans had no clue about, but which they would not manage without. Even if the Earth was saved from catastrophes and a third world war and even more misery, it would not be kept clean and beautiful and alive without the Nature spirits. When the poisons of humans take over, there can only be chaos and destruction. How can the humans deny the little ones "above and below the earth," and denote them as mere fairy-tales?

We had no answer to that question.

"No, I would have thought so, the answer is frightening and destructive," our dear vitrigo continued. "None of us wants to answer that question. None of us wants to think of it. Unfortunately, none of us knows how to tackle that question. We, who can't be seen by physical eyes, can walk right through a human without her noticing. Then how can we help her carry the incredibly heavy burden that the future brings? Still, that's exactly what we must try to do. We must find a way. The help must come from 'above,' as humans call it - and 'above,' that is us, and some others."

"I know there exists a group on another planet that I've visited before and that you can read about in a book called *Time Journeys to the Origins and the Future,"* I interrupted. "That group is carrying out a rescue action for the Earth. We also need to consider the Earth's karma, and therefore they're working in their own way. I want to call all the beings you see here the 'servants of the Earth.' But how are they supposed to serve Earth if it's destroyed? Will they witness the destruction from the planet that they've been evacuated to? Is that how you think when you evacuate them, Vrang?"

"I'm not managing the evacuations, dear Jan. I will also get evacuated, along with all of my dwarves, if I can't put a stop to it and come up with another solution. It's a desperate situation. The entire Earth will weep, because it is, of course, a living being."

"Weeping downpours and trembling from earthquakes," Lydia commented gloomily.

"We live on a planet where we are not thriving at all," Thesa interrupted. "We want to go back to Earth. We want to be a people there, a tribe, like we were so long ago. We're ready to help get the Earth on an even keel."

"It's the humans that need to get on an even keel, dear wife," interjected Balt. "There is some meaning to Janne's suggestion of putting love chips in their necks. However, they first need to get rid of their bad habits like violence, crazy sex, power abuse, hate, and jealousy, and all the other things that have brought them to where they are now. The worst case is the youth. So many adolescents need to understand that they're headed in the wrong direction. They think they can't do anything about it."

"They get tired and indifferent," Lydia said sternly. "They take after their parents' bad habits, or comfort themselves with alcohol and drugs. The government plucks money from the poor and gives it to the rich. New insights on a high level are needed all over the world. How will that happen?"

"Now you've seen what's behind the scenes and what good things the Earth is about to lose," Vrang said. "You must return to Mother Earth and tell what you've experienced. I must leave you, and I will take the unicorns with me, so you can dismount them now. Balthori will bring you back. Now you must say goodbye to the Invisible People who love the Earth and don't want to leave her.

"I'm now needed among the smiths in the mountain at home, but let me tell you, if you want to meet me again, just let me know. I'll be listening and will come when you call on me."

He embraced each and every one of us before we were even able to say our thanks. Then he mounted his unicorn and whistled for the others to follow. We kept our gaze on him until he had disappeared into the forest, at which point we looked back on the magnificent scenery with all the elementals around us. Leaving them was difficult. They waved at us, they sang for us, and the fairies caressed us with their veils. No eyes remained dry.

We stood close to each other and disappeared from this lovely place.

30. Back to Mother Earth's Cave

Soon we were sitting once again in Mother Earth's warm, cozy cave. When she had listened to our stories, she asked a question:

"What conclusions do you draw from everything that you have told me? Are the beings of Nature for real, or just in the imagination of humans? Can you convince the presently living humans about their existence? If you can't, they will disappear for good. What can you do about it?"

"Mass media," I mumbled. "The mass media have their destiny in their hands. The mass media must be convinced."

"Maybe it's better that the beings of Nature are kept away from Earth while it's cleaned up," said Mother Earth seriously. "What is required is a comprehensive cleaning. It has begun, and it will continue and become increasingly thorough. May I now get to know your results? When did the cooperation between humans and elementals come to an end, and is it still ongoing somewhere?"

Of course, Lydia wasn't slow to respond.

"It's different at different locations on Earth. If we paint all with the same brush, then the answer would be that the cooperation ended a few years after Christ (AD). But one can't put it like that, because cooperation between elementals and humans is still ongoing in the present time on Earth in Iceland and also in some places in the United Kingdom. Such tribes as the original Aborigines and the Maori have retained their awareness of the beings of Nature. The Native Americans have kept them in their own way, but they don't work with the same beings as we do.

"In Tibet, with the Hunza people, the collaboration was strong and thriving when we were there, but it has changed at the present day on Earth. In some places with the indigenous peoples of Peru it occurs, because their religion contains a lot of the connection with Nature. Yes, there is still at least an awareness of the beings of Nature with many indigenous people today, and we can only hope that the great changes on Earth will cause it to appear more pronounced."

"There, Lydia has said what we all wanted to say," smiled Balthori. "My wife and I, who have a lot of the beings of Nature within ourselves, will be located on the planet in which we currently live, but we are ready to move back to Earth with our sisters and brothers as soon as it becomes possible."

Mother Earth examined us quietly and intensively one by one, until we all fidgeted.

"You have done a good job," she praised. "I am proud of you, and I will pass it on to the highest level. You may not understand the importance of what you have accomplished yet, but we hope that many who read your medium's book, Jan, will come around. It comes down to reaching the humans. As a result of the beings of Nature being accepted and perhaps becoming visible again, the Earth can be saved. It's a sizable chunk of the pie, which indeed contains many rescue actions, but this is one of the most important.

"Now it's time to come up with your questions."

"May we learn more about Anu?" I asked. "You've promised us that, and I've got the idea that it's associated with our task here and now."

Mother Earth smiled and motioned for us to pay attention. Then she proceeded to tell us about the gruesome king Anu's betrayal of the humans.

"As I mentioned before, Anu, for instance, invented the talk about salvation and a savior to encourage humans to crave masters who can teach them resurrection, to be saved, to achieve nirvana, and to live morally in order to obtain eternal bliss. With humans longing for something unattainable, he had them in a more secure grip, as a longing that is not fulfilled usually will last for a lifetime.

"The spiritual and religious teachers are stuck in the same type of prison as all other humans. If any prisoners manage to free themselves and escape, guards are immediately sent after them to discredit them in everyone's eyes (the media!) and speak scornfully of supernatural nonsense and demons. All the other fellow prisoners must be incorporated into the thoroughly and securely crunching jaws of materialism.

"Of course, the prisoners don't understand that they are inside a prison, which has guards who are trained by Anu's minions. And they are many, and in high positions!

"However, Anu has enemies, strong ones. It's my Mineral Kingdom, Plant Kingdom, and Animal Kingdom that already have started to destroy parts of the prison, so that certain individuals from our spheres can regain their identities and establish a new image of the wholeness of freedom.

"Unfortunately, this is just a small part of the whole. Many want to remain in their own safety within the prison walls. They oppose the infinite greatness of the new freedom. For them, the channels of the ego are the most important thing, and of course, also the religious conviction.

"Others will easily accede to the new freedom. First they might be a little hesitant, as chicks when they try their wings. Then it goes quickly in the right direction. The first part of the process is important. If they don't want to risk flying into the prison wall repeatedly, they must arm themselves with an unconditional sense of unity, equality, and honest intent at all times. That is necessary in order for flying to become the life of freedom and love that it was meant to be."

"Has anything of what you have told us already begun?" I interrupted. Mother Earth nodded slowly several times.

"Oh yes," she replied. "Otherwise there surely wouldn't be any idea for me to tell you all of this. The fight for freedom has begun. I hope that your medium on Earth understands that this is the real Truth that will shake the world when it's confirmed, not only in words. It is already underway. Anu has pushed it so far that the humans now are in the process of wiping out my Earth. I won't allow that."

"Are you referring to the ongoing disaster of polar ice that melts?" asked Lydia.

"And all the wars in the southern countries, which only seem to get worse?" I added.

Mother Earth nodded again with a gloomy and sad look.

"If you think of the Earth as a body instead of my round, beautiful ball," she replied, "you can explain it like this: The brain in the collective system, the world community, is the banks. It assumes that life is money and money is life. As long as this is the case, it is satisfied. However, certain signals have arisen that scare the collective system. Certain things that happen in the world are predicting changes, and the changes are nothing that Anu likes. To prevent this, he resorts to things that can make people insecure, make them feel discomfort, and get nervous and inattentive. Overwhelmed with technology, as they are, they become scared and powerless."

"What happens now?" I quickly interposed.

"The collective system will fall. The body I just likened the Earth to will die! It might take many years, but in the meantime the humans must get used to the new body which is being set up that includes the new soul consciousness that makes them the right kind of soul carrier."

"Can you please explain in more detail how humans should behave in order to get started?" wondered Lydia, who liked to get the facts. "Isn't there any recipe?"

"Yes, the breathing," replied Mother Earth, smiling. "If they breathe like I'm going to teach you now, they will soon feel better. The exercise is called the Quantum Pause.

"It goes through four stages. Sit comfortably, with both your feet on the floor, and close your eyes. Choose a number from three to six, and use it when you breathe. I now choose the number three, so it will be easier to understand.

"1. Inhale through your nose while you count to three.

"2. Hold your breath while you count to three.

"3. Exhale through your mouth while you count to three.

"4. Hold your breath while you count to three.

"Repeat these steps three or four times in a row before you return to regular breathing. Then repeat the whole cycle 3-4 times. How often?

When you remember it and when you feel like it. Pretty soon it will become a habit that takes care of itself."

"That was an easy recipe!" laughed Lydia. The two elves looked at each other and smiled.

"It will probably be the most important part of Jan's medium's book," said Mother Earth seriously. "From my side, it's a proclamation to the world. A proclamation should not be complicated; it should be quick and efficient. Come, my beloved friends, now it's time for us to part. Thank you for an unforgettable contribution to the secret book of Nature!"

Being separated from Vrang had been difficult enough, but it was even harder to part with Balthori and Thesa. We belonged to the spirit world; they were living personalities. Yet all four of us knew that we would meet again. The elves were working for the Earth and they knew the group in another universe calling themselves the Wingmakers. The day would come when all four of us could work together there, with the exciting people who call themselves the Central Race. Our hope was with the Wingmakers, because we knew that the Earth was in the center of their duties (more information can be found at www.wingmakers.com).

"Farewell!" said Mother Earth, and she embraced us warmly. "I will not give any sermons or admonitions, I'll rather tell you that I have great faith that my beloved Earth will heal and improve herself in Beauty, Joy, and Love."

31. Home Again

It felt quite tough to return, even though we had accomplished an undertaking that provided knowledge about the Invisible People. Elementals seemed important, and they were present in our emotions and memories. Lydia and I were summoned to Melchizedek, and he embraced us warmly and sincerely.

"Your homecoming can only bode well," he exclaimed happily. "We've been following you from here, and we know that you have attained a new knowledge, a knowledge that all residents on Earth ought to have. Few will believe you, but a few is still better than none at all. A new era for Earth is at hand, when the beings of Nature no longer will be strangers or superstitions."

"How can you explain to a person that actually anyone can see a Nature spirit?" I asked.

"For those who want to meet a Nature spirit, you have to pay attention. Again, it's the power of thought that helps realize what you wish for," he answered.

"If you close your eyes and visualize an elemental intensely enough, you will be able to perceive it in some way," Lydia added. "These shy beings have different ways of showing themselves, and mostly it's only through snapshots. But they can also send a feather that shows up right in front of your nose, or steal an object and then return it in a completely different location after a long time has passed. They can appear in the shape of a bird and sing to you, and they can touch you, and maybe pull at your clothes, even though you can't see anyone around you. Pets have the ability to see them, so if you have any pets, pay attention to their reactions. Sometimes they will freeze in place and follow something with their eyes, something you can't see. Then try to see what the animal sees with your own power of thought."

Melchizedek nodded in agreement.

"The most important thing isn't to catch sight of a fairy or a gnome. What's important is to perceive their presence and try to purify your own life by staying as positive as you can and by helping others when it's needed. It's actually simple. It's a question of evolving your awareness. There's only one way to do it: the way of thought. If you think a lot about the beings of Nature in a friendly and accepting way, they will know. Then something positive will happen - sooner or later."

Suddenly my dwarf ring started to send out signals. Flashes were shot out of it, and Lydia's hanging opal did the same. A crash could be heard, and I noticed a broad smile upon Melchizedek's lips. There he stood, the highly beloved God of Nature: Pan!

"Surely I told you that I would contact you when you were finished with this journey!" he trumpeted with his enormous bass voice. "As usual, you've experienced many adventures, because it's always an adventure to seek out the past - and the future. Mother Earth has told me that you've done well in your mission and that more missions await.

"My subordinates are waiting for the humans. They're waiting for the humans to recognize them, to ask them questions, and try to meet them in their land - or theirs. Right now their life is way too turbulent, and most of them don't want to leave the Earth, even though they realize the necessity of doing so. Do you have any words of consolation, words of recognition, or any questions? Jan and Lydia could certainly arrange some space on the network that the humans are using so diligently. Such an interest would, at least for the time being, halt the emigration from the Earth - that's what my elementals are dreaming of.

"Farewell, my friends, and thank you for the work that you've carried out on making my Invisible People as visible as they can possibly be!"

He embraced us and disappeared as quickly as he had arrived.

Our last experience with all the Nature spirits, but also the meeting with Pan, had a deep impact on me. I would love to communicate these experiences to everyone reading this book. Try to evoke the Invisible People in your thoughts. Could you at least try?

See a flower, and a fairy leaning against it. See a butterfly flying with a sheer figure upon its slender back. See those alert eyes, which are squinting a little, looking out from the bark of the nearest tree. See a small gnome figure settling down in front of your fireplace, waiting for a nice fire. There's so much fun you can see, if only you want to. Maybe your images will materialize if you are thoroughly and sufficiently focused and intense in your thinking, your act of will. Try, my friend, try!

Now I, Jan, am being called out to new adventures, together with Lydia. We've been called to a meeting which implies a change for both of us, a development which could lead to evolution. We will help with a process that we hope can help the Earth to survive, to thrive again, and to once more give humans a paradise to live in. We are called to another universe, to the Central Race, to Prime Creator. I don't know when we will return, or even if we will return, but regardless, I still say:

Until next time!

Epilogue - Message from Pan

For several years, I have had a group devoted to spiritual development, where among other things, I channeled Pan, the King and Protector of Nature and the main partner to Mother Earth. As stated in the text that follows, he always makes his entry with a great fanfare and a bang. He always begins and ends by saying that he is Pan.

Please go ahead, dear readers - enjoy, laugh, or cry! You can hardly remain unaffected. This is Nature's greeting to you through me.

Mariana Stjerna

32. Channeled Messages from Pan — The King of Nature

A whole lot of what Pan has said, I think is worth forwarding. His advice and opinions are valuable, even if his language often is pompous. I would like to convey some of these channelings to my readers. They will be presented in their "original" condition, and not as I usually write.

Pan lives in Nature, not among humans. He wants to communicate something of the infinity and the stunning beauty that his - but also our - world has to offer. The love to his proteges, the animals, the plants, and all elementals, as well as his humility concerning what he tells, you can't mistake. The purpose is to get us humans to understand that we must take care of our beautiful Nature, help Mother Earth to the best of our ability, and become more humble before Nature's beauty and diversity, so that we may keep it.

Message No. 1

Pan: I wade in the water and there's seaweed around me - well, it's not the only thing that is here. I'm not walking *on* the water, I walk *in* it. It's not a problem for me. There are dolphins, sharks, and all kinds of fish here. They've joined groups around me where I stand on a coral cliff surrounded by seaweed. They have gathered here to bring complaints. They tell me that they're dissatisfied to be born on Earth in toxic waters and in an insecurity that really doesn't belong to their ocean world at all. The ocean world should be clean and rippling. It should "whiz," seethe, and surge around the fishes and other beings in the purest pearly, cobalt blue and turquoise water. Such clarity in the water, clarity in the springs that come via waterfalls from high cliffs! They're clean. It is, at least for the most part, clean water coming down.

But as soon as it comes down to the earth it gets poisoned. How are the fish supposed to live?

I see trap nets with weeping fish - trap nets where clear, beautiful fish eyes beg for help. What shall I do with all this? I have no place on Earth anymore, I'm driven away. Along with the entire sea, I'm driven away! Help! Let humans know about this!

Fish can cry as much as they can smile. There are so few who care about them. Therefore, they have no real support. I'm trying as much as I can, but now I am asking you for help as well. Help, so the nets will let go from the floundering, painful movements that our fins do! Help, so that the poison will not kill the little newborn baby already in the dolphin mother's stomach!

These are two small examples from a gigantic sequence of events that happen right now. The whole Earth must be renewed, and we need all the help we can get!

I am Pan, and I have a lot of magic to my aid, but I can't help against the evil, the thoughtlessness, or the violence! That's what I can convey to you today, here from seaweed and marine algae. Some places on Earth are still fairly clean, and we hope they will remain that way. But those places are far, far away at the Arctic and Antarctic. Things are happening there, too. Help!! Help! Come stand under our waterfall and send out help to everything that involves water! I beg of you!

I am Pan, and I am humble for once. Even though it's you who should be humble before me, I am the one who is humble before you!

I will return and I see you, I hear you, and I feel you.

Message No. 2

Pan: Here I, Pan, come. I would love to meet you under the waterfall, I want you so much to see the waterfall and to stand below it now when I come. And I really want to tell you how close you are to the beings of Nature, and how much they want to come closer to you, so that you can perceive their existence.

I think it's time for mankind to wake up. To be sure, she is still asleep, she is but a mountain of meat living in air. But there are others, too, like you. And for them, we are pleased. You might have thought of the climate right now. You might have thought that it is a beginning. It might never again be like it used to be. Something drastic might have to happen. We will soon not be able to breathe, those of us remaining on Earth. We can't breathe! Thick clouds sail around, brown and black, dark gray and gruesome, choking us.

I would love to be the Water Sprite, sitting by the stream and playing. But I am not that Water Sprite; the Water Sprite is a fairy-tale figure. Pan and the Water Sprite have always been considered to belong together, but we don't. I am the Father of Nature and I am the one the Nature spirits invoke. Every straw has a being and every straw is important. Even if it's stamped down, it has done its part. Every leaf existing on a tree radiates that which mankind needs, and when it dies, new leaves will emerge. And even if the leaves are mere buds - because I know that you have seen that leaves are buds which burst out in spring - there are salutary rays inside of these buds that radiate out from the trees. But not now. They don't dare to come out. There is too much rubbish in the air!

What is it you're doing, humans? Yes, we are so concerned, so very concerned. But I know that *you* are not part of this and I want to thank you, on behalf of my subjects, for all the work you put in to awaken humans. But believe me, you have to continue. It's not achieved in a couple of minutes; it takes time. But it all works out in the end. Every time you do something for us, something good will happen. Every time you think about Nature, a little being will open up its beautiful eyes and thank the Creator for its existence. You should know that if you sit down on a stone or a stump in the forest, you can talk to all the beings there. And they listen; I promise you that they listen.

I just wanted to come by to confirm that we are very, very much on our guard, at the same time that we are grateful for all your help. But we are awake and we are observing you, whether you want it or not. And we strike back. The last thing wasn't fun to hear, but there aren't that many fun things that we come up with now. But at least

I am glad that I've received this contact where I can scold a bit that which exists outside.

But that which exists inside of you, in your hearts, take care of that. I like to show myself here in this group and *I am Pan!*

Message No. 3

Pan: I greet you! I can't resist coming over for a little while. But I just wanted to say hello and tell you that the work you are up to is very much appreciated by all of us. The more you can communicate about Nature and about the beings that exist there, the better it is, because the animals are suffering.

Have you seen pictures of how they handle the large southern forests? Do you know how they handle them? They just go over them with their large vehicles, and animals are killed or hunted to places that don't belong to them and their lives, and where they can't continue living. Have you seen how the animal transports are killing the animals, all sorts of animals? Have you seen how they are treated? Yes, I know, Mariana, the trap nets, the seas are getting empty. I talked about it last time. Not only the fishes are crying, I am crying myself, and all of my helpers are crying. But what good is that? Tears can't shut down what's happening, the ravaging, the wild, horrible ravaging, the extermination of animals of many kinds.

A hunter would reply: "But if we didn't shoot down animals and if animals didn't die, there would be too many animals on this planet." And then I reply like this: "That is not the case!" And that wasn't the case in the hundreds and thousands of years when humans and animals lived together. Then there weren't too many animals on Earth, and now this is suddenly an argument. But that's not the case, I promise you that. Because regarding the animals, it is something that takes care of itself; the selection, the survival is in the animals themselves, in their cells, and we don't have to be concerned with that at all.

Blaming that there are too many animals, when in fact there are too many humans! Though they surely are animals, too, aren't they? Hum!

214

Yes, I get so angry when I see how you humans handle everything. But I like *your* work very much and I am so happy about it. And I am so happy that you include the animals when you write, think, and talk. So you have my love!

Continue with what you're doing, and we will help you as much as possible from our side.

I'll meet you under the waterfall! *I am Pan!*

Message No. 4

Pan: I want to say a few words. You should know that there still are elf kin on Earth. There are still hidden, human-like beings that don't dare to show themselves. There are still elves and fairies. There are still what you believe are fairy-tales, but they are reality.

But at the same time, they are partially hidden behind a veil, and they will appear when the time is right. Because these beings long for living in the bright valleys of this beauteous Earth again, in this beautiful world that they have been forced to hide from. They don't want to disappear.

They are hidden where you least expect them and where you won't search for them.

So don't come here telling me that so-called fairy-tale characters no longer exist. I exist!!! To the full! And I wish that you would accept the fact that you don't know the individuals who live lovingly, hidden in your forests, in your mountains, and under the sea.

I just wanted to tell you all that I think it's so sad to walk around being constantly denied. *You* don't deny me, I know that. So here I can speak freely with a good audience.

Thank you for listening, and farewell for this time.

Message No. 5

Mariana: Pan, I have written about you in my latest book manuscript.

Pan: I know. Don't you think I read what you write? It is necessary for me, because it is the children who I want to reach. Once upon a time I reached the children in England through the book of Pan, which didn't really portray me as I am, but which nevertheless portrayed the beings of Nature. That's the way I'd like it from now on. I don't want to be forgotten, I don't want to.

Mariana: But Pan, there are a great deal of cartoons, too.

Pan: Ha! Goosy! Goosy! So much stupidity. We are not as they portray us. No! The children have to understand that they should contact us by thought, and thereafter it can become more and more. If they think that they want to have contact with us while out in Nature, they will.

Mariana: Then I can take this time to ask you about R. Ogilvie Crombie's book Pan and the Nature Spirits *that I own. Is it true?*

Pan: Ha! Of course it is! Of course! He was indeed a proper gentleman. Do you think that he lies in that book? No, he had the gift of being able to see us, and we were very good friends, and we still are. Now he is on my side here, of course, the side that I find it easy to get in contact with.

But I want to get in contact with humans, do you hear that! I and the whole world of Nature spirits want to get in contact with you again and cooperate and feel that each and every one of us is meaningful for Earth. That's what we want!

This is what I wanted to say. I'll see you under the waterfall, my friends. I am Pan, and I love you humans! But I hate what you stand for these days!

Message No. 6

Pan: I come quickly and cheerfully to this company.

In the world of Nature, we walk around with a veil of sorrow, we surely do. There are many species which have come into existence through an amazing creation. But you should know that many species have also come into existence through degenerated species. So in my world there is both good and evil, as it is in yours. That was a new idea, huh?

Yes, this company needs some new ideas sometimes. Ha! Ha! It is I who shall convey these ideas, because it's messy here. We go around worrying about getting entirely obliterated. It's good that we - fauns, fairies, and my people - exist here, but soon we have to leave. We can't stand the atmosphere on Earth, and therefore I want to talk to you about what happens when we leave.

What happens to your vegetation? Surely we are there. What happens with your animal life? We are afraid of what I just mentioned: species that accidentally have created species that aren't good, and those species might get the upper hand. Many of these species do that sometimes, and already have. These are mostly insects of varying kinds. There are also other animals who aren't that good, but the insects have somehow gone awry. This has led to a situation where we aren't quite able to restrain them.

We don't know what they're after. That is not good. They are newcomers, but they affect the old original species in a negative way. If only you knew how much wisdom there is even among insects, you would be astonished. I mentioned before that fish can cry, even though you won't notice it due to the waters in which they dwell. It is the same with insects, though they can scoff instead and be driven by evil forces. But then they aren't driven alone, one by one, but in collections that can cause much damage. And that is ongoing and it's also part of the environmental hazard. It has probably already been noticed, and people have probably already started writing about it.

I wanted you all to know this. It is my message today, as I always have different messages for you. Thus, my message today is that you should notice this and use your thoughts; your thoughts are very useful indeed. Uh, yes, therein lies a great deal of work for you. I know that and you know that. But it must be done!

Group Participant: *May this situation be caused by these weird and unnatural insects that in some way have mutated due to the toxins that have been spread and made them more viable?*

Pan: Exactly so! Unfortunately, that's the way it is.

Group Participant: You often say that insects hold the frequencies in the air in the same way that whales and dolphins hold the frequencies in the waters. So do these insects cause negative energies in the air?

Pan: Yes! That is one of the things that happens. They can also cause attacks and stinging.

Group Participant: And with them follows illnesses and epidemics?

Pan: Yes, and they are spreading! That is why I brought this up today. It's a current topic. It might take several years, and it might come sooner. We don't know that.

Group Participant: Will it hit hard against the crops?

Pan: Yes, of course! It hits hard against both humans and crops. Everyone should actually have their own little garden patch, but I know that would involve quite an effort for you.

Group Participant: But maybe there won't be a choice in the end? Maybe we all have to return to small-scale agriculture?

Pan: It's probably true that it might get that bad. But in that case, that's for the better. Too much of this large-scale agriculture that's going on has invited these alien creatures. It's not possible to get control over the large areas currently being cultivated. It is possible to keep control over a small garden and to take care of it with love. But this here isn't a small garden, and it's definitely not about love; instead, bug sprays are being used, as if that helps. Even the poison from the bug sprays might be something that gets into insects without killing them, and then degenerate species are formed.

Group Participant: But don't even the fertilizers destroy, and all the additives?

Pan: Yes, of course. And that is what chases my people away!!! We don't want to be chased away; we have had the Earth allocated to us, and now we have to leave it!

218

Write, Mariana!! I know you're writing about me, I know you're writing about me for the children. Write, and make it clear to them that we exist. We are not fairy-tales! We are for real!! They must learn that a lot of what is called fairy-tales is reality and has been reality through the ages, even if it has gone so far that human eyes no longer can see what they should be able to see!

And so I am done for this time. Now you have some to think! I will return, and I love you.

Message No. 7

Pan: Now I come in my usual disorderly way, for you to understand that you have me to tussle with. You don't ask me that many questions, but I can talk all the same.

Mariana, I am so happy that you're working on introducing elementals in the right way into your children's book, or into your books as they now have become. Here you have my complete cooperation. The little faun that you have created who you call Laars, with two a's, he exists for real with me. I have many fauns who help me. They are very nice, humorous, happy, and kind souls who are keen to help, but who also are somewhat mischievous, and some mischief never hurts. I think you need that.

Some fun is always needed. You see, they are all so serious up there. But some of them, fortunately, have a sense of humor. Well, we joke here under the waterfall, but meanwhile, things are happening that aren't as funny. Too many trees are cut down, and too many toxins are coming out. There is so much killing in Nature that is both unnecessary and purely destructive. All this killing is wrong. And now I'm talking a great deal about the animalistic killing, the killing of the Animal Kingdom. Too much shooting is going on.

If you think about the first humans - okay, maybe they weren't the first; there were several "first humans," of course. Anyway, they got by on what they killed for their own living; they never killed for the sheer pleasure of it. To kill for sheer pleasure challenges all the negative energies of a human, it changes her and it makes her worse than she should be and needs to be. We don't like this killing at all. We get shy and worried, and we cry and we whine and we wheeze, because we don't have a chance to defend ourselves. We are innocent animals, we are animals who have formed families, and family members die and we can't do anything about it. How do you think it would feel if a shooter came up and just shot down a child here, a mother there, and a dad there among the humans, just because it's so amazingly fun to shoot?

We want to keep the forests in peace, the meadows in peace, and the waters in peace. Nowadays, we have to climb high up into the mountains to be in peace. All this is brought to my attention, every day and every moment I get to hear this kind of sad stories, and I am the one having to do something about it. How am I supposed to do that? I can't be responsible for your knives, rifles, and guns. You don't need that much. The meat rots for you. You have too much and you mistreat the cattle.

There must be a change on this globe. We want to return to the time when the beings of Nature dared to make themselves visible, dared to communicate with humans, lived in peace with them, and helped each other when needed. That's the way it has been and that's how we want it to be again, and we're working towards that goal.

I'm sorry if you think I'm being negative, but I'm just telling you the truth, and the truth in your current existence is negative. The truth is a horrible truth. You are living in a lie, you are surrounded by lies. Now, I don't talk about this group here, but what exists around you. There are just lies. Lies and damned lies!! We want to return to the truth and the love and the Divine selection.

And with that, my friends, you have gotten to hear a real lament, but it's also warranted.

Thank you for listening. You are my friends, and I love you! Do you have any questions?

Group Participant: If the elementals showed themselves, then wouldn't humanity get another attitude towards them?

Pan: Yes, of course. But in the current situation, they don't dare to. They only do it on rare occasions. Someone here in this group has probably sighted a glimpse of an elemental. But they can't show themselves if they don't feel complete trust for whomever they show themselves to. They will, however, do it, assuming that humans change their attitudes towards them. If no one believed in you, if no one believed that you existed, if everyone looked straight through you and you sat there being entirely visible, how would that make you feel? That's how my elementals feel. They can't stand the atmosphere here, either. They need it to be all clean around them, that is also an important issue.

Message No. 8

Pan: Nooow I am here again! We are all green friends, brothers and sisters, of course. And the green, that includes everything that has to do with Nature.

Mariana, I know you really are striving to work with us in the children's book *The Barrel Binder's Child.* We all study that one up here from other parts of Cosmos. We think it's funny, and we recognize ourselves in it. It's so nice to get to do that. You should see my little helpers, the fauns, who have small horns and a little tail, ha, ha, ha. They are so gorgeous and so childish, but in the right way. They're so blue-eyed, but at the same time they know the difference between good and evil, my fauns, and all my other beings as well that exist around here and that no one believes in. Ha, ha, ha.

Gnomes and fairies are familiar to you, and maybe the elf people, who had to move because you are so mean to them. Of course, there are a few remaining here, but they aren't many. The elves are as big as humans, just more transparent. But not so you can see what is going on inside their stomachs, and things like that. Ha, ha. That would be awful; it's not like on radiographs. But they are a bit "paler" than you are, so to speak.

I know you have talked about all the misery that is happening on

Earth today. Humans are chopping down the forests, and they fight each other. The land areas of southern countries, such as Iraq, Iran, and Afghanistan, where they are fighting now, are actually very fertile. There's a soil that actually could flourish and give harvests of fruit, flowers, and forests. Now there are only ashes, now there's just dryness, now the soil is totally destroyed, now the whole air is just a thick smoke, a thick smoke of war gases and such.

Do you understand how we feel? We want to remove all that, we want to sweep away all the humans who behave badly, and we want to put out growers, gardeners, and animals in rainforests. We want to place an ocean of flowers there. Do you understand how we're all crying; even the worms are crying, because neither do they have anywhere to be.

Thank you for still being keen on listening to the birdsong. Now there is a lot of birdsong outside. What I wish is for you to listen even more to birdsong. Even if you don't have a clue as to what birds are singing, it doesn't mean a thing. The birds around you will tell you things with their beautiful voices, and their energy will flow into you like music. You will feel very good if you lovingly stretch your thoughts towards the birds, if you feed them and if you really, really listen. It only takes a little while; you can have your door or window open or you can be out walking. Listen to the birds, because through the birds I will direct power to you. See, that was something new and exciting.

That was my message for today. Any questions?

Group Participant: But Pan, Mother Earth is fooling us slightly here. The weather is getting warmer. As it is now, we're getting too much heat. That means that the flycatcher, for instance, will arrive on its usual date and miss a part of the dinner table. The birds are being fooled, and thus there will be less birds of the insect-eating kind.

Pan: Things will go slow, but my advice is to listen to the birds, and then there will still be places with lots of birds where they sing a lot. So if possible, you should be in the woods.

If the weather changes - and so it does, of course - then it is because the Earth is changing. Why do you think we are in such a hurry to teach you??? Why do you think we're working as we do? Simply because of the urgency!!!

So just work on with the indications that you have received. Now I'll go back to the waterfall and splash a little healing water on you.

Message No. 9

Pan: Oooh well, now I got the chance to speak. Thank you very much for that. You do know that I am Pan, don't you!!!?? Are you afraid of me, are you? What?

Group Participants: *Yes, yes and no, no.*

Pan: That is good, because I have horns and I have claws. Sometimes I appear in hooves; sometimes I have big whopper feet. Well, you probably know that it is a difficult time you and we are living in. I will tell you that we, the beings of Nature, are wondering every day how it will look like on Earth in a while, and not a long while. How will it look like for us?

We are not visible, but we exist here, to be sure. This is our home as much as it is yours. We have hoped to once again become visible and once again get the opportunity to speak, perhaps even co-exist, with you humans. But not yet. We know that we are welcomed in a sphere like this, but if we would enter a shopping mall, which you have a lot of, and show up there visibly and say, "Hello, hello, here I am, here is Pan. Observe us now!" and if I would have my little fauns around me and some dancing fairies, what do you think they would do at the shopping mall? They would believe that it is some kind of holistic invention, a hologram, and it's not everyone who could imagine even that.

We believe the children would welcome us with delight. Sometimes we show ourselves to children when we know they are special children. We hope that parents who hear their children say, "I have seen a strange man with horns in his forehead sit out there on a stone," don't get scared. But most parents would say, "You have so much imagination. You have read too many fairy-tales."

We don't like to be fairy-tales anymore, that is not who we are. We work as much as you, and we work behind the scenes. Because, do you know what, there wouldn't be as many healthy trees and healthy, blossoming flowers and bushes and all that is sprouting now, unless we had been there. If we had abandoned you completely, which we really had a strong desire to do for a while, then there wouldn't be so much sprouting.

But we want the Earth to reclaim her rich vesture. We want humans to enjoy Nature that has been created for us to take care of, and to enable it to be a joy for all eyes, both visible and invisible. We also love Nature, and we, just like you, see lakes, mountains, trees, and meadows that bloom and water that murmurs. Nature is not just for you. It is for us, too, and we don't want it destroyed.

We know what is about to happen, and we have sent down people who will tell you. We want humans to receive one reminder after another concerning what is about to happen. It's just too much of that.

So continue, Mariana! We know you are writing about us. But it's not us and our performance that is important. The important thing is to save the Earth for all children who are growing up. We love the children and we exist for them, too.

I really wanted to say these things to you. I am so happy that you want to listen in this group. We need the listening of all our hearts. We will help to ensure that you in this group work for us in a very satisfying way.

So just return to the waterfall. In there under the waterfall you shall emanate light rays of energies that are strong. And why should you be under the waterfall? Well, because you have a tendency to spread your thoughts and on the whole be a bit thoughtless and a little annoyed and a little like, you know, yes, there is a buzz around you. It buzzes like when bumblebees are buzzing, but that is nice, of course. Yes, you should be under the waterfall, because there you won't have the chance to be unfocused. It is for the purpose of concentrating that we put you under the waterfall to meditate, so now you know that.

So, take a little look at what I have said before, put one and two

together, and emanate good loving energies to our beloved Earth. Now
I am finished. Any questions?

*Group Participant: I recently observed a cross-breeding between a fieldfare
and a ring ouzel, as I assessed it. Is there a special message in that?*

Pan: Yes, it is a message that there can't be any criticism or reluctance
against cross-breeding of any kind. Because one of the difficult things
that are happening now is not only that you humans look down on us
beings of Nature, you look down on each other also. It is alternately
black, white, and yellow and it can seem so kind, so genuine, and so
nice. But inside black, white, red, and yellow there is a battle. Oh yes.
So it's just the surface that appears nice, entertaining, and well, but
inside wines a wind of reluctance and condemnation.

*Group Participant: What do you say about these clonings that occur when
it comes to the animals?*

Pan: I say it's a damned way!!! I damn them!!! They should not exist!!!
Now I have answered that. See you again.

Message No. 10

Pan: (making a noisy entrance) Don't think you will get rid of me
that easily!!

Mariana: Oh my! That really scared me!

Pan: I 'm just kidding with you. Am I not allowed to do that? I'm sitting
here by a waterfall that is so ragingly grand, and I'm thinking of you.
I'm thinking about Nature, I'm thinking about all of the interesting
and joyful visits to the world of Nature with the elementals that I want
you to do, and which Mariana is currently doing as she writes about us.

I'm thinking about all the things that are happening right now to
my subordinates around the world. The animals, as well as the plants and
the minerals, belong to my world. There are terrible things happening.
I'm beyond upset when I sit here in peace and quiet, gazing out over

the Earth. It hurts so much. But still the undines and the salamanders are dancing. Still my elementals dance in many, many places.

We who are here, among Nature's phenomena, we have decided that now is the time to release a communique about us. About us, yes, yes. We're tired of the silence, we're tired of hiding, and you know that I'm a man of action, so that's why I was trying to frighten you when I did my entrance, because I thought that maybe you would pay attention. I know you do. I joke around all the time.

But we want to be seen. We want to be heard. We want to let you know that we exist. We won't show ourselves now, because if we do, we would be destroyed by you humans. We get killed, we get poisoned, we get pushed around like cattle. To think that the day would come when I had to say this! No, no sorrow, no moping here. Now we're moving onwards! Could you make a movie about us?

I want some sort of breakthrough. I'm Pan. I rule over Nature. And, I've had enough. Don't be scared. It's not you that I'm turning against. Your country is very unreceptive, even though you have a Nature that many, many would envy you for, if they knew what wonderful Nature you've got. In the Nordic is where we want to be, where we want to thrive, in the Nordic is where we exist and occasionally can be seen. If only there were humans who would dare to tell that they've seen us, because there are humans with the ability to do so. But they don't dare to speak about it!

The beings of Nature are rebelling and demonstrating! Whoever sees us will see us, and those who don't will at least know that we exist. So be it, and so it will become. I've decided that now. Well, that's what I wanted to say here today, and perhaps it wasn't that little.

Nooow I must go, I'm being called now. I bid you farewell for today. I am Pan, the King of Nature and the Love in Nature!

Message No. 11

Pan: Fiiiiinnnaaally! How terribly long you have been going on. I've stood here and stomped, and I am wet, so I'm treading water, because I have just taken a bath in my own personal river. Good to see you again!

Mariana, I would like to thank you for the book that you have written about us. I'm fully satisfied with it, because I'm also part of it. I know that humans don't believe in the beings of Nature. They are fairy-tales, all of them are fairy-tales, it is believed. But have you thought of fairy-tales about dragons, trolls, fairies, fays, and gnomes and all such, have you thought of the fact that these concepts could not arise out of the blue?!

It was actually so that when we started to become uninteresting to humans and couldn't cooperate with them anymore, then we pulled back. We are not those who want war or who mess with humans. We found a path to remain as the Invisible People, Mariana, but that path is in decline now.

I love you! But that doesn't get me any farther. Here I stand in my dimension, staring at your stupidities, at the same time as I maim my poor elflike brain. How will I make them understand?

Mariana: *But haven't you noticed that there are things happening on Earth pointing in the right direction?*

Pan: Yes, I've noticed that humans are beginning to wake up, and they awaken ever more, but certainly not when it comes to the beings of Nature. Fortunately, the interest in Nature is awakening, however we have immense difficulties in taking care of certain areas that are poisoned and destroyed. In these areas there are namely no elementals anymore. They have left. Maybe they will return the day you understand that you shall restore order in the Nature Kingdom.

I always get to chide and mess with you, even though I love you so much. I'm always permitted to say that you shall do this and this and complain about what stupid things you are doing with Nature. But there are also such things that are good. There are still so many beautiful plants and so many beautiful animals left. There's so much to rejoice about. And the more you rejoice at what you see, the greater chance it has to be further developed and to be enlarged, being materialized, and get the help that it needs.

So don't stop walking out into Nature to enjoy it. Every enjoyment you experience is like a caress of Nature. A caress over the fairies' thin green veil of hair, a caress over the sheep-like backs of the fauns, a caress over the woolen caps of the gnomes, a caress over the fays' sheer veils and the thin arms of the undines, where the water pearls shiver in rainbow-colored cascades.

We need caresses, we need love; the more the merrier. Exactly like you. And that I can't stop trying to make you understand. I won't leave you. I'm the captain of this ship, and whatever happens, the captain stays by his helm. Bind beautiful flower crowns and feel how the summer cradles you in her womb. The days when it's cloudy and not raining too much, go out and enjoy! Give the days of your own love, pleasure, and joy, and then they will get better.

Yes, I've come here as usual with my pointer. You will have to put up with that, because that's why I'm here. I'm not here to praise you for being so good with your gardens and whatever else. I'm here to give you a feeling for the entire world of Nature. I represent everyone and everything in Nature, and that's what you need to feel and that's what will give you the strength to go out and feel all the wonderful things that are on the ground, in the air, and in the water.

Now I've finished talking, haha, for now! Farewell, and see you soon, because I will always return. Take care! I am Pan!! Don't forget it, I have power, but I have a good power.

Message No. 12

Pan: Yees!! Finally!! Now it's my turn. What kind of gene are you talking about? That is something that we, the beings of Nature, don't know anything about. We don't speak much about genes. But, while we're on the subject, I would like to tell you that we miss our friends, brothers, and sisters, the elves, immensely. They are so human that they have certain genes.

But when will they be allowed back on Earth? Well!? You banish them and you banish us. There are many flower species and animal species that have bid their farewell. "Well, I'm off. There's nothing left to gain here. I can no longer thrive here; in this place I'm being treated like shit!" Yes, I use real words, I do. And, I don't "beat around the bush" all fancy like some others, I simply don't.

However, I know what Love is, and at least there's an overabundance of Love among the beings of Nature, yes, yes. They know of nothing else. They do not fight each other, because they've got to stick with their species and work on evolving it. If you work on evolving your own species, you don't fight others. It's as simple as that. What if a fir tree and a pine tree would start fighting? Can you imagine that!? It wouldn't work. Or, what if a monkey and an elephant would start fighting? No, that wouldn't work either.

No, no, no. It's that simple if you just stick to your species and work to evolve it and just try to make it better and better. Then there would be no need for disagreements.

I know that you are deeply entrenched in the Wingmakers. I also know that you've been wondering about what the Wingmakers have to say about the beings of Nature. They don't say anything, they don't. But they are completely aware of us; the thing is, it's not yet time to bring us forth into the daylight, because people don't believe what they see. I think that if a fairy would show up right in front of the nose of a human walking down the street, that human would say, "What is this nonsense!? Shoo!" They wouldn't believe what they saw. That's how it is with a lot of things for you humans, and that's why I'm needed!! Yes!!

You're needed, but we're also needed, and that's why I'm raising the banner up high and coming to you every time you meet, for you may not forget me. The day I will not come is the day that you will cry - that day all of Nature will cry, all of the animals and all the plants. That day must never come.

No, I feel at home here with you. I know that you appreciate me and what I stand for, because it's important that you continue doing so. That's why I make these small, quick visits, to make you understand that you must be very aware of my presence when you're out in Nature.

I bid you farewell for now! I looove you!

Message No. 13

Pan: Now I think I've had enough of standing here stomping. Will I not get any chance today, me? I think you have talked and talked and talked ... and no one has mentioned the word Nature or PAN or elementals, or climate changes. Whew!! That's what is associated with all of this.

The unity, it is completely right, but where is it? I think this whole weather situation is like a long wooden trunk that is being cut lengthwise. Out of the first half there comes rain and out of the other half there comes sun. It has become like this because humans keep cutting and cutting.

The weather situation doesn't only affect your globe, it also affects a lot outside your globe, maybe invisible to you, maybe to some extent visible. We, of course, need people of all kinds that can work also with the environment, which is what I stand for and that you can't forget about. It's easy to forget it when you speak about what you have spoken about now, no one has mentioned the environment. We need groups who work for this also. It would be a good idea if you could find out if there are any such groups. We haven't noticed any benefit from these groups, if there are any.

We think that things are starting to get really messy now, and I don't accept that. I don't accept that my beloved Earth is being destroyed!! Life is for living and to be lived, not for killing and to be murdered, which is now occurring. You see, I saunter around in the forests, I run up a mountain and stand there looking, and what do I see? I see lakes that are shrinking, seas that are shrinking. Where will this end? I see so much misery within the landmarks of Nature that I get really sad. The leaves cry too often, they do. The sun has difficulties getting rid of his morning clothes. I will assure you that he fights, the sun. He fights all he can to shine in the right way. At the same time, he has become a bit too strong.

There is so much that needs to be corrected. From where do I get that help? Who helps me? That is what I want you to find out. I want you to find out if the Wingmakers, who have such resources and have possibilities for cosmic exchange, somehow stand up for us. I think they do, but I can't reach them. Not yet, but I really would like to. You can tell them that. I think I've said what my heart wanted to communicate. Give me back life, the health and the beauty. There are such large pieces of Nature that are wasted and are being destroyed.

But what I can tell you is that if a meadow with beautiful flowers becomes built upon with a nine-story-high stone house and then a storm arrives that destroys that stone house, and the stones are spread all over the meadow, well, then it's going to take some time - but that time will come - before the grass grows over the stones. It takes some time, but the seeds that are lying there sprout and grow up to become flowers, and moss grows on the stones. The meadow will return, it will, but not if another stone house is built upon the ruins. That's what I want to tell you.

I am Pan, and I say farewell, for this time. I love you, and all of my Nature spirits greet you. Don't you hear how they murmur, don't you feel how the wind sweeps its softest mantle around you to tell about my love for you? Farewell! I am Pan, the ruler and God of Nature, and no one plays with me!

Message No. 14

Pan: Well, now it's my turn! Finally! I'm a bit bilious, well not bilious, but impetuous. I'm impetuous, and it suits me, and you have to accept that. Ha, ha, ha, ha. A little rough sometimes, a little rough, yes.

I am so sick and tired of the development worsening, and that what is good environmentally is accepted, but postponed for the future. What future? We have no damn future to look forward to. Yes, I swear a little bit sometimes, you know that, but you can't help it when you are in a situation as bad as mine. Hum! I really like you a lot, and I think it's very funny to come here. I like to see that you're listening and that you're trying to convey what I want to have conveyed, trying to think of what I say sometimes, what is memorable - well, it might not be that often, but it does happen. (Laughs)

I guess we'll see what happens. I believe in humans, nevertheless. I believe in everyone who loves Nature and the animals. At least, there are many who do that. I believe that if you ask the children in a school class to raise their hands if they like Nature, most of them would do it, and we have to work on that. The children are vastly important, as small Nature reserves. Hum! That's what they are. We have to try to work on that.

So tell all the children you know that Nature is incredibly important. Feel free to tell them about me, I like children. Please tell them that I have little fauns running around in the woods that would like to talk to the kids. Some children see more than what they dare to talk about, I promise you.

But I've got a rival in Harry Potter, because children who seek out the dark don't have a big chance of being convinced that fauns exist. Children who get the dark inculcated in them from the time they are small are damaged by it. They need bright children's books that are as exciting as Harry Potter, but which tell about the light and the joy. There may certainly be some conflicts between good and evil, because we can never escape the fact that good and evil exist on the same road. But the good shall prevail, and it was damn long before it did in Harry Potter. Hum. Hum.

I have to keep myself up to date with everything earthly, so I have someone who has told me how it is.

We need to spread enlightenment about our world, and I hope that you help to spread the word the best you can, but now you're all so busy, so we have to be patient a while longer. It is wrong that children get exposed to so much scary stuff in their lives, through mass media, for example. And all this terrible stuff a little child mind is supposed to take in and think about and turn and twist, and not really understand what is up and what is down.

Actually, I think you all know how I feel, and now I must return, return to my water and to my forests, as long as they still exist. Return to my thickets of wild roses and my fragrant mosses, which I like to bury my face in when I feel lost. For I do so as the Pan I am, and then

I take a large piece of moss and put it against my face and I draw in the scent, because then comes the clarity, an outstanding clarity. Think about that. Moss can be used for much. Now I say goodbye, for it's time.

Message No. 15

Pan: Yes, now I'm here. Now I'm heeere and it is me, Paaan, with my usual violence. But it's not violence, it's a loving violence, I am the bringer of storms in your life right now.

Have you figured out why there's so little written about the Nature Kingdoms in the Wingmakers material, have you done that?

Group Participant: Yes, we have looked at it. We were told that the Wingmakers would like to work with the root of evil, in this case the humans, and to concentrate on it in order to bring order to the humans and their thoughts, actions, behavior, cooperation, and consciousness. In the next step comes, as a natural consequence, the great Nature Kingdom.

Pan: I understand, I understand precisely, and that's good. I just wanted to know that you had understood how it all works. But we don't have the same kind of patience as humans, we're a bit restless. There are so many sad things happening. More and more forests disappear, and with them, the species who live there. It's not that we want to create new species, both in the Plant Kingdom and Animal Kingdom, but we want for the old species to have as good an environment as they've always had.

There has been a huge disparity, and I am very worried that the last rainforests - and on the whole, all forests - will disappear. Because then, dear humanity, things get bad for you, too. That's what I'm trying to make you understand - that when you take Nature to you and let yourselves become a part of it, then it makes you feel good. But when you push away Nature and cut the threads binding it together with humanity, that's when it goes bad for humans. Before too drastic things happen, we would need help. But I don't know how, because it's not my business. I can't do anything, because if I show up in town with bare feet, horns in my forehead, and my shaggy body, people will think that there's a masquerade underway. Or they will think that they're being pranked and cheated, because they're so used to being cheated, but so are we at this point. We get cheated, so very cheated.

Remove all the disturbances in Nature, remove the chainsaws, remove all packaging. Hell's packaging. Nature's gifts don't need to be packaged; a bunch of grapes or a few apples can be sold as they are. You can bring your own bags. That's one of the thousands of suggestions that I can give you.

What are you doing with the fish? Where's it going? You keep fishing, so the fish become extinct. And what do you do with the poor animals that you drag away to kill, just so you can get an overabundance of everything? There are no limits, and you waste everything in abundance, and what do you do with the leftovers? For there's a huge amount of it. You who sit here don't know it, but I do. It becomes trash, which then is thrown in those places where it decomposes and turns into poisonous fumes, which then spread.

I don't know what you can do, I only know that I want to stand on top of a high mountain, in the Himalayas, and yell at the top of my lungs so it can be heard all over the world: "Change your minds, think again!! Don't let waste rule over your lives. Don't let waste destroy the Earth that was given to you by the Creator with the purpose of becoming the jewel in the cosmos." That's what I want to say. You probably won't hear much else from me besides complaints about how my people and I are being treated. But at the same time, I have hopes that enough humans will understand that something needs to be done, and soon!!

Yes, I am Pan, and I bid you farewell, for I love you and wish to return to you. It's nice that I get to speak my mind about how I feel and get to tell about it to those who can hear me, because there are so few!! Farewell for now.

Message No. 16

Pan: Now I am here again, I am Pan!!! I can see that you look a bit tired, but I don't have any medicine to give you, I only have complaints.

Ugh! How horrible it is all around. Look how people behave towards the animals and Nature. Oh, how difficult this is.

Do you know that every time a tree is being cut down it feels a terrible physical pain? You didn't know that, I guess. Therefore, you should speak with the trees before you cut them down, if you have to do that, and explain why you do it. Ask them for forgiveness and give them love so that they feel they are getting love. That is important.

It is actually the same with all plants, but of course, when you are out picking flowers you can't ask for forgiveness every time you pick a flower. But I don't ask that of you, either. Only when you cut down a big plant such as a tree. You see, in every tree there lives a deva (tree spirit), and the devas of the trees also feel this pain. When you go over an entire woodland and just cut the trunks as if they were matches all falling, then the devas have to make it out of the trunks, otherwise they also will get killed. How are they supposed to keep up with that, and if they do, where should they go?

There are, of course, places that accept them. You have organized societies, but you can't guess how organized some life is in Nature, such things as are not visible to humans. You see, there are actually groups that take care of despairing devas and fairies and other elementals that have lost their footing due to their settlements being devastated and they don't have anywhere to go. But they do, actually; it is organized just like an employment agency. Yes, I know it sounds funny, but it's actually almost like that, and it's necessary. Now the situation is desperate, because the groups that take care of their own kind and send them in the right direction, to get back their dignity, are overcrowded. Overcrowded, I said!

One tends to believe that there is infinite room in the air, but there is not, because the space is divided into dimensions in such a way that there is room only to a certain limit for certain things. You don't believe that, of course, because you thought that all such things are infinite.

There are also some that are taken care of and are getting healed. They can have lost a foot, an arm, a leg - yes, even a head. Then they get healed. We can heal such things, yes we can. And sometimes I can join in to help when there isn't enough power to heal them. Then they, of course, call on Pan, and I come and help them because I love them, my people. I want them to feel good, but how are they supposed to feel good now?

Look at the plant life and look at the wildlife. Ow, ow, ow, that's not good. But now I have whined enough, and you have been told a bit about how things are. These dimensions, you see, are situated close together, and it's not so damn easy to be sluiced from one dimension to another.

You have no idea how much life there is behind this life, and you have no idea about that life. But it exists just as strong and vigorous, and in a way, physical. I call it the physically unphysical. Good, don't you think? I think that's a good expression: the physically unphysical! Very good! I think you can add that to you vocabulary.

Yes, I believe I've said what I wanted to say. I have whined enough now. So, is there something you want to ask me? Well, how terrible quiet it became, ha ha.

Group Participant: You gave me a bad conscience, Pan; sometimes I cut down a tree or two. But when you remove small trees you do it in order to save the trees around that tree, so it won't die by itself.

Pan: I agree with that. This is not the kind of trees I am talking about.

Group Participant: You mean large clearcuts?

Pan: Yes, I can't imagine that you devastate. I just think you are cleaning, and that is a completely different thing. Anyone else who wants to say something?

Group Participant: I cut the peaks of the birches here in my garden, so that they wouldn't rise too high. What impact does that have? It didn't feel especially fun to do that work.

Pan: Yes, of course, you did it for esthetic purposes.

Group Participant: We wanted the sun to shine in here.

236

Pan: Well, then it's forgiven, but before you do such a thing, you have to speak to the tree. You can even pat the tree, if you are really kind and understanding. Did you do that?

Group Participant: I had an inner communication, at least.

Pan: You had that. That's good,

Group Participant: But it didn't feel especially nice to perform the job.

Pan: I understand that, and it also hurt the birches a little bit, but the devas remain, since they remain as long as they have something to take care of, and they still have the birches, of course. Then it's no danger. We can even be nice and say that sometimes you need to cut your hair, and that you cut the hair of the birches. A poem came up in my head:

> *I become a foaming lake.*
> *I become a woolly cloud.*
> *I become a proud tree that stretches its crown towards the woolly cloud.*
> *I become a fragrant soil under your feet.*
> *But I can also become freezing snow.*
> *And I can also become snow-covered mountain peaks.*
> *And I can also become an ocean that is contaminated.*
> *And I can also become an iceberg that is about to melt.*
> *And I can also become a wild animal that will soon be eradicated*
> *   by the humans.*

Farewell, my dear friends! See you soon again!

Message No. 17

Pan: I am Paaan and I can't see more than three persons here, but it doesn't matter, for we can have a really cozy chat. Ha ha ha. While the snow lies heavy on the roofs, I am awake. I must function in snow, in fog, and in rain, as well as in fair weather. Because under the snow there it buds, under the snow grows the beauty and the power. And that is perfectly fine. I wonder if you've been thinking about something you want to ask me about?

Group Participant: We have previously talked about Ambres and he says, among other things, "Humans are a natural disaster, a terrible natural disaster."

Pan: Ha ha ha. That was a very good and humorous perspective. Ha ha ha.

Group Participant: When I heard it, I thought of you, Pan, and what your kingdoms must go through because of humans.

Pan: Yes, that's the way it is. But what can I do about humans, more than to meet natural disaster with natural disaster? Do you understand?

Group Participant: Yes. Force and counter-force are equal and oppositely directed (a physical law).

Pan: Yes, and almost every day you see in the media what happens on Earth, like floods and other things. That's because we repay.

Group Participant: It's the pendulum that's swinging back.

Pan: Yes, and we're ready to start from the beginning, if needed.

Mariana: What do you mean?

Pan: Start from scratch with the Earth, clean up humans, clear the flowerbed. The flowerbed exists, and it's the human who is the weed. We are starting to get tired of this, very tired. We know that one or two persons can't accomplish that much. But think about it, can't you do that, nevertheless? If words can accomplish something, then of course you have them. If one begins, perhaps the others will follow. But we dare not believe in it either, because now it's beginning to go too far with the whole thing.

Now the snow covers your beautiful country. When it has melted, other times will arrive, and I will not call them wonderful. I want to call them the times of miracles, because there will be major changes on Earth when the snow has melted.

Group Participant: Will it be an awakening or disasters?

Pan: Both.

Group Participant: *We may hope that the love virus we talked about earlier tonight can save some of the disastrous aspects within humanity.*

Pan: If it's finished by then, it will not be soon. But we in the other dimensions indeed constitute a very numerous cheering section. So we hope for changes, not just those that we achieve ourselves, but we hope to meet changes of an entirely different nature.

Sweden is a very beautiful country. I really like floating around in your country. I think of all the high mountains, I think of all the wild waters, I think of all the greenery, of all the animals. Yes, it would be sad if Sweden was to be uprooted and become a gravel heap.

Mariana, I have sent some signs for you, do you know that?

Mariana: *Deer?*

Pan: Yes, precisely. I know you are very fond of deer, so I have sent them to you now and then.

Mariana: *I've noticed that.*

Pan: They are signs that we are listening within my department, in my dimension, that we are listening more than you think. They are also signs of protection. Have the rest of you seen any deer?

Group Participant: *I have also seen deer. Just a few weeks ago, when I was out walking with our dog, three of them stood still under a spruce and watched wide-eyed just 10-15 yards away from us.*

Pan: Deer are very good emissaries for us. Their graceful beauty and their ability to appear before humans without in any way being captured or destroyed - unless there are hunters out there, of course - means that we like to send deer as good tidings. So think of that when you see them.

Group Participant: *They represent the gentleness.*

Pan: Yes they do, love and gentleness. It's a very loving animal.

Well, I don't know if there is anything more I have to say to you.

We are stalling at the same spot every single time we meet, and that spot is not with you, but with the whole of humanity right now. But there are many things afoot, and you have learned about that tonight, and we are pleased to inform you. It's always nice to carry a hope in your heart. As long as you hope for something good and joyful, you don't feel bad.

I am Pan, and I bless you, my friends and messengers. My link to humanity is people like you. I love you! Farewell for now.

Message No. 18

Pan: You have talked for such a long time today, and I have been standing here, waiting and waiting. You have talked about epidemics and about all sorts of things that will happen on Earth. To me, every hole in the Earth, yes every hole, is filled with pain. I guess there is need for a restart, as you say.

But then I want to be involved, because then it will be a replanting as well, do you understand?

Then I want all humans to sow seeds in the earth - of course, they shouldn't be forced to do it, but they should themselves realize the benefits of it. All should have plants that they planted themselves in their homes, both nutritious and beautiful ones. Plants which they can enjoy, which they can exchange with each other and take care of, and which make them understand that their hands must handle the plants with care and be loving during the planting. They also must understand that they should talk with the plants, both with the kitchen plants and with the ornamentals. Hmm. Then their talking will radiate love to the plants.

Here is my personal advice to all humans:

Every time you sow a seed or set a plant, keep in mind that the elementals are with you and help to make it successful. Please, say a little prayer about it in your heart. When you buy a houseplant, surround it with elementals that receive your love for the growing. The plants can hear you, be assured of that!

240

It doesn't have to be many pots with plants, but I would like it to happen in every home and that the children learn how to handle seeds from the beginning; that they already in school get the opportunity to plant and learn more about the plants, including what different plants can be used as remedies.

We haven't spoken about this before, but I, Pan, am also the doctor of the world, hmm! I am such a good doctor, you see, that there is no one better. I have all the medicinal plants at my disposal, and I know how to use them. I believe that such medicines that are made of plants from my garden that heal human diseases should be the only medicines allowed on Earth. Here you manufacture so much trash with so many side effects and with so much shit. Hhuu!

You say that you have laboratories that are so amaaazing. Hhuu! (Laughter) They have an environmental impact that is purely filthy. I have painkillers as well as stimulants, I have medicines for precisely every damn disease that exists on this planet, even against HIV and cancer - yes, everything.

What do you care about that - you prohibit medicines of this kind, you prohibit educated doctors from working with such things. Certainly there should be doctors, but they should work with the medicines of Nature. There is nothing of the medicines of Nature that doesn't help, but you have invented an awful lot of artificial products that of course also heal, but that also have side effects of different kinds. Most of them have side effects.

There are radiations in Nature; there are radiations that are wonderful, ohhh, what beneficial radiations we can achieve. But you haven't even been bothered to discover them yet. So I guess I have to take one of my "slaves" - no, I don't mean that. There are no slaves around here - I am just kidding with you - but I guess I have to take one of my colleagues here and send him or her off to you. Then you can learn how to make radiation that is not harmful. Would you be willing to do that?

Group Participant: Oh, yes. I seem to sense that type of radiation from crystals.

Pan: Now you are getting into something really good. It's not just the plants that have a healing power, but also the stones. There are so many remedies in Nature that you haven't the slightest idea. But when it comes to radiation, the crystals are, of course, a good starting point.

Yes, there are many things that you haven't thought about that I have opened new windows for here. I really like you a lot, yes, I do like all five of you a lot, and I am so happy that you do the work you do. I think that you, in a not too far distant future, will come up with a model of everything that we have taught you and which you can use on the outside world. Because you think, and not everyone does that. Do you have any questions for me?

Group Participant: Pan, last time you talked about cleansing in the flowerbeds.

Pan: Yes that's true, but then I didn't speak of these small flowerpots that I have spoken of today. The purpose of these small flowerpots is to open certain channels inside the human. Have you ever worked with a seed, put a seed down in the soil, without feeling the participation of the heart, thus thoughts of love?

Group Participant: And the expectations of watching a seed grow up into a sprout. That is so much fun. You are there poking and poking.

Pan: Exactly! That is how we want it all over the world.

Group Participant: That knowledge was taught in elementary school many years ago. You even got to plant your own apple trees, I remember, and bring them home.

Pan: Things were better back then. It has slowly been downhill from there.

Group Participant: Back in the old days we lived of what Nature had to offer, now we live of what the supermarket has to offer.

Pan: And that is mostly chemicals and things that are developed in those terrible laboratories.

242

Group Participant: *There are many synthetic additives that the human body can't absorb; instead it is being destroyed. They pass straight through the human body and enter into a stream of water and remain there.*

Pan: Yes, and the treatment plants you have are not always of the best quality. It's exactly the same way when a cow go to slaughter. All of her body knows that she will be slaughtered and eaten by humans, and these negative emotions remain in the cow meat that humans eat. That's why I ask you humans to stop eating meat. All animals have such emotions. Every time an animal weeps before its own slaughter, me and my brothers also weep. (sighs deeply)

A long time ago, and even nowadays in small groups in hidden places in the mountains, animals are kept, not to be eaten, but to produce milk and to offer their strong, powerful mane of hair and to be ridden on. These animals are having a good life; they are loved and they give off as much as the humans manage to receive. This is how it was meant to be from the beginning; this is how things should be when the upheaval arrives. The upheaval must remove all the artificial, all the toxic, all this evil.

Well, then I, Pan, bid you farewell for now. I am happy every time my little garden here is blooming in front of me.

Farewell, farewell. I am Pan, at your service. I love you!!!

Message No. 19

Pan: Here I am! And I am just as angry ... as last year. (Laughter) Yeah, you can put it like that, and I am also just as happy to be here as last year. And this year you will need me, that's the way it is!! You will need me and I will stand up for you.

I have been thinking about what I shall help you with. First and foremost, I shall help you with the energies, because they are necessary for you to have. To amplify them with the power of Nature, that's not so bad, huh? If it's not me, it's one of my colleagues who does it.

I'm starting to lose patience, and I begin to understand that what will happen to Earth now is the best thing that can happen, namely, changes in both land and water.

Heaven you have where you have it. The air you have where you have it, but you have learned that the air contains much more than you ever imagined. But the Earth is mine, and here I rule, all the way into the center of the globe, to the heart of the Earth.

And you don't know that around the heart of the Earth it is inhabited. I can't call them humans, but I can call them elementals. There are lots of elementals inside the center of the Earth, elementals that are actually quite human-like, at least some of them. They are there, live there, and help Mother Earth.

Group Participant: But certainly they live in harmony with the Earth?

Pan: Oh yes, they live in harmony with each other and the Earth, not with humans. It happens that they catch a peep at humans, but they get very sad over what they see. Yes, I am always in contact with them.

Group Participant: But now, when there will be such great upheavals and floods, where will the animals go, all the terrestrial animals? They won't get enough space and they will drown?

Pan: (sighs heavily) Yes, that's indeed part of the sorrow in our Nature Kingdom.

Group Participant: So there will be even fewer animals?

Pan: There has to be. There has to be, but we shall probably try to retain large tracts of land.

Group Participant: So that will mean that many species become extinct?

Pan: Absolutely, unfortunately. But there will be humans who will deal with this problem. There will be humans who were present when all these species existed here.

Group Participant: Who have a gene pool?

Pan: Yes, you could say that. What I want to get at is that these humans, who at the same time often are scientists, will do what they can to maintain the genes and then recreate the animals. But land will sink and land will also rise up. At the poles there will be land as we now see it.

Group Participant: What happens at this latitude?

Pan: The latitude that you live in - do you mean the Dalarna landscape here in Sweden? Dalarna will remain. That's why I have worked so intensively with you and tried to make you understand that you shall plant a little bit sometimes. You can do that now when the spring comes. You shall rejoice in the landscape you have. Dalarna, and also Varmland, will remain. And the mountain range ... Don't worry for that which disappears, because it can't be helped. The land areas will not disappear forever, but as I say, some will dry up, some will rise up. I will make sure of that. I need a lot of land. I want to rule over as much as possible of both fauna and flora.

But this issue with the animals, as I said, it worries me. A large part of them we have to transfer to another planet; we can do that also. We can take genes of the animals on Earth and move them to another habitable planet, so they don't disappear. We don't want that.

Group Participant: Then I will take the opportunity to ask, do the animals have a group soul?

Pan: Yes, most animals have a group soul, especially smaller animals, but there are actually animals that have their own soul - the dolphins, for example. One's own soul is thus a fragment of a group soul when it comes to the animals. That also applies to pets like cats and dogs.

Group Participant: To be specific, I saw a TV show where a woman claimed that the horse that she had owned many years ago had returned to her. She recognized some behavioral patterns of the horse.

Pan: That can happen. It happens that animals that have been very strong intertwined with their owner - master or mistress - enter again in a similar creature and relationship. Sometimes they develop in a different way, from a lower animal species to a higher, and so on, but such things as you told may well happen. Yes, we have a lot to deal with and we have five years ahead of us that will be tremendously dependent on the humans who are helping. Energies are more important than anyone suspects. There must be order in the energies that we send out, and I believe that you can achieve that. They must be incredibly strong and incredibly concentrated.

Yes, you have much to do, you already have much to do, and you will have even more to do. Ha, ha. It will be fun when you come so far that you can see us with your physical eyes. I know you can see us with your psychic eyes, but when you can see us with your physical eyes, then we can communicate in a completely different way.

Then you will see what an amazing order there is in the Kingdoms of Nature. You have no idea how incredibly well structured everything is, and balanced. Together with the beauty, there is Love. It's everywhere. When you destroy the plants and the vegetation, then you destroy a piece of Love. Now I've said a great deal of what I wanted to say. Now I will sit down at the top of a foaming waterfall and go down the slide, and therefore, I say goodbye!

I am Pan, and now I sit on the highest waterfall I can find. Farewell for now. Now I am with you, now I and my colleagues stay in your energies, remember that!!

Message No. 20

Pan: I think you have talked about very good things, for I, too, have had such a concern for all those wonderful things that exist underground, that you can't see, and which want up and out. I have such concern for the dirty waters. We need a massive cleansing of the waters. Sounds crazy, don't you think? Cleaning the water! The water that comes down contains so much dirt today. There are still, high up in the mountains, pure, clear springs that you can drink from directly. But that's all.

Yes, you have probably seen it, and I can tell you that we take a peek at your TV sometimes, because we must know what you are doing, so we have our scouts that tell us what is happening.

In a newspaper you can read that this issue with the environment is exaggerated; everything is all natural. It says that it's only natural that a poor polar bear slips around on an ice floe without coming to its coast, to its permanent dwelling, etc., etc. Then in another newspaper it says that now it's time, now it's terrible, now we are facing an environmental disaster. What are you poor humans supposed to believe? We wonder about that here.

I have here behind me - do you see, Mariana; look, Mariana - a whole army of elementals that represent different things and that are terribly upset. I said "terribly," but I was about to use an even uglier word. I won't spoil you with overly ugly words; then you will just think that it's funny.

Yes, I have this crowd behind me that Mariana can see, but now she is so far away that she can't communicate with you, and it is, my dear friends, a crowd of rebellion. It's a demonstration, you see, it's a demonstration of the beings of Nature that you haven't previously had on Earth. A real demonstration, where you walk around with flags and look very, very angry. Most of them do that.

This demonstration would probably very much like to materialize itself, but it can't at the moment. It will be able to do it eventually, and then it will be no fun for humans if you don't change your ways. Yes, I shall not continue to hold on and yell about the environmental disasters, which are most definitely there lurking behind every corner, that you read about every day and that you see on your screens.

Shooting is completely reckless. Those who shoot for shooting's sake should be shot themselves; it sounds cruel, but it ought to be like that. Such humans should either be removed or totally change their opinion.

That poor polar bear mother is really standing on a small ice floe, and she can't reach her children, because they are on another small ice floe. How do you think it will turn out? The animals are helping us, and that can't be said of humans.

So my message to you today is that the crowd of Nature spirits that I have behind me is prepared to step in. Though they can't themselves do anything physical, they can - through their ability to speak with the animals and other parts of Nature, even with the Plant Kingdom - provide warnings, and this was certainly such a warning.

I will not stay that long today; I just wanted to tell you about the crowd I have behind me, that they actually are fully prepared to act through the Animal Kingdom and the Plant Kingdom. I think it's important that you got to hear this, because it allows you in a completely different way to understand things that are happening, don't you think? So, my friends, with this completely fresh knowledge, I leave you for now. I can tell you that this crowd behind me raises a hope in the entire Nature Kingdom. They have had enough, and they act. But not against you, my friends, because you are my beloved friends, and I tell you about these things to help you.

I am that I am, that I am, that I am!! Pan I am.

Message No. 21

Pan: Yes, here I aaaam! Pan is here and greets all his dear friends. I wonder if you have any questions for me in the golden-red light of the autumn. It doesn't seem so.

Yes, now we're moving towards a time that is getting more and more humid, cold, and foggy, only to later change into pure cold. Then it's time for you to live at least partly in my country, in my Nature, and in that Nature that you can create around you, inside of you. Because outside of you there is a completely different kind of Nature.

You also must learn to understand what the kind of Nature that you meet now can do for you. What does it have in store for you, and how should you approach it? Was it actually meant from the beginning that the sun shouldn't shine every day? That all leaves should blow away from the trees and all flowers stoop to the ground to enter their next incarnation? Was it meant that the autumn should come and change into winter and cold, so that humans would begin to feel uncomfortable with themselves and what they have around them?

Yes, it was meant that there would be different climates and that they should evolve in different ways in different countries, but it wasn't meant that humans should disagree, feel uncomfortable, or simply detest the time that arrived, but every season should have its own charm.

That's what you have to realize. I don't just live in my garden, in my waterfall, in my sunshine. I wander around and I see exactly what occurs on the Earth I'm walking on.

It's not just nice things, it's not just fun things, it's huge disasters going on and it's immense difficulties of various kinds that are happening now and will do so in the future. But all that happens is good. Somehow it's actually good.

If you think of the time you live in as a good time, because it's a time of development, enlightenment, and Love above all, then maybe your life will take a different direction. Yes, I preach, of course, as usual when I come to you, because I really want you to be able to visit me sometimes, visit my Kingdom. Live with my beauty. I'm not talking about my appearance; I'm talking about the beauty around me. Well, I believe that you do so very often.

I really like this group, because you somehow live along inside of me.

You live along in what I do, and what I want you to do, and you live along on an Earth that is about to be destroyed. You live along on an Earth that is about to evolve towards the next era of beauty, the next period of a completely different beauty. The outer beauty, but above all the inner beauty, will grow. The more the outer beauty disappears due to war, destruction, and environmental disasters, the more the inner beauty will grow. That is necessary in order for you to get back the outer beauty, and then the inner beauty quite simply must make some great achievements. We hope for that.

I just wanted to visit you for a little while today to say that I love you and that you are my friends. I am with you every time your thoughts touch the slightest of that which has something to do with Nature. Then comes a lightning with Love from me that strikes you.

If you feel that, then you know who it is. Thank you for today! Thank you for existing, and thank you for letting me come here.

I am Pan, and I say: See you later!

Message No. 22

Pan: Oh, that was about time. Here I stand, waiting and waiting and waiting!!! So many people! I hope all of you like flowers and animals!

Group Participants: Yes, we do.

Pan: You do - how nice, because it's them I am in charge of. I presume all of you know who I am? I am Pan.

And there sits my old friend since childhood. She has been given the gift of receiving my complaints and my praise. You see, I praise and complain alternately. She has been given the gift to communicate what I want to say. She helps me to reach out to you. Well, here I sit in my garden, enjoying the sun and all the beautiful flowers. Do you know that flowers and animals actually exist on other planets as well, though they don't look the same? But a whole lot look the same - for instance, moss. Moss we have on a great many planets. It is a little different in color, though.

We have mountains on very many, well most, or all planets. Mountains with different components, rock types that are dangerous to you humans, and wonderful rock types and gemstone rock types, which you would love to access. (Laughter) But we will make sure you don't succeed with that. Yes, there are a lot. When I was standing here outside, I heard that you talked about space and space visitors and such things.

I have been allowed to help a great number of elves and devas and different figures that belong together with the vegetation, but also those associated with the animals. I have been allowed to help many across a border, so they have been able to settle down in a different location. For it is beginning to become dangerous to be on Earth. The Earth begins to eradicate one after the other, both animals and plants. Who is to blame for that? You can't take advantage of the beauty that is offered to you.

Initially, the Earth was a lush garden. Then it was summer, and there were lakes, there were waterfalls, and there were oceans. There was also a completely different kind of beings than the naughty boys who live there now. I think you are very naughty - not you who are sitting here, but not all humans are kind. What have they done with the animals? They have bred both the one and the other. I think they should stop doing that, I do. Hum!

There is scrap and nastiness afoot on Earth, but it's not such things we are going to talk about. We will talk about what is nice and beautiful. It is autumn with you now, and the autumn is nice. The leaves are colored yellow and shiny and have a message for you:

"Now we sink down and turn into mold, but in spring we let our buds burst open and bloom again to give you joy. It's our task," says the leaves. That's the way it is and the way it was, even in the beginning when Earth was created, and even when humans were created. For when humans were created, it was intended that they would be blessed with a birth and a death that was not a death, but a rebirth that was visible and understandable and not like now, terrifying.

That's the way it is and that's the way it has been, and I have been here from the beginning and seen it all. Maybe I am using some rude words and thoughts sometimes, but that is to wake you up. I want you to be awake for Nature more than you currently are. You don't have time together with Nature anymore, you put your nose in your books or you sit and stare at that screen you have, the TV. You stare at it and you stare at your computer, and then you sit there on your backsides and never get any further.

Get your butt out in Nature, that's what I say!!! Go out much more than you do, and when you get out, become aware!!! You have Nature all around you, do you ever think of that? No, you go there and think about what you will cook for dinner! Ha!!

When you go there, ideally on a forest road or a road that's not so busy and where there's Nature all around you, when you go there, take a little closer look at the leaves. Look a bit at the grass that you trample down. Every blade of grass belongs to the grass soul; every leaf belongs to its soul group. You don't currently think of that.

Enjoy it, take a leaf from the tree and caresses it, look at it. "Oh, how beautiful you are," you should say. "How fine you are, thank you for existing." Then you can let it go, because then you have given Nature a kind word and it needs that now, the way it is treated.

Yes, that was actually my little lesson for today. I've maybe said something along those lines earlier, but there are so many new ones here who also need to get to know Nature.

And the animals - there are fewer and fewer of so many species. But when you see a beetle on the road, well, it moves as fast as it can; bend down and caress it gently with your index finger and say, "How cute you are, little beetle." Is there anyone who does that? Nah!

Group Participants: *Oh yes!*

Pan: There is? I am glad to hear that, that really makes me happy!
Because in the tiniest of all, the greatest of all exists. Remember that.

I love you all with Nature's unspoiled Love! I am happy to meet you today, and I will see you soon again. We'll meet in your dreams and we'll meet in your reality.

I am Pan! Farewell!

Message No. 23

Pan: I am Pan, and I am happy to see you again. There's a lot that you need to learn, and now it's the season that is hard to live through, up here in the Nordic region. You have no heat, you have slush and dirt, and you have a hard time making your way through sometimes. But don't complain, because I can comfort you that *beneath* all of this, spring is sprouting. There the vegetation sprouts and there the animals are waiting for their little cubs that will be born in spring. It's so wonderful with all this life that is not visible, but is in full swing. That is what you shall think about now; you shall think about the life that exists beneath your feet and that is pure, brilliant, and new. Newborn, like a little baby that will grow up beneath all of this.

In your country and many other countries, the trees have to lose their leaves and the grass has to be weighed down by snow. That happens where you live, you have to accept that. But I also understand that when it's hard to walk, your thoughts get a little heavier.

Therefore, I want to cheer you up by thinking of the light beneath your feet. That light is so important; it's a light that you carry with you all the time. That you must not forget. Absolutely not. The light, which exists beneath that dirty puddle of mud mixed with snow that is so nastily disgusting, is pure and nice. Beneath all this, a frantic activity is going on.

You can be sure that if you dig a little into the soil, all the root men and root women are busy down there. The fairy people that live underground have a lot to do, and they enjoy the life they have underground. When everything grows upward, they will follow with, and dance around the plants.

But now they are forced to groom the roots and take care of everything, otherwise there will be nothing beautiful in spring. Think of spring, think that there is being prepared a spring beneath your feet. If you think so, if you think that the light exists beneath your feet, then I think you are doing very, very well.

For I am Pan, and I know what I'm saying. I really want to help you. Do you have any questions for me? - Not today. Well, then I will say farewell to you. I have seen you for a while and I have talked to you and I have told you that the light exists beneath your feet. That was today's message from me!

I am Pan, and I really want to get back to you. Farewell for now.

Message No. 24

Pan: Yeeeeees, here I am: Pan!!! I say heeellooo to you. Have you stomped hard on the ground and felt that it sprouts beneath?

Group Participant: I've thought about it. The light beneath the surface of land.

Pan: That's good. It's important, and you can continue with that occasionally. Yes, there's a lot that you have been through, and there's a lot that you're about to go through. There is a lot I have to give you of love, of flowering, and of joy! For joy plays a very large role - if you feel happy, everything is much easier.

You must feel happy when you're a human and have contact with Me. Ha, ha, ha!!! With Me! (amusement) You should be happy that you're born to Earth that is sprouting around you, even beneath the snow.

You should be happy that you have the chance to learn so much about what exists beyond the Earth portal.

You should be happy that I like you so much and that I want to give you so much. So much seed that it grows everywhere among you.

I want to give you seeds to grow further; I want to give you seeds to form roots beneath the soil. I want to give you seeds to sing, sing beautiful, lovely songs.

Music, I want to give that to you. I want to give you the music of Nature. The music that you listen to when you walk in a rose garden, it is so beautiful.

I am Pan, so I can make music all by myself. I have a pan flute, and when I play, the flowers stretch themselves, the leaves on the branches bud into green, lovely cones. I have very much music to give you. Play if you can, and if you have a pan flute, play it and listen to how it sounds.

Group Participant: I have a pan flute, but I can't play it. Maybe I should try.

Pan: You don't have to play yourself; you can listen to recorded pan flute music, or try to whistle a bit of it yourself.

Group Participant: I will try.

Pan: Ha, ha. Yes, I'm trying to get you to realize that you should feel joy. Even if death is near, it is not black and unkind, but bright and loving. I promise you that next year there will be a lot of changes for the better. There will be positive changes, both to each one of you and for your group and for all of us who work for a better environment. A lot will happen next year, difficult things will happen too, but that is to clear the way for the good things.

I can predict that, even though I am not exactly a fortuneteller. I might - and I really hope so - be able to take you to the land of mists that surrounds my own Eden. Through Mariana, we might be able to take a walk there in the new year and smell the scent and see all the beautiful flowers and other beautiful plants that exist in my own garden.

I would like you to follow me on a really pleasant walk there. But we won't do that today, because it takes some time. Today I will just tell you to be grateful and happy that you are alive and healthy, that you find the roots sprouting beneath your feet, that you're moving towards a brighter time, no matter how you behave, and even if you think it is dark around you, you're moving towards brighter days. That's what I want to give you today, a winter solace. You probably need it, and I hope that you will receive it.

Group Participants: *Thank you, thank you.*

Pan: Now I send out the winter solace's wonderful, lovely vibrations and energies over you.

I am Pan, and I say farewell for now. See you again soon. I am Pan, and I love you!!

Message No. 25

Pan: Yeees, to well, what you're talking! I am Pan, and I also want to take part and talk! Yes yes, hahaha!

I think it was a long time ago since I saw you, so do you have any questions for me? I know that you think about Nature; I actually have been present in the background earlier here today. Perhaps you finally are beginning to understand that Nature is the most important factor on Earth. Nature came into existence before humans and animals. Nature is the foundation of the Earth, of the flowering, of the food. Without Nature, you can't live!

It's very important for me to get a place in your hearts, and I believe I have that.

It's also very important for humans to learn that I exist, because they don't think so. I am a fairy-tale figure. Yes, let me be a fairy-tale figure in the tales, but in reality, in that reality that you are working with now, I exist to the full and I have a structure that is very human.

Humans have somehow created a picture of me, that because I belong to Nature, then I must have cloven hooves and horns. Just to joke with you, I've shown myself like that to you many times, but in reality I am equipped exactly the same way as our friends in Wingmakers, The Masters, we can call them. I actually look like a human. Were you disappointed now?

Group Participant: *(laughing) Yeeees.*

Pan: I can take shape as Pan too. (Laughs)

Group Participant: *Don't you even have a tail?*

Pan: I have if I want to. (Laughs) I can create a tail. But actually, I wonder what to do with it?

Group Participant: *To wave with and to whisk away the flies. (Laughter)*
Pan: Surely, we have dogs that express their joy with their tail, but I can show my joy and my community with you by talking with you and giving you various small missions such as this, with putting your feet in the ground and feeling how it grows under the soles of your feet. It was one of those pictures that I hope you get back to a little now and then and make use of. It's an important picture that can create much goodness inside you.

Nature is on its way back. I actually don't think it will take as long a time as I previously thought, before Nature has become what it really should be. Nature should be in tune with humans and not be destroyed by them. That's what is on its way back now. We are working tremendously with Nature, and humans are getting a bit environmentally conscious - well, more and more for each day that passes.

It is very important that all children, all young children, become aware of Nature and the gifts of Nature. Therefore, my mission to those of you who have grandchildren or small children around you is to tell them how important Nature is and how much it means. You're welcome to paint for them the picture of the kind Nature God Pan as you want. I need the children to help me.

The children must not turn away from Nature, because then what's going to happen will get even worse, but the kids can have a Nature God to turn to as well. I love the children. They are buds that might develop into something good, but perhaps also into something toxic or contaminated.

You must not forget Nature. Please, talk to Nature; it perceives what you say. Talk to the trees; even if the snow lies thick, they will listen, I promise you. Talk to the flowers, yes, with all that is Nature. Talk to the grass you walk on. Yes, you can talk to the snow, too, if you wish, but I don't think you'll get as much response then. I would somehow like to strengthen your awareness of Nature; that is why I come to you.

I hope that you, even though you are about to celebrate Christmas, where nothing but the Christmas tree is from Nature (and actually a fictive Nature, since it nowadays is mostly plastic), sit down during Christmas and think about a summer meadow. Enjoy the summer meadow; send love to it, to the birds that sing, and the deer grazing on it. That's my advice to you today.

I am Paaan and I bless you and I send you my love and my joy. Farewell for today.

Message No. 26

Pan: Yeeees, Heeere IIII aaaam and it was soooooooooo loooong ago since I got the chance to speak to you. How are you, my friends? Have you come up with anything that is important and meaningful to you? Do you have any questions for me? I have a feeling that you do.

Group Participant: I have a question that Mariana has conveyed. You have mentioned to Mariana that you would like to see a webpage with the material you want to spread. Has Mariana got this right?

Pan: Ha, ha. Yeees. Well, I have told Mariana that I would like to be on a webpage. I would like to express a lot of my ideas, so that humans understand them and see them. I would like to remind humans how important Nature is, tell them that they have to be careful with it, feel love for it, appreciate and value it as long as there is such a beautiful Nature like the one you have around you. All the things that I want to say don't reach out to them; it is nothing but words so far. When it appears on a webpage, it can at least be read and understood by people. That's my wish.

I didn't say that I want my own webpage; it might be too much to ask for. I have said that I want to be part of a webpage.

Group Participant: *Then I think I have a proposal to work on. I think it can be arranged in a good way on a webpage.*

Pan: That would be nice. I am very grateful, really. I want so many flowers on it that the webpage flourishes and some animals that pop out from time to time! That is what is so important for me. Maybe we can talk more about it the next time we meet. It's not that easy to talk about flowers and animals when the snow lies around the doorstep.

Group Participant: *We had two deer here outside our house just a moment ago.*

Pan: What a joy! Every time you see a deer, you should think: It is a sign, it is a friendly gesture from Pan. Because it is. That is what Mariana does and that is what I want you all to do; deer and hart are actually God's children, if you allow me to express myself in that way.

Since we don't speak about a God, but about the force, the love, and the beauty in the cosmos, I can tell you that it exists in these wonderful animals and many more besides; the dolphins, for example, and many others. Then there are many animals that have been created by mistake on your Earth, that weren't supposed to develop the way they have. There is, of course, also a risk that humans develop in the wrong way, so why should it always go right when it comes to animals?

In contrast, when it comes to plants, there is no chance that they can become incorrect or that they develop in the wrong way. Plants have a different kind of life, and they are faithful guardians to humans, which humans do not at all expect.

But you haven't understood that. The trees are guardians, and it is wonderful with trees - for example, oaks and willows, yes, all sorts of trees you see around you. Even the conifers that of course sting you, but if you caress them the right way, they are like silk. This is something that is very important for you to think about.

Every time you look at a tree, even if it is snow-covered now, think: "Thank good God for having a tree standing there." You know that I don't at all like when people cut trees. Sometimes you have to do it, but then the tree cries. If you haven't told the tree that it will be cut down, then it cries. Then the deva of the tree can't survive. It is very sad, and it occurs a lot on your Earth.

But now we are not going to speak about boring things, we are only going to speak about all the beauty, all the beautiful things that await us. You have winter, not in your hearts, but around you. But it won't be long before you can see the brown soil and the green grass and hear the gravel crackle when you walk on it. Then comes the time when humans come to life and enjoy themselves, and then a lot of things will happen that have to do with the development of humans.

For now is a transitional period, you know that, you have already heard that elsewhere. This time will bring both good and bad things. It goes without saying, a transitional period must always do that, but when all is completed, then things will be in a very good order on Earth. That is what we hope for and work for.

Now I will go home to my waterfall and sit down and play, and think of you, my friends, who really know that I exist and know what I wish and dream about, and who don't want it to remain just fantasy that the Earth will thrive again.

I bless you and will see you soon again, all my dear friends. Farewell for now. Thank you for being here for me!

Message No. 27

Pan: Hello, I knew very well that I'd be welcomed here. Yes, I am Pan indeed, and I've asked you questions and asked for your help. Do you have anything to say?

Group Participant: *Yes, both Mariana and I have been in contact with this lovely woman who gladly takes in materials from you on her web site, which is fairly well-established, but most of all, it's pure and nice.*

Pan: Hurray! I'm so happy to hear that! Then, let's get started as soon as possible, there's not that much that is needed each time. It's important to have flowers and plants and trees and grass and soil and water, all of this is important because it's me and it's the Earth. I want to communicate Nature to humans so that they can feel Nature penetrating them and making them filled with a happy soil that sprouts a growing and vigorously developing plant. That's what I'm going to do.

Thank you! I'm so happy about this! I will try to give humans spring in a new and more captivating way! Then you know where to find me. I take joy in this cooperation and I thank you for welcoming me here and letting me come and talk about how wonderful Nature is that I represent, including the animals.

I give you my thanks and I leave with joy and prepare this in my thoughts.

Farewell and thanks! I am Pan, and I love humans, even though they don't believe it or know it!

CPSIA information can be obtained
at www.ICGtesting.com
Printed in the USA
LVHW012350160322
713569LV00012B/1272